Praise for *Bringing Down the House*

"Perfect for a read on the plane down to Vegas."

—*The Vancouver Sun*

"In this high-octane tale with rich, sharp dialogue bordering on Elmore Leonard turf, the plot races by at a NASCAR pace and the characters on both sides of the table are as real as an inside straight, making their moves and planning their scores like a croupier on speed. Take the odds, bet the bank, and stare down the dealer. *Bringing Down the House* is a can't-miss deal."

—Lorenzo Carcaterra, author of *Gangster* and *Street Boys*

"[*Bringing Down the House*] will grip anyone who has ever hoped to break the bank at Monte Carlo."

—*Booklist*

"Ben Mezrich takes us where every man dreams of going but precious few ever have—beating the casino. In this rollicking truth-is-stranger-than-fiction tale, Robin Hood meets the Rat Pack as the hero steals from the rich and gives, um, to himself. Odds are you'll love it."

—Michael Capuzzo,
New York Times bestselling author of *Close to Shore*

f **P**

ALSO BY BEN MEZRICH

Skin

Fertile Ground

Threshold

Reaper

AS HOLDEN SCOTT:

The Carrier

Skeptic

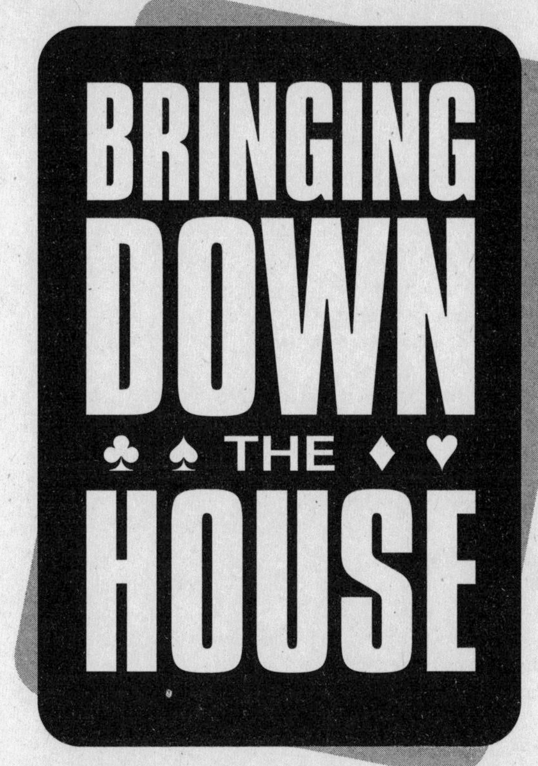

The Inside Story of Six MIT Students Who Took Vegas for Millions

BEN MEZRICH

FREE PRESS
New York • London • Toronto • Sydney

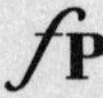

FREE PRESS
A Division of Simon & Schuster Inc.
1230 Avenue of the Americas
New York, NY 10020

The names of many of the characters and locations in this book have been changed, as have certain physical characteristics and other descriptive details. Some of the events and characters are also composites of several individual events or persons.

First Free Press trade paperback edition 2003

FREE PRESS and colophon are
trademarks of Simon & Schuster, Inc.

For information about special discounts for bulk purchases,
please contact Simon & Schuster Special Sales:
1-800-456-6798 or business@simonandschuster.com

Designed by Dana Sloan

Manufactured in the United States of America

20 19 18 17 16 15

The Library of Congress has catalogued the hardcover edition as follows:
Mezrich, Ben.
Bringing down the house: the inside story of six MIT students who took Vegas for millions / Ben Mezrich.
p. cm.
1. Cardsharping. 2. Gambling—Nevada—Las Vegas. 3. Gamblers—Massachusetts—Boston—Biography. 4. Massachusetts Institute of Technology—Students—Biography. I. Title.

GV1247 .M49 2002
364.1'72'0922—dc21
[B]
2002072218

ISBN 0-7432-2570-8
0-7432-4999-2 (Pbk)

CONTENTS

ACKNOWLEDGMENTS		ix
ONE		1
TWO	Boston, Present Day	5
THREE	Boston, June 1994	11
FOUR	Atlantic City, June 1994	17
FIVE	Boston, September 1994	35
SIX	Boston, October 1994	44
SEVEN	Boston, October 1994	53
EIGHT	Las Vegas, Present Day	60
NINE	Thirty Thousand Feet, November 1994	68
TEN	Las Vegas, November 1994	75
ELEVEN	Weston, MA, Thanksgiving 1994	91
TWELVE	The Double Life, 1994–95	97
THIRTEEN	Chicago, May 1995	107
FOURTEEN	Boston, June 1995	114
FIFTEEN	Foxwoods Casino, Present Day	121
SIXTEEN	July 1995 to October 1995	128

SEVENTEEN	Boston, Halloween 1995	135
EIGHTEEN	Boston, November 1995	139
NINETEEN	Las Vegas, Present Day	154
TWENTY	Las Vegas, Fall 1997	161
TWENTY-ONE	Boston, Fall 1997	173
TWENTY-TWO	Las Vegas, Present Day	183
TWENTY-THREE	Boston, Valentine's Day 1998	189
TWENTY- FOUR	Las Vegas, President's Day 1998	193
TWENTY- FIVE	The Bayou: Shreveport, LA, 1998	199
TWENTY- SIX	Boston, Spring 1998	209
TWENTY-SEVEN	Boston, Spring 1998	213
TWENTY- EIGHT	Boston, Spring 1998	219
TWENTY- NINE	Boston, Spring 1998	227
THIRTY	Las Vegas, Memorial Day 1998	235
THIRTY-ONE	Boston, June 1998	240
THIRTY-TWO	Las Vegas, Hard Rock, Present Day	246
HOW TO COUNT CARDS AND BEAT VEGAS	An Essay by Kevin Lewis	252

ACKNOWLEDGMENTS

My deepest thanks to Dominick Anfuso and Leslie Meredith, my spectacular editors at Simon & Schuster. Thanks also to Dorothy Robinson for keeping me focused throughout the editorial process. I am indebted to David Vigliano, my superb agent, as well as Mike Harriot and Jason Sholl at Vig's agency. Thanks to Brian Lipson at Endeaver for shepherding the project through the Hollywood machinery, and to Jay Sanders at Eagle Cove Entertainment for truly understanding what this book is all about.

Furthermore, this book could not have been written without the incredible support and expertise of my card-counting friends here in Boston. Thank you for introducing me to a side of Las Vegas most people never get to see.

As always, I am grateful to my parents and brothers for their continued support. And to Tonya Chen: Beautiful, you glow like neon in my eyes.

BRINGING
DOWN
THE
HOUSE

ONE

It was ten minutes past three in the morning, and Kevin Lewis looked like he was about to pass out. There were three empty martini glasses on the table in front of him, and he was leaning forward on both elbows, his gaze focused on his cards. The dealer was still feigning patience, in deference to the pile of purple chips in front of the martini glasses. But the other players were beginning to get restless. They wanted the kid to make his bet already—or pack it in, grab the ratty duffel bag under his chair, and head back to Boston. Hell, hadn't he won enough? What was a college senior going to do with thirty thousand dollars?

The dealer, sensing the mood at the table, finally tapped the blackjack shoe. "It's up to you, Kevin. You've had a hell of a run. Are you in for another round?"

Kevin tried to hide his trembling hands. Truth be told, his name wasn't really Kevin. And he wasn't even slightly drunk. The red splotches on his cheeks had been painted on in his hotel room. And though thirty thousand dollars in chips was enough to make his hands shake, it wasn't something that would impress the people who *really* knew him. They'd be much more interested in the ratty duffel bag beneath his chair.

Kevin breathed deeply, calming himself. He'd done this a hundred times, and there was no reason to think that tonight would be any different.

He reached for three five-hundred-dollar chips, then glanced around, pretending to look for the cocktail waitress. Out of the corner of his eye, he saw his Spotter. Red-haired, pretty, wearing a low-cut blouse and too much makeup. Nobody would have guessed she was a former MIT mechanical-engineering major and an honors student at Harvard Business School. She was close enough to see the table but far enough away not to draw any suspicion. Kevin caught her gaze, then waited for her signal. A bent right arm would tell him to double his bet. Both arms folded and he'd push most of his chips into the betting circle. Arms flat at her sides and he'd drop down to the lowest possible bet.

But she didn't do any of these things. Instead, she ran her right hand through her hair.

Kevin stared at her, making sure he had read her right. Then he quickly started to gather his chips.

"That's it for me," he said to the table, slurring his words. "Should have skipped that last martini."

Inside, he was on fire. He glanced at his Spotter again. Her hand was still deep in her red hair. *Christ.* In six months, Kevin had never seen a Spotter do that before. The signal had nothing to do with the deck, nothing to do with the precise running count that had won him thirty thousand dollars in under an hour.

A hand in the hair meant only one thing. Get out. Get moving. *Now.*

Kevin slung the duffel bag over his shoulder and jammed the purple chips into his pockets.

The dealer was watching him carefully. "You sure you don't want me to color up?"

Maybe the man sensed that something wasn't right. Kevin was

about to toss him a tip when he caught sight of the suits. Three of them, coming around the nearest craps table. Big, burly men with narrow eyes. *No time for niceties.*

"That's okay," Kevin said, backing away from the table. "I like the way they jiggle around in my pants."

He turned and darted through the casino. He knew they were watching him from above—the Eyes in the Sky. But he doubted they would make a scene. They were just trying to protect their money. Still, he didn't want to take any chances. If the suits caught up to him—well, everyone had heard the stories. Back rooms. Intimidation tactics. Sometimes even violence. No matter how many makeovers the town got, deep down, this was still Vegas.

Tonight Kevin was lucky. He made it outside without incident, blending into the ever-present flow of tourists on the brightly lit Strip. A minute later, he was sitting on a bench at a neon-drenched cabstand across the street. The duffel bag was on his lap.

The redhead from inside dropped onto the bench next to him, lighting herself a cigarette. Her hands were shaking. "That was too fucking close. They came straight out of the elevators. They must have been upstairs watching the whole time."

Kevin nodded. He was breathing hard. His chest was soaked in sweat. There was no better feeling in the world.

"Think we should quit for the night?" the girl asked.

Kevin smiled at her.

"Let's try the Stardust. My face is still good there."

He put both hands on the duffel bag, feeling the stacks of bills inside. A little over one million dollars, all in hundreds: Kevin's bankroll, partially financed by the shadowy investors who recruited him six months before. They had trained him in mock casinos set up in ratty apartments, abandoned warehouses, even MIT classrooms. Then they had set him loose on the neon Strip.

Most of his friends were back at school—taking tests, drinking beer, arguing about the Red Sox. He was in Las Vegas, living the high life on a million dollars of someone else's money. Sooner or later, it might all come crashing down. But Kevin didn't really care.

He hadn't invented the System. He was just one of the lucky few smart enough pull it off . . .

TWO

Boston, Present Day

Twenty-five thousand dollars in hundreds, strapped to each thigh. Another fifty thousand in a Velcro bag taped to my chest. Fifty thousand more stuffed into the pockets of my jacket. A hundred thousand nestled against the small of my back.

I felt like a cross between the Michelin Man and a drug dealer. Bulging and nervous, I pushed through the revolving glass door and entered Logan Airport. Refrigerated air smacked me full in the face, and I paused, getting my bearings. Terminal B was bustling with college kids fleeing town for the long Memorial Day weekend: backpacks, baggy jeans, baseball caps, duffel bags. Everyone moving in every direction at once, the unchoreographed ballet of a modern American airport. I took a deep breath and joined the flow of people.

I kept my eyes low, watching my scuffed dark loafers pad across the tiled floor. *Act casual, think casual, be casual* . . . I tried not to think about the new BMW strapped to my back. I tried not to think about the down payment for a two-bedroom condo nestled in my jacket pockets. I concentrated on looking like everyone else; maybe not a college kid, but perhaps a grad student, a teaching assistant—someone's older brother here to help with the luggage. Just part of the cacophony, a statistic in Logan's weekly FAA report. *Act casual, think casual, be casual . . .*

Suddenly, the modern equivalent of Stonehenge loomed in front of me: two airport metal detectors standing side by side, flanked by waist-high conveyor belts continuously feeding into boxy steel X-ray machines. My pulse rocketed as I mentally checked myself. No bills hanging from my sleeves, no glimpses of green sticking out through the buttons on my shirt. I stepped into line behind a pretty brunette in low-riding jeans, even offering to help her hoist an oversize, sticker-covered suitcase onto one of the conveyor belts. *Act casual, think casual, be casual . . .*

"Next." A tall African-American woman in a grey Logan uniform beckoned. There was a name tag on her right lapel, but I couldn't make out what it said because of the sweat stinging my eyes. I blinked rapidly—but casually—and stepped forward through the disembodied door frame. The invisible rays sliced and diced my entrails in search of metal. Just as I started to breathe easier, a high-pitched mechanical scream tore through the dead air. I froze.

The woman with the name tag pointed me back through the machine. "Empty your pockets of any metal objects and try again."

My throat constricted. My hands jerked instinctively toward the bulges beneath my jacket. Above the stacks of hundred-dollar bills, I felt something shaped like an enormous suppository.

Shit. I had forgotten about my cell phone.

My fingers shook as I reached into my coat and fumbled for my Nokia. I could feel the woman's eyes on me. If she asked me to take off my jacket, I was dead. She'd see the bulges and all hell would break loose. I'd spent the past six months researching stories involving attempts at sneaking undeclared fortunes through airport-security checkpoints, and I knew all about customs law.

The security agents can detain you for forty-eight hours. They drag you to a windowless room, sometimes handcuff you to a chair.

They call in agents from the DEA and the FBI. They confiscate your stake, sometimes without even giving you a receipt. It will take lawyers and letters and appearances in court to get the money back. Maybe six months, maybe a year. Meanwhile, the IRS will descend on you like grey-suited locusts. It will be up to you to prove you weren't planning to trade the cash for little bags of fine white powder. Because to customs agents, money smells like cocaine. Especially hundred-dollar bills. I've read that 95 percent of the hundred-dollar bills in circulation have minute traces of cocaine embedded in their fibers. That means those specially trained customs dogs can sniff out a professional blackjack player faster than they can spot a drug courier. To the dogs—and the customs agents—they both smell the same.

Fear soaked my back as I handed the woman my cell phone. She looked at it like she'd never seen one before. She turned it on, turned it over, then handed it back. Behind me, a kid in a tie-dyed sweatshirt tried to shove a potted plant onto the conveyor belt. The woman with the name tag rolled her eyes. Then, thankfully, she waved me past.

"You're okay. Have a nice flight."

I was barely breathing as I stumbled toward my gate. America West, flight 69. Boston to Vegas direct, the Friday-night neon express. A line of people had already formed by the check-in desk; boisterous, drunk, mostly male, palpably eager.

Kevin Lewis was waiting quietly near the back of the line. I spotted him immediately. Tall, athletically built, but with a slight, shy stoop to his shoulders. Dark hair, dark eyes, a wide, boyish face beneath a mop of dark hair. Vaguely ethnic, but beyond that, indeterminate. His roots could have been Asian, Latino, even Italian or Russian. Like me, he was older than most of the college kids boarding the flight, but he easily fit in with the crowd. He could have been twenty-one, twenty-six, or thirty-five. Wearing a jeans jacket and a baseball cap, he could have passed for a BU frat boy. In a suit and tie, he would have blended in on Wall Street. At the moment, he was wearing an

MIT sweatshirt and baggy shorts. The classic MIT stereotype, right out of his parents' dreams.

He saw my flushed cheeks and smiled. "That's what it felt like. Every day."

The bravado seemed incongruous with the shyness in his shoulders. In many ways, Kevin *was* the classic MIT stereotype. His résumé was perfect: a math-science whiz kid who'd graduated at the top of his class from Exeter, the exclusive New Hampshire boarding school. An electrical-engineering major with an incredible affinity for numbers, a straight-A student who'd covered all the premed requisites—partially to appease his father, partially because the challenge excited him.

But Kevin's résumé didn't tell the whole story. There was another side to his life, one written in neon signs and purple casino chips.

In Boston he'd earned straight A's at MIT.

In Vegas he'd partied with Michael Jordan, Howard Stern, Dennis Rodman, and Kevin Costner. He'd dated a cheerleader from the L.A. Rams and gotten drunk with *Playboy* centerfolds. He'd been chased off of a riverboat in Louisiana and watched a teammate kicked out of a Las Vegas casino. He'd narrowly escaped being thrown into a Bahamian jail. He'd been audited by the IRS, tailed by private investigators, had his picture faxed around the globe by men with shadowy reputations and guns holstered to their waists.

Along the way, he'd amassed a small fortune which he kept in neat stacks of Benjamins in a closet by his bed. Although nobody was quite sure how much money he had made, it was rumored to be somewhere between one and five million dollars. All of it legal, none of it spawned from his perfect, stereotypical résumé.

Shy, geeky, amiable Kevin Lewis had led a double life for nearly four years. Now I was going to tell his story.

"The Velcro's starting to itch" was all I could think to say as I shook Kevin's hand. "There's got to be an easier way to carry your stake."

He grinned, his head cocked to one side. "Sure. Fake umbrellas. Phony laptop computers. Plaster casts and hollow crutches. We went through a gadget phase. You know, James Bond kind of stuff. But hollow crutches are a lot harder to explain to the FBI than Velcro."

If there hadn't been a quarter million dollars taped to my body, I'd have thought he was joking. But Kevin was dead serious. He was keeping his part of our bargain, disclosing the secrets no one on the outside had ever heard before.

I met Kevin Lewis nearly seven years earlier, in a local Boston bar. I had graduated from Harvard a few years before he left MIT, and we shared a few mutual friends as well as a few minor interests: sports, late nights at college pubs, widescreen TVs. I was a fledgling writer at the time of our introduction, just about to publish my first novel. As far as I knew, Kevin was employed by some sort of computer software firm, something he had never explained in detail—probably because I had never been interested enough to ask.

Kevin seemed too much the typical MIT grad: a true engineer at heart. As my writing career began to take off in the years that followed our first meeting, we rarely crossed paths. It was almost six years later that we ran into each other at a Super Bowl party in an apartment located a few blocks from Fenway Park. Kevin had just flown in from a "business" trip to Las Vegas. During the game's halftime show, I found myself alone with him in the kitchen. After a quick exchange of pleasantries, he surprised me by lowering his voice and beckoning me in close: "I've got a great story for your next book," he began.

I immediately thought about edging toward the exit. Like every other writer, I had heard this opening a thousand times in my career. Everyone had a story he believed worthy of a best-seller; for me, reality was rarely interesting enough to take the place of fiction.

But as Kevin began to open up to me, I felt the hair rising on the back of my neck. Unlike the thousands of other cocktail party stories

I had heard, Kevin's tale had all the elements of a high-concept, cinematic thriller—but it was *real*. Everything Kevin was relating to me had actually happened. He had lived it, every minute of it, and he was willing to let me get it all down on paper.

"Why?" I had asked, amazed.

Kevin never answered my question directly. Over time, I've tried to piece together an answer of my own.

Kevin had been part of something incredible. He and his friends got away with one of the biggest schemes in Vegas history—and nobody knew a damn thing about it. Telling the story was his way of reliving the experience in a public forum. It was a way for him to prove to himself and to anyone who cared that it had actually happened.

More than that, it was a way for Kevin to come to terms with the choices he had made, the decisions that had led him to his double life. Many of those choices might have seemed immoral to the outside world. By telling his story, Kevin could explain himself to those who believed that what he did was somehow wrong.

In other words, his story was part boast, part confession. For me, this was too good a story to pass up.

As the Super Bowl played on in the other room, Kevin made me an offer. He promised to tell me everything, to give me access to his contacts and his lifestyle. He promised to teach me his system and show me the key that could unlock the casino's coffers.

In return, I would give him his moment.

The deeper I delved into Kevin's double life, the more I realized how far I had come out ahead in our bargain. When I finally sat down to put the words onto paper, Kevin's story flashed by my eyes in Technicolor as bright as a Vegas marquee . . .

THREE

Boston, June 1994

In the beginning, there was sushi.

Five neat little rows lined up across the glass coffee table like a battalion of squat, brightly-colored soldiers. Above the battalion, the strong scent of seaweed and raw fish spread out in a fog to fill the cramped, seventies-era high-rise apartment. Beneath the table stood a pyramid of discarded cardboard cartons from Toyama, the late-night Japanese dive located a few blocks away in Boston's moderately European Back Bay. The dive wasn't a favorite but an expedience, one of the few restaurants open past midnight on a Sunday in a city that still clung to antiquated blue laws and Puritanical facades—despite playing home to one of the largest, rowdiest college-age populations on earth.

The sushi was part of a weekly routine. As usual, it was well after two in the morning, and Kevin Lewis was crashed out on the worn futon in the middle of the sparsely furnished living room. The TV was on with the sound turned down, and Kevin was half asleep. His body ached from two hours at the MIT gym, and his mind was numb from a long day spent sequestered in a chemistry lab at one of Boston's top hospitals. It was two months into the summer after his junior year, and he had spent so much time surrounded by test tubes, he was beginning to identify them by name. The daily grind at the lab was made worse by the fact that he no longer had any interest in medicine as a career; he just hadn't figured out how to break the news to his parents. His father was still trying to convince him to quit the MIT Swim Team so he could spend more time on his research. More time with the goddamn test tubes.

Kevin had just turned twenty a month before and he was old enough to make his own decisions about the direction of his life. But like most twenty-year-olds, he had no idea where he was heading. He knew only where he *didn't* want to end up. It was 1993, the dawn of the Internet revolution; many of his MIT classmates were already conceiving start-ups in their dorm rooms, conspiring to turn the high-tech skills that had made many of them pariahs in high school into launchpads for their billion-dollar dreams. The kids who weren't dissecting microprocessors in their bunk beds were set to ride the tried-and-true waves of Wall Street. Venture capital, investment banking, tech consulting—MIT, along with Harvard and the other Ivies, was one of the main feeders to the vast money-making machines fueling the revolution. If the eighties had made greed acceptable, the nineties had elevated it to an art form.

Medicine, academia, science for science's sake—these were not compelling choices in the tornado of options swirling around a campus such as MIT. But unlike many of his classmates, Kevin didn't see himself being satisfied by a life on Wall Street or a smoke-and-mirrors sojourn into Silicon Valley. He didn't think of himself as some sort of saint: He was as addicted to the notion of unfettered greed as the kid on the next bunk over. He just hadn't yet found his drug of choice.

At the moment he didn't want to think about his future, or his father, or the test tubes in his lab. He just wanted to sleep. But the sushi waged war with his senses. He reluctantly opened his eyes and watched as his friends descended on the coffee table.

Christ, the jackals.

He was immediately struck by the contrast in physical geometry. Jason Fisher's hulking form cast a boxy shadow over the rows of sushi. Six foot one, two hundred and twenty pounds, Fisher was built like a heavyweight boxer. His shoulders were huge, his head square, and the muscles beneath his MIT T-shirt rippled like a plastic trash can left out in a heat wave. Kevin had met Fisher in the gym after bravely offering to help the former MIT student load plates the size of manhole covers onto the bench press. He had been surprised to learn that Fisher, several years older, was a similar mix of ethnicities; part Chinese—you could see it in his eyes, narrow drops of oil beneath a ridged brow—part Brazilian. Two days later, Fisher introduced Kevin to his cohort and roommate, Andre Martinez. Slicked-back hair, flashy silk shirt, shark tooth necklace, bushy eyebrows, and impossibly wide teardrop eyes. Martinez was barely five foot four and couldn't have weighed more than a hundred and thirty pounds. But his reputation more than made up for his size. Kevin had been hearing rumors about Martinez since freshman week.

The standout genius at a school filled with geniuses, a kid so smart he had scared the math professors into accelerating him to graduate-level courses on his third day on campus. Whiz Kid, Boy Wonder, the pride of MIT—until, one week into his sophomore year, Martinez had suddenly left school. In the six months they'd known each other, Kevin had never asked why—and Martinez had never volunteered.

"I think it's awake," Martinez said now as he flipped a piece of sushi into his mouth. "Jab it with a chopstick to make sure."

Fisher complied, poking Kevin in the forehead. Kevin grabbed for his wrist, knocking a sushi roll across the living room. Martinez laughed a little too loudly, and Kevin realized they were both drunk. Less than an hour ago, Fisher and Martinez had landed at Logan, and it looked as though they went through most of the beverage cart during the five-hour flight. Kevin tried to hide his distaste. It had been like this all summer. The two of them gone every weekend, then spending the week sleeping late and drinking early—and dropping in on Kevin without regard to the hour. They never went to work, never seemed to do anything at all, while Kevin slaved away in the lab.

"A couple of slackers," Kevin said, shoving two rolls of sushi into his mouth. He was channeling his dad, and it bothered him. Why should he care how his friends spent their time?

"We choose to think of ourselves as emancipated," Fisher said. "We're working our way up to slacker."

Kevin shook his head. Everything was a joke to them. They existed entirely in the present, no responsibilities, no conscience. Kevin couldn't imagine living like that. Everything in his life had always been planned out. Exeter, MIT, his part-time job at the lab. Even with the plans, he agonized over every step. Fisher and Martinez didn't agonize over anything. They didn't seem to have a future, and they didn't seem to care.

Neither of them had even graduated from MIT; both had simply left. At least Fisher's reasons had been noble; his sister, Josie, had been injured in a car accident, and he had dropped out to help with her recovery. Since then he had been hanging out with Martinez full-time. "Hanging out" was a good way of putting it, because neither of them had ever held a job, set an alarm, or worn a tie.

And yet the money never seemed to run out. In fact, they had enough money to travel to Las Vegas nearly every weekend. Why Vegas—almost *always* Vegas—Kevin hadn't yet figured out. He had never been there himself, had only read about the "city of sin" in paperback novels and seen it on prime-time TV. Although the bright neon lights and massive resorts were compelling enough, he couldn't imagine vacationing in the same spot over and over again. Throw in a few topless showgirls, and it made a little more sense. But Fisher and Martinez weren't exactly casanovas. Neither of them had kept a steady girlfriend longer than a carton of sushi lasted in the refrigerator.

"If I didn't know any better," Kevin grunted, reclining back onto the couch. "I'd think you guys were selling drugs."

"White slavery," Martinez responded, fighting Fisher for the last piece of fish. "You're just lucky you're a Chink like the rest of us." He crossed his eyes. His mother was from Singapore, his father from Cuba. His family tree was made up of so many different races, you needed a pie chart to buy him a birthday present.

"Seriously," Kevin said, his eyes half closed. "What the hell do you guys do on the weekends? You've been gone every Friday this summer. Not that I'm complaining. The only problem is that you keep coming back."

Fisher started clearing the coffee table, using the sleeve of his sweatshirt to catch the crumbs. Martinez seemed suddenly interested in a smudge on the seam of his silk shirt.

"I guess it's 'need to know,'" Kevin surmised.

Martinez looked at Fisher, who shrugged. Martinez reached into his back pocket and tossed something onto the table. It landed with a soft thud.

Kevin's eyes widened. A stack of bills about two inches thick bundled together by a strip of colored tape. Kevin reached for the stack and saw that the top bill had a picture of Benjamin Franklin in its center. A warmth moved through his cheeks as he fanned through the rest of the stack. Hundreds, all of them. He wasn't Rain Man, but he could count. A hundred hundreds. *Ten thousand dollars.*

He was wide awake now. "What are you guys into?"

Fisher smiled. There was mischief in his narrow eyes. "Why don't you come with us next weekend?"

Kevin couldn't stop fanning the stack of hundred-dollar bills. He had never seen this much money in his life. They could pay their whole summer rent with the stack and have enough left over for sushi every night.

"To Las Vegas?"

Martinez held out his hand, gesturing for the cash. "Not Vegas. Atlantic City. The Holyfield fight at the Tropicana, Saturday night. A friend of ours is hooking us up."

Kevin had never been to a professional boxing match. He'd heard that the tickets for a Holyfield fight were almost impossible to get. Not only were his two slacker buddies hooked up, but Martinez was walking around with ten thousand dollars in his back pocket. Kevin felt like he was on the threshold of something he couldn't define. The mystery of his friends' carefree existence was about to be revealed.

Kevin knew what his father would say. "I'm supposed to be in lab on Saturday."

Fisher gave him a patronizing look. "Take a day off. The test tubes will be there when you get back."

Kevin didn't like Fisher's tone. Fisher could be a jackass—it went hand in hand with his size. His words felt like a macho challenge. But Kevin *was* curious. He'd been following a straight line all of his life. Nearing his last year at MIT, he was on the cusp of a time of confusion, searching for a future that was both satisfying and compelling. Maybe Fisher and Martinez could show him something more fulfilling than the world which had been painted for him. And bottom line—he'd always dreamed about seeing Holyfield fight.

What did he have to lose?

Kevin tossed Martinez the stack of hundred-dollar bills. "Do we have good seats?"

FOUR

Atlantic City, June 1994

Five days later, Kevin exited Newark Airport through an automated tornado of revolving glass, just as a Mercedes limousine slid to a stop in the passenger pickup lane in front of him. He had to shield his eyes as the bright sunlight flashed off the car's sleek black curves, and he glanced back toward Martinez, who was working his way through the revolving door behind him. Martinez already had his sunglasses on, a wide smile on his narrow face. The crazy fuck still looked drunk, though it was nine A.M. and they had spent the past hour circling ten thousand feet above northern New Jersey.

Martinez moved next to Kevin on the sidewalk, slinging his backpack over one shoulder. "So, how do you like our ride?"

Kevin raised his eyebrows. He turned back toward the limo. "That's for us?"

He watched the rear passenger door swing open. An unusually tall man in a slick grey suit uncoiled onto the sidewalk, pausing to adjust a jet-black ponytail against the nape of his neck. The man caught sight of Martinez and sprang forward, hand outstretched.

"Welcome back, Mr. Kim."

Kevin stared as Martinez shook the man's hand. *Mr. Kim?* There was a jangle of metal emitting from the man's wrist, and Kevin glimpsed a tacky gold bracelet wound around an even tackier gold watch. The man's face was smooth and tan, his eyes set close together above a sharply tapered nose. His expression was somehow obsequious and terrifying at the same time.

"And this must be your friend," the man continued, still vigorously pumping Martinez's hand. "I'm Dino Taratolli. I'm Mr. Kim's host at the Tropicana. Any friend of Mr. Kim's is a friend of our casino."

He gestured toward the limo, then took Martinez's backpack off of his shoulder and galloped toward the trunk. When he was out of earshot, Kevin grabbed Martinez by the elbow. "Mr. Kim?"

Martinez laughed, leading him forward. "Oh yeah. I forgot to tell you. I'm Robert Kim this weekend."

Kevin followed Martinez into the cool leather interior of the car, quickly noting the crystal-appointed minibar and the twenty-inch television mounted on the rosewood divider that separated them from the unseen driver.

"You're Robert Kim. And who am I?"

"You're still you. But we're both Eurotrash millionaires."

Kevin wasn't thrilled that the weekend was starting with invented identities. His suspicion that his friends were into something illegal was only growing stronger. But he decided to play along. They *were* sitting in a limo with a TV and a minibar.

He heard the trunk slam shut, then glanced back at the airport terminal. The sidewalk was nearly empty; it was a Saturday morning, and you had to be crazy or drunk to fly to New Jersey on a Saturday morning. *Or a little of both.*

"And what about Fisher? Where the hell is he?"

Fisher had headed to the bathroom right after they had exited the airplane. Kevin had assumed he'd meet them outside, but he hadn't yet appeared.

"He's going to meet us later," Martinez said. "He had to make a phone call."

Kevin felt a nervous shiver move through him. He'd expected the weekend to be an adventure, but he had to ask himself: How well did he really know these guys? He'd met them just four months ago. Before that, he'd known them only by reputation. Two college dropouts with mysterious means of income and nonconformist lifestyles. Warning bells were going off, but Kevin was doing his best to ignore them. He reminded himself that he was there to see the fight, maybe get in a little gambling. Besides, the warning bells had been installed by his parents. Maybe it was time Kevin started to take some risks with his life.

"So Fisher's not taking the limo with us?"

"He's got his own ride," Martinez said, falling silent as Dino Taratolli climbed into the seat next to him and shut the passenger door. The lanky man tapped on the rosewood divider with two ringed fingers, and the limo pulled away from the curb.

The scenery outside was mostly highway, chemical plants, and industrial warehouses, so Kevin had little to distract him from the two wild cards seated across from him. It was obvious that Martinez and the casino employee had spent a fair amount of time together. From what Kevin could gather through their staccato patter, Dino had been Martinez's *host*—that word again, pregnant with meaning Kevin didn't pretend to understand—at Caesars Palace in Las Vegas until six months ago. Then Dino had been *bought out* by the Tropicana in Atlantic City and had brought many of his *high rollers* with him.

Evidently, Martinez—or Kim, as Dino knew him—was one of these high rollers. Certainly, Martinez seemed to have the jargon down pat. It was as though he and the host had a private vocabulary, rife with words like *comp, whale, action,* and *RFB.* After twenty minutes, Kevin couldn't stifle his curiosity any longer.

"What exactly does a host do, anyway?"

Maybe a little blunt, but it seemed like a good place to start. Martinez didn't seem to mind the interruption—it gave him a chance to take a closer look at the minibar. Dino offered a smile, not exactly condescending, but it was obvious he had pegged Kevin as a sidekick, nothing more.

"We do whatever it takes. We make your stay as pleasant as possible. We bring the big players to our casino—and we make sure they keep coming back."

Simple enough. Maybe Kevin was making an idiot of himself, but he had been brought up by a scientist and born with an engineer's mind. He liked to ask questions, and he liked to be thorough.

"And what's a big player?"

Martinez had a bottle of vodka in one hand and was searching for orange juice in the refrigerator beneath the bar. If he was concerned by the conversation, he wasn't showing it.

"That depends on the casino," Dino answered. "Usually, there's a sliding scale. If you're betting twenty-five dollars a blackjack hand—or a roll of the dice, a pull on the slots, a spin of the roulette wheel—you get a special room rate and a smile from the desk clerk. Seventy-five bucks a hand, you might get a free room. A hundred and fifty, maybe RFB—that's room, food, beverage. But if you're a high roller—betting five, ten, twenty thousand a stay, you're going to get the full treatment. A ride from the airport. A bucket of champagne waiting for you next to your Jacuzzi. And a guy like me to make sure everything runs smoothly."

Kevin whistled. *Five to twenty thousand dollars a trip.* His slacker buddies, sleeping until noon every day. Blowing five grand in Vegas every weekend. Maybe they had rich uncles he didn't know about. *Or a stash of cocaine under the sink.*

"So the hosts seek out the high rollers," Kevin said, "give 'em free stuff to keep them at the casino. When you move casinos, you take your players with you."

Dino nodded as Martinez fixed himself a screwdriver. "That's the idea. Each one of my high rollers understands the sort of service I can provide. Whatever it takes, I'll keep them happy. And who knows, maybe they'll hit it big, turn into a real live whale. Right, Mr. Kim?"

Martinez looked up from his drink. "A great white one, Dino."

Outside the window, the industrial warehouses had given way to cottage-styled houses packed closely together. Beyond the houses, Kevin saw the bridge linking them to the ten-mile sandbar that housed the largest gambling center west of Nevada.

Growing up on the East Coast, Kevin shared the common "local" view of Atlantic City: an experiment that had never quite lived up to its expectations. In the late seventies, the necklace of casinos along the country's most famous boardwalk had opened its doors to much hype, but the dream of a Vegas of the East had never quite materialized. Despite the fact that the casinos themselves had intermittently flourished, the surrounding city had deteriorated in rapid fashion. Over the past two decades, Atlantic City had become a textbook case *against* legalized gambling in urban centers.

The much-published hype/hope was that the casinos would create jobs and bring in a high-class tourist population from nearby Manhattan. But despite private investment of more than six billion dollars, the area surrounding the casinos never experienced the expected economic resurgence. Speculation in properties and the demolition of existing buildings to make way for the casino hotels led to abandoned structures and the closure of nearly 35 percent of the city's existing businesses. Unemployment surged and crime tripled, while 25 percent of the city's population left for greener pastures.

Atlantic City had the glitz and glamour—weighed down by crime and poverty.

As the limousine rolled across the bridge to the sandbar, Kevin tried to smell the ocean. All he got was car leather and exhaust.

"What's a whale?" he asked finally.

Martinez clinked his glass against the window. "A whale is someone who can lose a million dollars at cards—and not give a damn."

High rollers don't take cabs from the airport. They don't carry their own bags. They never wait on check-in lines. They stay in rooms with Jacuzzis, circular leather couches, wide-screen televisions, and views of the beach. And evidently, they wear whatever the hell they want, no matter how ridiculous they look.

Martinez came out of the bathroom in an electric-blue shirt and matching jeans. He had exchanged his sneakers for shiny leather designer boots, and his hair was slicked down with so much mousse that the outline of his skull was visible. The effect was disorienting—actually, in a way it was *orienting*. With the hair and flashy outfit, Martinez looked more Asian than Latino; he easily could have passed for a rich kid from Korea or Japan on his way to a trendy disco.

Kevin laughed out loud, his feet up on the glass coffee table in the center of the lavish living room. The suite was bigger than any hotel room he had ever seen before; two thousand square feet, with wide picture windows and plush cream carpeting. The windows overlooked the boardwalk, and from twenty floors up, the beach was so beautiful it was hard to believe they were in New Jersey.

"Nice duds," he commented. He was still wearing shorts and a sweatshirt. He had an oxford shirt and khakis in Martinez's backpack, but he hadn't planned on changing until they were on their way to the fight. "Does the casino have some bizarre dress code I should know about?"

Martinez ignored the query. He was busy fishing around the inside of his shirt with both hands, and Kevin wondered if he was looking for his sunglasses. Certainly, they'd finish the look. Then he heard the distinct rip of Velcro, and Martinez's hands reappeared.

Kevin's heart thumped as he saw the roll of bills. At least four inches thick, twice as large as the roll Martinez had shown him back at their apartment. And again, the visible bills were hundreds. As much as twenty grand taped inside his shirt. Had Martinez worn the money on him the whole trip from Boston? Through airport security, through the metal detector—shit, the kid hadn't even raised a sweat.

By now, Kevin was beginning to realize that Fisher and Martinez were, at the very least, serious gamblers. Was it possible that they had made all their cash playing casino games?

He knew there were people who made a living at cards—hell, there'd been movies about it, books, even newspaper articles. But he understood from what he had read that professional gamblers usually just eked out a living, playing carefully for tiny odds. Wads of cash and huge VIP suites were for people who lost—not for those who won. Unless Martinez had gotten lucky at a slot machine, how did he and Fisher support all those weekends in Las Vegas? Why was a guy like Dino Taratolli whisking them past the registration desk and up into a suite like this?

Kevin was dying to know the truth. "That's quite a stake. It's going to be fun watching you drop it at the tables. What do you play? Craps? Poker?"

Martinez smiled, jamming the stack of bills into his shirt pocket. "Blackjack. It's the only game worth playing."

Kevin rose from the couch. Blackjack? He would have guessed poker. It seemed more Martinez's style. He was crafty, smart, and judging from his shifting appearance, quite a chameleon. Kevin would have thought those skills to be best utilized in a game where you faced off against other players. Blackjack, you played against the house; really, it seemed like you played against the cards. What good was personal style in a game like that?

"Okay, blackjack. But shouldn't we wait for Fisher?"

They'd been in the suite for twenty minutes. Kevin wondered

what was taking Fisher so long. *Probably stopped at the hotel gym for a few bench presses.*

"Don't worry about him," Martinez answered. "We're here to have fun."

Kevin started to protest, then thought better of it and acquiesced. Fisher was a big boy. There was obviously some reason he was dragging behind. Worst case, they'd meet up before the fight. Kevin hadn't seen the tickets yet, but Martinez had promised him that the seats were so close, he'd need a raincoat to keep himself from getting drenched with blood and sweat.

"There's nothing more fun than watching a guy in a shirt like that lose some money," Kevin joked. "So let's hit the tables."

Martinez shook his head. "First, we check out the pool. The showgirls hit the pool early. Then we attack the buffet. Can't play on an empty stomach."

He looked back at Kevin, patting his bulging shirt pocket. "And then we're gonna *kill* the tables."

It was two in the afternoon by the time they stepped over the threshold of the casino floor, and Kevin was feeling mildly lethargic, the result of a heavily laden VIP buffet and forty minutes on a lounge chair in a private pool cabana. He hadn't seen any showgirls, but he had been lucky enough to watch an extremely pale family from Passaic play water volleyball against a group of Japanese tourists.

The floor was crowded, equal parts tourists in shorts and T-shirts wandering in from the boardwalk and well-heeled weekend warriors from Manhattan, some in suits and ties. Despite the fiercely air-conditioned ventilation, the air stung with a blend of sunscreen and cigarette smoke. Kevin and Martinez paused at the entrance, getting their bearings. Slot machines fanned out on all sides, the blinking lights and spinning wheels wreaking havoc on Kevin's senses. The tables were spread out across the center of the long floor, blackjack felts and craps stations intermingled with roulette and stud poker. Crowds three people deep gathered around each of the tables, and Kevin didn't see a single free stool. For a moment he wondered if they'd even get to play. Then Martinez pointed at a raised section of the floor, separated from the main tables by three steps and a velvet rope. There were a dozen tables behind the rope, and only a smattering of players.

"High-stakes room," Martinez said. "Usually I like to play the main floor, but there are too many civilians here today."

Kevin followed Martinez toward the high-stakes tables, winding through the crowd. The crush of "civilians" energized him; so many smiling, laughing people, so much gambling adrenaline flowing through the room. He found it hard to catch his breath.

When they reached the steps to the quieter tables, Martinez yanked the stack of bills out of his shirt pocket and casually split it in half. "You've played blackjack before, right?"

Kevin looked at the bills in Martinez's hand. Sure, he'd played before—a few times on vacation with his family, once or twice at Foxwoods, the Indian casino in Connecticut. But the most he'd ever bet on a single hand was five dollars, and the most he'd ever risked in a night was a few hundred. He wasn't stupid, he knew that the house had an edge at the tables. *Every player is a loser eventually.* He'd gambled a few times for fun, but never seriously.

"I'm no expert, but I won't make a fool of myself."

Martinez pointed toward the nearest empty table. A frizzy-haired dealer in a dark blue shirt was standing behind the horseshoe-shaped felt, hands behind her back. Six decks were spread out on the table in front of her, faces up. The empty plastic shoe—rectangular, two feet long, uncovered—sat waiting, hungry for their action.

"So you know basic strategy."

Kevin shrugged. He knew how the game was played. The dealer

dealt you two cards, you added them together and tried to get closest to twenty-one without going over. If you wanted another card, you pointed at the table. If you wanted to stand, you waved your hand. If you got over twenty-one, you busted, and the dealer took your money. If you hit twenty-one on your first two cards—a blackjack—the casino paid you one and a half times your bet. The player went first, the dealer second. The dealer's play depended on the casino, but usually he would hit until his cards added up to seventeen—or until he busted. When you got pairs of the same card, you could split them and have two bets going on separate hands. Again depending on the casino, you could double your bet—double down—on your first two cards, taking a single card in the hopes of beating the dealer for more money. The rules were fairly simple, as card games went. But the strategy seemed tricky, and Kevin was by no means an expert.

"I know the books say you're supposed to keep on hitting until you get seventeen, if the dealer's showing a high card. When the dealer shows a weak card—maybe a five or a six—you usually stick with your first two cards. And I know you double down on an eleven, hoping to draw a face card for a twenty-one."

"That's a start," Martinez said. He extended his hand, offering Kevin half of the bills from his stack. *Ten thousand dollars, cash.*

"Are you sure this is a good idea?" Kevin asked.

Martinez waved the money at him. "Don't worry. I'll be right next to you. I'll let you know when you're making a mistake."

Kevin's cheeks burned as he took the bills and followed Martinez to the table. *Christ, this beats sitting in the lab.*

Kevin lowered himself onto a stool next to Martinez and watched as he peeled twenty bills off his roll and laid them on the felt. Kevin carefully did the same and waited nervously as the dealer counted out twenty black chips for each of them. Then she swept the cards off the table and began to shuffle. Her hands danced gracefully through the choreographed ritual shared by blackjack dealers the world over. By the time she rolled the deck, aiming it at Martinez for the cut, Kevin was bouncing off his stool.

Here we go. He moved a black chip onto the betting circle in front of him. He would have liked to have started lower, but the table minimum was a hundred. He noticed that Martinez had started with two chips. His friend seemed completely calm, smiling as he made small talk with the dealer. Her name was Brett, she was from Delaware, she had two kids and an ex-husband, and no, she'd never been to Korea. Kevin didn't think Martinez had ever been to Korea either, but what the hell, it made for good conversation.

After the first few hands, Kevin's nerves settled, and he began to enjoy the highs and lows of gambling. Hand by hand, the chips lulled him into forgetting how much money he was playing with; instead, he concentrated on making the right plays. He'd never studied any books on basic strategy. But he knew about BS from a television special he had seen on cable: a framework of proper plays based on what the dealer was showing, developed first—in a flawed but thorough form—by four army engineers who played tens of thousands of hands and published their results in the September 1956 edition of the *Journal of the American Statistical Association.* BS was then thoroughly reworked in the early sixties by a UCAL and visiting MIT math professor named Edward Thorp, then tweaked numerous times over the years by experts with access to IBM computers. Kevin had never bothered to study basic strategy because he gambled only occasionally—and he wasn't really sure how much of a difference it made, anyway. Was skill really that much of a factor in blackjack? Didn't it all boil down to a matter of luck?

Martinez obviously took basic strategy extremely seriously. Whenever Kevin paused, trying to figure out whether to take the next card or stand, Martinez was ready with quick advice. The dealer didn't seem to care; in fact, she lent her own expertise. Kevin usually deferred to Martinez, since it was his money they were going to lose.

As for Martinez, he played smoothly, barely looking at his cards, tossing chips into the betting circle with seeming abandon. He kept his bets around two hundred dollars, but every now and then he jumped up to five hundred, and once he even laid down a thousand dollars at once, getting lucky with a pair of kings. He never celebrated when he won, never complained when he lost. In fact, he didn't seem that interested in the game at all.

His play seemed to follow BS, except for a few noticeably odd executions. Once, with a two-hundred-dollar bet on the table, he hit on a sixteen against a dealer's two. Luckily, he drew a two for an eighteen to win the hand. Another time he doubled on an eight, managing to draw an ace. Toward the end of the shoe, he began raising his bet, taking advantage of a hot streak of good hands. Kevin began to win himself, drawing three hands of face cards and ending with a natural twenty-one. He was grinning at his good fortune when the plastic shuffle card came out, signaling the end of the shoe. The dealer raised her hands, announcing that it was time to shuffle up.

"That went well," Kevin said. It looked like he and Martinez were up a few thousand dollars. Most of it was stacked in front of his friend, but at least five hundred dollars of pure profit was in front of him. It was the most he'd ever won in his life. He thought it was time to get a drink and celebrate. He was about to search for a cocktail waitress when he noticed Martinez trying to catch his eye.

As the dealer rolled the cards into a tall pile, preparing to shuffle, Martinez leaned toward Kevin, lowering his voice. "You see that last run of cards?"

"We got really lucky. A lot of high cards. Kings, queens, a couple of aces. We both did pretty well—"

"Actually," Martinez interrupted, "it was nineteen face cards and three aces set among eight unremarkable lows."

Kevin stared at him. He hadn't noticed Martinez paying such close attention to the cards; he hadn't written anything down or whispered to himself.

"So?"

"So you know that right now, near the top of that stack of unshuffled cards, there's a string of predominantly high cards, about thirty deep."

Kevin looked at the stack, watched as the dealer split it into two equal-size piles. In a few seconds the rituals of her shuffle would begin, the cards cut together again and again until they were thoroughly mixed.

"I'm not sure I follow you."

Martinez sighed, impatient. "You're aware that high cards favor the player, right?"

Kevin remembered the television special. "Sure. Because the dealer has to hit up to sixteen, with more high cards, she'll bust more often."

"That's one reason," Martinez interrupted again. "There's also a higher chance of hitting blackjack, which pays one and a half times your bet. And there's a better chance of drawing into a double down. There are other reasons, but those are good enough for now."

He paused, jutting his chin toward the dealer, who had finally begun to shuffle the cards together. "So if you knew that a run like that was about to come out of the deck, couldn't you take advantage of the situation? Raise your basic bets, change your strategy a little, win a lot of hands with a lot of money on the table?"

Kevin squinted. In theory that made sense. But the stack of high cards had already come and gone.

"If you knew that sort of run was coming. But she's shuffling the cards."

Martinez smiled. "Right in front of us."

Kevin realized that Martinez had been watching the dealer shuffle while they were whispering back and forth. Kevin shook his head. Martinez had to be joking.

"There's no way you can track those cards."

"There isn't?"

Martinez recentered himself on his stool, still watching the shuffle. Kevin continued to stare at him.

A few minutes later the dealer finished, letting Martinez cut. Then she restacked the cards in the shoe and began to deal. Hand after hand, the play went by quietly, and both Kevin and Martinez remained about even with the house. As the shoe reached the halfway point, Kevin began to relax, assuming that his friend had indeed been screwing with him. He put another hundred on the betting circle—and watched as Martinez suddenly raised his bet to a thousand dollars. He coughed, and Martinez looked at him, then smiled at the dealer.

"Feeling the lucky spirits, Brett. In Korea we listen to our spirits."

She laughed, dealing out the cards. Both Kevin and Martinez drew twenties, kings and queens. The dealer drew sixteen, then busted with a ten.

That was just the beginning.

Over the next four rounds, there were twelve face cards and two aces. Martinez won nearly six thousand dollars, and even Kevin made a killing, winning three hundred more.

After the shoe emptied out, Martinez scooped up his chips and stepped back from the table. Kevin followed him, his head spinning. When they had passed out of the high-stakes area, he grabbed Martinez by the shoulder.

"How the fuck did you do that?"

Martinez signaled a passing cocktail waitress, taking two vodka martinis off of her tray. After tipping her a five, he turned to Kevin.

"It's not magic. Just math. It's called shuffle tracking. It's a basic probability-distribution exercise. You can even calculate the percentage of low-card infiltration into the run, caused by the dealer's shuffle. After that, it's just a matter of practice. Really good players can track a group of fifteen cards through a six-deck shuffle without breaking a sweat."

Kevin sipped his martini, amazed. Martinez was right, of course. It was more math than magic. But it was still incredible to watch.

Altogether, they had made close to ten thousand dollars—in under an hour. And it hadn't been simple luck. Martinez had truly tracked that dealer's shuffle.

"I'll explain more later," Martinez said, pushing forward through the crowd. He was heading toward another blackjack table situated at the edge of the main floor. There were two overweight women sitting next to each other on the last two stools, watching the play. Across from them, in the first-base position, was a familiar, bulked-up shape with dark pinpoint eyes and a crew cut. Fisher had finally arrived.

As they approached the table, Martinez touched Kevin's arm.

"There's one other thing. When we reach Fisher, act like we don't know him."

Kevin rolled his eyes.

"Okay, Mr. Kim."

"I'm serious," Martinez said. "Just stand behind the table and watch. I promise, it will be a good show."

From the moment they arrived at the table, Kevin could see that Martinez had been telling the truth. The two overweight women were jabbering to each other in loud voices about "the damn fool" sitting across from them. As Kevin watched, Fisher made some of the strangest blackjack plays he'd ever seen. For the most part, he kept hitting like a madman, taking as many cards as he could—even busting with four cards after hitting on a seventeen. After each hand, the two women chided him for making such obviously stupid moves.

"What the hell is he doing?" Kevin whispered to Martinez. "Trying to lose?"

Martinez shook his head. "Look at how he's betting. Just ten dollars in the circle. He doesn't care about these hands. He's playing a part, trying to establish himself as a wild player. At the same time, he's running the cards, counting down based on the deal. He's trying to control the deal so that a specific card is dealt to him."

Kevin narrowed his eyes. "A specific card? What do you mean?"

"He's sitting at first base—the closest seat to the dealer. Sometimes, with some dealers, you can see the bottom card when they roll the deck after the shuffle. If they let you cut the deck, you can cut to an *exact* point, maybe one deck's length—and when they stack the deck into the shoe, that card you just saw ends up at *exactly* the cut point—the fifty-second card. If you're good, really good, you can get the dealer to deal you that specific card."

Kevin laughed out loud. One of the overweight women glared at him, then turned back to the table. Kevin looked at Martinez.

"That's crazy. And even if you *could* get the dealer to give you a card you already saw, how much difference would it make?"

"Depends," Martinez said, watching Fisher hit on another seventeen. "If you saw an ace, it's over a fifty-percent advantage. That means on average, you bet a thousand dollars on that hand, you get more than fifteen hundred back. How many ten-dollar hands would you lose to get one fifteen-hundred-dollar hand?"

Martinez paused as Fisher suddenly pushed a stack of black chips into the betting circle. The two women went dead silent. The dealer, a tall Latino with an earring in one ear, glanced back at a man in a suit standing a few feet behind him in the pit—obviously his boss. The suited man looked over, seemed to recognize Fisher, then nodded. He'd seen enough of Fisher's play to know that he wasn't a threat. *Another rich kid doing something stupid.*

The dealer dealt the first card to Fisher—and there it was, an ace of spades. The two women crowed, jabbering about the crazy fool's luck. The rest of the cards came out: Fisher's second card was a nine, for a soft twenty, beating the dealer's seventeen.

Fisher swept up his winnings and stood, smiling at the two women. "Thank you for your help. I think I'm finally starting to get the hang of it."

Then he walked right past Kevin and Martinez and headed for the pool.

They found him stretched out on a lounge chair, hands behind his head. His dark eyes were shielded by wraparound sunglasses, and his biceps bulged beneath a tight white T-shirt. Martinez pulled another two chairs next to him, and Kevin sat heavily, still bewildered by the display he had just witnessed. He was beginning to see his two friends in a different light. He'd always known they were math whizzes—Martinez was legendary, and Fisher followed closely behind, having honored in molecular engineering before leaving MIT to be with his sister. Obviously, they had decided to use their skills in an innovative way. They had learned some fantastic card tricks, and they had parlayed these abilities into a moneymaking scheme.

"Now I know how you afford all those weekends in Vegas," Kevin said, kicking off his shoes. "Those were some pretty cool stunts."

Fisher adjusted his shades. "Circus acts, Kevin. Shuffle tracking and cuts. They give you a nice advantage over the house, but they can't be used too often. Usually, we only pull that shit out when we're on vacation. Walking-around money, that's all. The real action is a lot more consistent—and a lot more lucrative."

Kevin was both intrigued and disturbed. He glanced across the pool at the sun-splashed boardwalk and the postcard-perfect beach. Then he looked back at Fisher and Martinez, splayed out on plastic chairs, cash bulging in their pockets. He thought about how hard he'd been working—in the lab, at school, at home. *It just doesn't seem fair.*

"So you guys cheat at cards?"

Martinez sat up, indignant. "Absolutely not. We don't alter any of the rules or fuck with the nature of the game. We use our brains to take advantage of arbitrage opportunities. Blackjack is beatable—so we beat it. We beat the hell out of it."

Kevin was fairly sure it wasn't as innocent as that. After all, Martinez had checked into the hotel under a fake name, and they were pretending that Fisher was a stranger they had met at the casino. But Martinez was right; what Kevin had witnessed wasn't exactly cheating—was it?

He remembered something he had read in the school paper, sometime during the first semester of his junior year. An article about a blackjack club at MIT. Ten or fifteen kids, mostly seniors, who spent their time practicing some highly technical method of counting cards. But he'd always thought it was just some campus exercise, one of the many geeky extracurriculars you saw advertised in the student lounge. He didn't think it had any real-world application—that anyone had actually tried it out in a casino. And he never would have guessed that his friends were involved in something like that. It seemed too organized for a pair of anarchists.

"It's an MIT club, right? I think I read about it in the paper. A bunch of geeks who play cards all night in the back of the library."

Fisher laughed. He might have been able to bench-press two-fifty, but he knew the truth: They were *all* geeks. Even the jocks at MIT had aced the math portion of their SATs.

"Well, it started out that way. A sort of club sport, with team sweatshirts and everything. But it's gotten a bit bigger than that."

Kevin wiped sweat from his forehead. The sun was beating down on him, but he didn't care. He'd come to Atlantic City to see his first professional fight—and at the moment, he couldn't even recall who was fighting. He felt like his friends were about to open a door, and he was eager to see what was on the other side.

"How much bigger?"

Fisher raised his sunglasses, blinking his oil-drop eyes.

"Bigger than you can imagine."

FIVE

Boston, September 1994

Kevin's lungs burned as he pushed his body through the water, each stroke stretching his exhausted muscles closer to their failure point. His world had narrowed to a tiny point of blue, just a few feet in front of his eyes. He was totally focused, swinging his arms gracefully like his father taught him, chasing that arbitrary point with an athlete's determination. All his life, he'd been able to find this place, this mental and physical state of *burn*. Lap after lap, he had been coaxing his body through his daily routine, and he'd go until he couldn't swim any farther.

It was late September, and school had been in session for nearly three weeks. Kevin's summer had ended as uneventfully as it began; after the weekend in Atlantic City, he returned to his test tubes and swimming. He had gained a new respect for Martinez and Fisher, and a new fascination with their way of life; but after the thrill of the weekend wore off, he felt reluctant to pursue the issue. Alone in the MIT library, he'd done a little reading into blackjack theory—and had confirmed much of what Martinez and Fisher had told him. The game *was* beatable, and there were people who made a good living playing cards. They were called card counters, and they had developed numerous systems to give themselves a slight edge over the casinos. But even with this edge, it didn't seem that a professional could ever attain the sort of success that Martinez and Fisher had suggested was possible.

In Kevin's mind, there were two major problems with card counting. First of all, your percentage over the house was too damn low. Even the most complex systems seemed to aim at an overall edge of around 2 percent; to make any money at all, you needed an enormous stake, and moving that kind of money around would draw attention. Which led to the second problem: It seemed too easy for the casinos to figure out what you were doing—and stop you from doing it. They couldn't arrest you, but in Las Vegas, they could kick you out of the casino. In Atlantic City, the law was a bit different: They had to let you play, but they could screw around with the deck, shuffle at will, change betting limits—in short, make it impossible for you to win. In the end, card counting was a neat parlor trick, but it just didn't seem like a reasonably effective way to make money. At least not the kind of money his friends threw around.

Which meant that either Fisher and Martinez were lying, or they had figured out some new system that nobody else was using. Kevin didn't put either possibility past them. They were smart enough to have invented their own technique. And they were crafty enough to lie convincingly about anything.

Either way, he had finally decided it was best to put thoughts of blackjack aside, and had gone back to the steady monotony of his life. He had finished his work in the lab, moved back into a campus apartment when school started up, and even begun dating a girl he met at the library. Felicia, who was five-six and wore glasses, had a swimmer's body hidden beneath MIT sweats and a healthy, preppy upbringing. She came from a grounded family, was majoring in engineering, and would fit wonderfully at his parents' table next Thanksgiving. If his father, a geologist at a British research firm, hadn't been in Ecuador on a geological project, Kevin would have already brought her home for dinner.

But he wasn't thinking of Felicia at the moment. He was concentrating on that pinpoint of blue. His body trembled as his legs kicked back, his hands cutting forward, just one more lap, one more lap—

And finally, he hit the wall—physically and figuratively. He flung his arms over the ledge and pulled his shoulders up, resting his chin on the concrete as he fought to catch his breath. He was so worn out, it was a full minute before he noticed the two pairs of feet right in front of him. He looked up: Martinez and Fisher were standing over him, grinning.

Kevin shook water from his ears, shocked. He hadn't seen or heard from them in weeks. They both looked tan, though Martinez had his hair combed down all the way to his eyes, obscuring most of his face. Neither of them seemed uncomfortable, but they were both out of place. Martinez because he looked like he'd never swum in anything deeper than a bathtub; and Fisher because he had once been a part of the swim team before fate had taken him out of school.

But nobody else was around to greet them. It was well after nine at night, and practice had ended nearly two hours before. The pool was deserted, the coach already home with his family.

Kevin pulled himself out of the water, standing on rubbery legs. "Look what the cat dragged in."

Fisher shook Kevin's hand, then wiped himself dry on Martinez's terry-cloth shirt. "Do you have a moment?" he asked.

Kevin shrugged. He was tired and hungry, and there was a pizza waiting for him in Felicia's room. But who knew when he'd see these two again?

"Sure. What's up?"

"There's someone we'd like you to meet."

The classroom was located halfway down the Infinite Corridor, the long hallway of institutionally styled rooms that ran through the center of MIT's main campus. Fisher and Martinez remained silent for most of the walk, and Kevin resisted the urge to pelt them with questions. It was obvious they were enjoying the drama, and he didn't want to ruin their fun.

Just as they reached the classroom, the door opened from the inside. Kevin recognized the room from his freshman year; he'd taken multivariable calculus and linear algebra one after the other, sitting in the same seat two semesters in a row.

He followed Martinez and Fisher in. The first thing he noticed was that the window shades were pulled; the orange fluorescent ceiling lights struggled to reach the corners, bathing the walls in strangely shaped shadows. Someone had rearranged the wooden seats into a tight semicircle in the center of the room, facing the blackboard. A chart filled with horizontal rows of numbers occupied most of the board. The chart was a work in progress: an angular man with curly, jet-black hair and a poorly fitted shirt had his back to the room, a piece of bright blue chalk gripped in his thick fingers. He turned just as Kevin entered.

"Welcome to Blackjack 101, Kevin. We're all thrilled to finally meet you."

Kevin turned his attention to the semicircle of chairs. Seven faces stared back at him; a few he recognized from various classes, most he did not. Two were classmates: a petite, pretty young Asian woman named Kianna Lam, a transplant from Taiwan who shared his major in electrical engineering; and Michael Sloan, a blond tennis jock who lived in the same building as Kevin. A third he had met in physics class: Brian Hale, an emaciated but brilliant senior who, like Kevin, was a local boy, having grown up in the nearby suburb of Waltham. The others were four male strangers who looked to be college-aged. Two wore glasses, and three were Asian, probably Chinese. They all had that MIT aura about them; studious, awkward, but also slightly superior, as if each was used to being the smartest kid in the room.

Kevin shifted his gaze back to the man at the blackboard. Unlike the others, he was definitely not a student. He looked to be in his late thirties or early forties. He was dark-skinned—either Persian or Latino—with a sharp, triangular face and pronounced cheekbones. He wore thick glasses with obtrusive plastic frames, and his teeth were horrible. They jutted out from between his lips, and it was impossible to tell if he was smiling or snarling. His clothes were almost as bad as his teeth; his shirt was two sizes too small, and his jeans were stained and frayed at the ankles, as if they had gone unwashed for a long, long time.

"Kevin," Martinez said. "This is Micky Rosa. He used to teach here, back in prehistoric times."

Micky nodded as his audience laughed, his hair flopping over too much glistening forehead. Kevin watched him with a new respect; he'd seen the name before. Two of the card-counting books had mentioned the former math prodigy—one of the youngest MIT graduates in history, matriculating at the age of sixteen—as a master of the sport. But the man was at least fifteen years older than Martinez and Fisher. What was he doing in a room full of college kids?

"I still teach here," Micky said, leaning back against the blackboard. Bright blue chalk was getting all over his shirt, but nobody said anything. It was obvious in the way they looked at him that his audience revered him. "But now I teach for profit. For me, and for my students."

He waved his hands at the kids seated in front of him. "Kevin, this is the MIT Blackjack Team. It's been around—in one form or another—for almost two decades. Recently, we've taken things to a whole new level. And we want to invite you to come aboard."

Kevin opened his mouth, but he couldn't think of anything to say. He looked at Martinez and Fisher. Martinez was smiling. Fisher was busy making eyes at Kianna Lam.

"Why me?" Kevin finally managed.

"Because you're smart," Micky said. "You've got a good work ethic. You're good with numbers. And you've got the look."

Kevin pawed the floor, pensive. Obviously, Martinez and Fisher had been cooking this up for some time. They had been feeding Micky Rosa information about him, sizing him up for their team. The trip to Atlantic City was a test of sorts, and he had passed.

"What do you mean, the look?"

Micky waved his hands again, tabling the question for later. "Kevin, we count cards. Are you familiar with the practice?"

Kevin nodded. "I've done a bit of reading on the subject."

"Good, good. So you must have heard of the hi-lo method of counting, right?"

Kevin nodded again. His memory wasn't photographic like some other MIT kids he knew, but he retained things fairly well. He knew that the hi-lo method dated back to 1962 and the publication of Edward Thorp's groundbreaking best-seller *Beat the Dealer*. In the book, Thorp outlined a simple counting method that allowed players to keep rough track of the number of high cards left in an unplayed shoe. Instead of counting individual cards, players simply kept track of a single number, the *running count*. This number was added to every time a low card came out of the deck, and subtracted from every time a high card hit the table. The more positive the running count, the more high cards were left in the deck—giving the player an advantage and inciting him to raise his bet. When the running count went negative, the player lowered his bet, expecting to lose more hands. Depending on the initial stake and the number of hands played, a player could reap a positive advantage with very little effort.

"Well," Micky said, stepping away from the blackboard. Chalk dust sprinkled the floor behind him. "You must also realize that the standard hi-lo technique of counting has a few major flaws."

Kevin had already gone through this in his head, after his trip to Atlantic City.

"I can think of two," he said, feeling the need to impress. Everyone in the room was looking at him—a sensation he enjoyed. "The percentage advantages are usually so small, you need an enormous stake to make any real money. And it's too easy a technique to spot. To take advantage of the highs and lows, you have to drastically raise and lower your bet. It's simple for them to catch you just by watching your bet."

Even Fisher looked impressed. Micky's lips shifted back, showing all his frightening teeth.

"We've developed a system that takes care of both these problems," he said. "We're going to hit Vegas—hard—and we'd like you to come along."

Kevin looked around the room at the cabal of young blackjack players. When it was just Martinez and Fisher, it seemed seedy but manageable. Two rebellious geniuses siphoning money from the casinos. But this was something else—organized, calculated, put together by a charismatic adult with bad teeth and a brilliant pedigree.

"I don't know," Kevin said. "It sounds kind of shady."

"Shady?" Martinez broke in. "We're freedom fighters, Kevin. We liberate money from the hands of the oppressors. We're Robin Hood, and the casino is the sheriff."

"And you give all the money to the poor when you're finished?"

"We give most of it to Toyama in exchange for sushi," Fisher said. "And Kianna spends the rest on shoes."

Kianna tossed a crumpled piece of paper at Fisher's head. Then she turned to Kevin and said, "Seriously, the casinos have been screwing people over for years. The games are set up to give the house a hefty advantage. Anyone stupid enough to sit down and play is paying for all that neon, all those free drinks. If anybody's cheating, it's the corporations that own the casinos. They set up the rules so that they always win."

"Almost always," one of the other three Asians added.

Kevin thought about what Kianna had said. "So you have a system that really works?"

Micky nodded, his hair flying everywhere. "Blackjack is beatable. Unlike just about everything else in the casino, it's a game with a *memory*. It has a past—the cards already drawn; and a future—the cards still to come. If you're smart, you can use this to put the odds in your favor. Thorp proved it forty years ago. We've been following his example for decades. And there's nothing illegal about it. You can call up the Nevada Gaming Commission yourself."

Kevin still felt uneasy. Even if it was legal—it *seemed* wrong. But it also thrilled him—deep down, in that part of his personality he usually kept buried. He knew his father would never approve. But his father was in Ecuador for the next two months. He'd never have to know.

"What can they do to you," Kevin asked, "if they catch you?"

Micky shrugged, waving his hands for the third time. It was a strange mannerism, regal and schizoid at the same time.

"They can ask you to leave. And you know what you do? *You get up and leave.* Because there's another casino across the street. And another one a block away. And another on a riverboat in the Midwest, and another on an Indian reservation in Connecticut. Pretty soon there will be casinos in every city on earth. Ripe for the taking."

Kevin touched his lips. "How much money can we make?"

Martinez clapped a hand on Kevin's back. "Now you're talking my language."

"Our group is made up of investors and players," Micky answered. "Martinez, Fisher, and myself—along with a few others who wish to remain behind the scenes—fund the team at the moment. Kianna, Michael, Brian, Chet, Doug, Allan, and Jon here are our present roster of players. The team's investors are guaranteed a certain return based on the amount of time the team gets to play—at present, our return is set at twelve percent. Beyond that, player pay is based on expected return per hand. Not actual return; it doesn't matter if luck swings one way or another, if you hit a losing streak or a winning streak. You earn what our charts say you're supposed to earn, based on perfect application of our system."

Kevin tried to digest what Micky was telling him. Investors earned 12 percent of their investment—*12 percent,* not 2 as he had read in the card-counting literature—and players earned cash based on how many hands they played, regardless of whether they won or lost. It sounded impressive. Still, he wanted something more concrete. He turned to Fisher.

"How much money have you made doing this?"

Fisher glanced at Micky, who nodded. "Martinez and I have made more than a hundred grand each in the past six months. When we started, we were just players. Now we've got a piece of the action."

Kevin whistled.

A hundred thousand each.

Playing cards.

"Okay," Kevin said. "I'm game."

"Wonderful," Micky said. "First there's something you need to do."

"What's that?" Kevin asked.

Micky offered a smile or a snarl.

"You need to pass the Test."

SIX

Boston, October 1994

Kevin had to pass three tests, actually.

Or a single test split into three parts, each corresponding to a different playing role on the MIT team. After the class ended, Martinez explained the details during the short walk across the Mass. Ave. Bridge to Felicia's apartment complex.

"When card counting was first developed, the idea of team play hadn't yet evolved. Bald white guys with glasses huddled over blackjack tables, eking out their tiny two-percent advantage by estimating how many highs were left in the deck. Sure, over time you could make money. But sooner or later the casino would spot you and burn you out. Once you were burned out of all the casinos in town, you were finished, extinct. A dinosaur."

Kevin smiled, his wide face lit by the Boston skyline on the other side of the Charles. Ahead, the low town houses of the Back Bay squatted beneath the twin shadows of the Prudential and the Hancock. "You get burned out, you become a dinosaur. Cute. So how does team play work?"

"Division of labor," Martinez responded. "The team is divided into three types of players. You've got your Spotters, your Gorillas, and your Big Players."

Kevin watched a bus rumble down Massachusetts Avenue, headed toward Harvard Square. "Fisher's obviously a Gorilla."

Martinez ignored his comment. "Everyone who joins the team starts off as a Spotter. A Spotter's job is to find a good table with a hot deck, then call in either a Gorilla or a Big Player. On most blackjack teams, Spotters do this by back counting. They stand around the casino, looking over players' shoulders, counting the cards as they come out of the deck. We've innovated a bit on this—because back counting is too damn obvious. Walk around any casino in Vegas, you'll spot the amateurs trying to back count. Sooner or later, they end up getting caught."

"But you guys don't get caught?" Kevin asked.

"We do it a little differently. Our Spotters sit at the tables, playing the minimum bet as they count. Nobody suspects them because they're just like everybody else. Losing a bit, maybe getting lucky—but never varying their bet. When the count goes good, the Spotter signals a call-in. Then the Gorilla or the Big Player sidles over to the table, and the real fun begins."

They reached the other end of the Mass. Ave. Bridge and stopped at the intersection. A group of rowdy frat boys waited on line at a dive bar across the street; Kevin could smell the dollar drafts contaminating the cool fall breeze.

"Gorilla play is the next step after Spotting. A Gorilla is just a big bettor. It's more acting than anything else. He gets called into a hot deck, stumbles over like a drunk rich kid, and starts throwing down big money. He doesn't think for himself—he lets the Spotter tell him when the deck goes bad. He's just a Gorilla, brain-dead. But depending on how high the count is when he's signaled in, his percentage advantage can be staggering. He doesn't count, he just bets and bets and waits for the seated Spotter to signal him that the run of good cards is over. Then he gets up and wanders off in search of his next call-in."

Kevin felt a sense of wonder. He was beginning to understand. Individual card counters had to wait for the deck to get good; then they would raise their bet. With Gorilla play, you were betting *only* when the deck was good. You'd win most of the time, and nobody would be able to peg you as a counter—because you *weren't* counting.

"And a Big Player?"

"A Big Player," Martinez said as they crossed the street, "does it all. It's acting and counting and betting, it's tracking the shuffle and cutting to aces. It's the toughest role and the most important. You carry the big money, and you get yourself known by the casino personnel. They comp you the big suites because you're betting a thousand dollars a hand. You get called in by the Spotters, but then you take over the play. You do things the Gorilla can't, like raising the bet as the deck gets better—but you have to do it with style, so the casino doesn't nail you. You have to look the part."

Kevin thought about what Micky had said when Kevin had asked why they'd chosen him: *you've got the look.* Did they mean he was capable of being a chameleon, like Martinez? Or that he was partially Asian, like most of the team? He wasn't an actor, he'd never tried to play a part before. Maybe Martinez and Fisher saw something in him that he did not.

"So you have three tests to take," Martinez continued. "First, you need to master basic strategy and a simple count—the tools of the Spotter. Then you need to learn how to use counting indexes to vary your play—and your betting—based on the count. That's good enough for Gorilla play. Finally, you'll have to pass the last exam. That's a full-scale test in a casino environment, where you'll take on the role of the Big Player."

"Where do you get a 'casino environment'?" Kevin asked.

Martinez smiled. "You just worry about the cards. We'll handle the rest."

That night, after a short visit with Felicia to apologize for missing dinner, Kevin sat on the floor of his bedroom, dealing to himself from a pile of cards six decks deep. At first he was simply practicing basic strategy. Micky Rosa had given him a booklet full of BS charts, which he had memorized while eating pasta in front of the television.

Kevin hadn't found the charts intimidating; he had spent most of his life submerged in complex math formulas. His father had quizzed him, even as a kid, on the basics of physics and chemistry. Unlike much of higher physics, basic strategy coincided with common sense.

Contrary to what many novices believed, the goal of blackjack was not to get the best hand possible; it was to beat the dealer's hand. The key to basic strategy was to understand that the dealer's advantage was based entirely on the fact that he drew *after* the player. Everything else in the game favored the player. The dealer was constrained by the house rules, which meant he was usually forced to hit until he either reached seventeen or busted. Therefore, the player's strategy was to try to calculate what the dealer's most likely hand was going to be, and then draw until his own hand was higher. If the dealer was most likely to bust (and the dealer normally busted 28 percent of the time), the player simply needed to stand on any two cards over eleven.

The player's calculations were based on the information he had available: what the dealer had showing. If the dealer had a strong card showing—like a ten or an ace—then the odds were high the dealer had a good hand and wouldn't need to take a third card. That meant the player had to keep hitting until he had a strong hand for himself. If the dealer had a weak card showing—like a six—he would most likely take a third card from the deck. Therefore, his odds of busting were high, and it made sense for the player to stand.

Proper strategy became a bit trickier when it came to splitting pairs and doubling down, the two moves that gave the player a chance to increase his odds against the house by raising his bet. With splitting pairs, the player could create two hands against the dealer's cards. This allowed the player to double his bet—but he was also doubling his risk. So the only proper time to split pairs was when the dealer's hand would be weaker than each of the players' two new hands. A standard set of rules for splitting had been devised by previous blackjack experts using computers running millions of virtual hands. Kevin found it easier simply to memorize the tables than try and work them out. The same went for the rules of doubling down, and the proper play for *soft* hands—hands with an ace, which could be used as either a one or an eleven.

Altogether, it had taken him under an hour to get a good feel for basic strategy. After dealing blackjack hands to himself for a few more hours, he switched over to learning the basic running count.

The hi-lo count was perhaps the simplest counting method one could learn. Low cards—two through six—were assigned a point value of positive one. High cards—ten through ace—were assigned a point value of negative one. When Kevin went through a deck, adding low cards and subtracting high cards, he came out to zero. It felt foolishly simple, going through the six decks again and again, flipping one card at a time. But it became progressively more difficult, the more cards Kevin flipped at once. In a casino environment, he'd have to be able to count the whole table in a matter of seconds. So he took advice Micky had given him on his way out of the classroom: *Match 'em up.* High cards and low cards canceled each other out. By seeing the cards in pairs—or even foursomes—of matching high and low cards, he could speed up his counting time geometrically. Pretty soon he could get through the six decks in a few minutes.

When he finally went to sleep, cards spun through his dreams. He was hooked. It wasn't just the potential for money; there were a lot of ways a kid on the honors track at MIT could make money. It was the pure mathematical *beauty* of counting that turned him on.

Over the next few weeks, his love of counting expanded. Micky and his crew guided Kevin through intense practice sessions, mostly sequestered in classrooms with the window shades drawn—both for effect and to simulate the often poor lighting one found in smoke-filled casinos. After mastering a simple count, Kevin learned how to estimate the number of cards left in the shoe by sight, then used this skill to turn the running count into a more accurate number called the *true count*. The true count was based on the statistical fact that the fewer cards there were in the deck, the more significant the count became. For example, a count of positive ten—ten extra high cards left in the shoe—had more value when there were only fifty cards left than when there were three hundred.

Five hours a day, seven days a week, Kevin matched high and low cards, then divided by the number of decks left in the shoe. Over and over again until the technique became more instinct than skill. Running count to true count, the number then applied to the index charts lodged in his memory that taught him how to vary his play based on the new advantage or disadvantage (derived, again, from thousands of hours of computer analysis and decades of play by MIT blackjack alumni).

Midway through October, Micky, Martinez, and Fisher subjected him to the Spotting and Gorilla tests. Both took place in Martinez and Fisher's apartment. Martinez dealt from a regulation shoe while Fisher counted alongside him, making sure he got it right. By the end, Kevin was playing two hands, calling out both the count and proper play whenever Micky tapped his foot. There was no betting involved yet; that would be saved for the final exam. But he was asked to run through the Spotter's signal list:

"The deck's warm," Micky called out. Kevin folded his arms in front of his chest.

"The deck's turned hot," Fisher said. Kevin folded his arms behind his back.

"Even hotter," Martinez added. Kevin's hands went into his pockets.

"I need to talk"—Kevin touched his eye. "Get over here"—Kevin lowered his head to his folded arms. "What's the count?"—Kevin scratched his ear. "I'm too tired to play anymore"—Kevin rubbed his neck. "I'm getting heat from the pit boss"—Kevin moved his hands to his forehead. "Something's wrong, get out now!"—Kevin ran his hands through his hair.

When he was finished with the physical signals, Kevin was asked to repeat the oral count signals, to be used when calling in a Big Player. These were all simple words that could be used in a sentence, right under the nose of a dealer, or pit boss. They seemed arbitrary at first, but they were also mnenomics:

Tree: the signal for a count of +1, because a tree looked like a one
Switch: +2, because a switch was binary, on or off
Stool: +3, because it had three legs
Car: +4, four wheels
Glove: +5, fingers
Gun: +6, bullets
Craps: +7, lucky seven
Pool: +8, eight ball
Cat: +9, lives
Bowling: +10, strike
Football: +11, because "11" looks like goalposts
Eggs: +12, a dozen
Witch: +13, witchy number
Ring: +14, fourteen-carat gold
Paycheck: +15, because you got paid on the fifteenth
Sweet: +16, sweet sixteen
Magazine: +17, the name of a teen magazine
Voting booth: +18, the age you could vote

Sometimes Kevin found it hard to think of a sentence under pressure, but Martinez assured him that even nonsense worked in a casino, because nobody was really listening. "This stool is killing my ass" meant the count was three, and "I'd rather be bowling" meant the count was ten. "My room upstairs is the size of a fucking voting booth" meant it was time to bet the mortgage.

Exhausted after three hours of testing, Kevin collapsed on the futon while Martinez and Fisher went out to pick up an order of sushi from Toyama. It was the first time Kevin had ever been alone with Micky, who was seated awkwardly on a beanbag chair in a corner by one of the stereo speakers. He was wearing a hooded sweatshirt and baggy shorts, dressed like a college kid, his posture clumsy and disarming. But Kevin knew the master card counter's looks were deceiving. Behind the thick glasses, his eyes were piercing, and he had one of the sharpest minds Kevin had ever known. His blackjack team was more than a lark—it was a shrewdly planned business, run almost like a cult. Everyone revered Micky; even Kevin found himself in awe of the man's abilities and charisma. When the team came together, any dispute was immediately deferred to Micky. Every decision about the team's structure seemed to come directly from him. Even Kevin's recruitment, though obviously spurred by Martinez and Fisher, was played off as Micky's idea.

Kevin didn't know how much money Micky had invested in the team, but it was obvious that he was its de facto boss. He was the link to the past decades of MIT blackjack, and he was guiding the future. Without him, there was no team, just a group of overintelligent rebellious kids.

"Kevin," Micky said now, peering at him through those thick glasses from the corner of the South End apartment, "I think you're ready."

Kevin felt a rush of adrenaline. It was the same feeling he got when his father approved of something he had done. His father would not have approved of Micky, an adult who hung around brilliant kids, turning them into gamblers. Kevin's father never would have understood. Card counting *wasn't* gambling. It was arbitrage.

"Saturday night," Micky continued. "Martinez will give you the address. If all goes well, you'll be able to join us in Vegas at the end of the month."

Kevin exhaled, hungry. He wasn't thinking about sushi.

Saturday night he was going to take the Test.

SEVEN

Boston, October 1994

Kevin squinted through the darkness as he moved nervously down the narrow, poorly paved alley. There weren't any streetlights to help him navigate between the murky puddles of unknown liquids seeping up from beneath the cracked asphalt, nor was there any way to avoid the minefield of broken glass that littered the curb. He was glad he was wearing his thick Timberland boots, though he was beginning to wonder if sneakers might have been more appropriate for this part of town. Judging from the boarded-up storefronts and decrepit tenement buildings that lined either side of the alley, there was a good chance he'd soon be running for his life.

Certainly, he'd never been this deep inside Chinatown before. This wasn't the quaintly ethnic, westernized row of dim sum restaurants and fortune-cookie take-out dives that characterized the touristy zigzag of streets bordering the financial district on one side, the theater district on the other. This was a part of Chinatown the college kids and guidebooks never heard about. A spiderweb of one-way streets, winding alleys, and dead ends, where nobody spoke English and nobody looked you in the eye. It reminded Kevin of the stories his father had told him about Hong Kong. These five square miles were a foreign country, and despite Kevin's Asian blood, he was the stranger here.

Thankfully, the alley seemed devoid of life. Kevin kept his head low, checking the numbers on the buildings with quick flicks of his eyes.

A blue awning caught his gaze, and he stopped, one foot in a viscous puddle, the other balanced on the curb. Beneath the awning was a small grocery store; a row of strangled chickens dangled behind the plate-glass storefront, next to a cardboard sign covered in Chinese writing. Beside the window was a wooden door painted the same blue as the awning. A number was scrawled across the center of the door in dark green ink.

Kevin checked the number twice, then shrugged: *Forty-Three Wister Street*. This was the place. He moved up the front steps and pressed a buzzer on the door frame.

There was a momentary pause, and then he heard shuffling from somewhere inside. Metal scraped against metal, a latch was undone, and the door swung inward. The grocery was to the right; directly ahead was a staircase rising steeply into near darkness. An elderly Chinese man in a white undershirt was standing on the bottom step, beckoning Kevin forward. "You Kevin? You Kevin?"

Kevin nodded, glancing into the grocery. The place was deserted, the scent of dead fowl overwhelming. He turned back to the man. "Yes."

"You follow."

The old man turned and started up the steps. Kevin tried to calm his heart, then moved after him. As he rose higher into the building, he began to hear noises drifting down from somewhere above. It sounded like a party: laughter, clinking glasses, high heels scraping against wood. Kevin's anxiety lessened. *How many people get mugged at parties?*

The stairway ended at another wooden door. The old man pushed through, and a blast of orange light poured out around him. Kevin took the last few steps and entered a long, rectangular room with low ceilings and no windows. His eyes widened as he counted three blackjack felts, a roulette wheel, and two craps tables, all regulation size, as if stolen straight out of a casino. There were at least twenty people in the room, about half of them Chinese. The rest looked to be businessmen in their thirties and forties, many of them dressed in jackets and ties. There was a bar running along the far wall, and cocktail waitresses in black dresses moved through the crowd, carrying trays littered with various concoctions.

An underground Chinatown casino. Kevin shook his head, amazed. He'd heard that places like this existed. He searched the room and finally caught sight of Martinez and Micky sitting next to each other at one of the blackjack tables. His first instinct was to go over and say hello, but then he remembered what Martinez had told him before giving him the address: *This is a dress rehearsal. Play by the team rules, or don't play at all.*

Kevin moved quietly through the crowd. He kept his gaze on Martinez but stayed at least ten feet away, first pretending to watch the action on the roulette wheel, then leaning over the craps table, minding the dice. The other gamblers didn't even notice him; just another Asian kid wandering the room. He kept his head low, chin almost at his chest. He didn't even raise his eyes when he saw Martinez fold his arms over his chest—signaling him in.

Here we go, Kevin said to himself. He nonchalantly crossed the room and lowered himself onto the empty stool at the far end of the table—third base. Neither Micky nor Martinez acknowledged him. Micky was sipping a carbonated drink through a straw lodged in a gap between two of his teeth, and Martinez was chatting with the dealer, a grey-haired Chinese man in a light blue jacket and khaki pants. When the man smiled, Kevin saw that his teeth were almost as bad as Micky's: His gums were the color of licorice.

Kevin reached into his pocket and pulled out a roll of twenties. Fisher had loaned him the money that morning, before heading to the gym to work out. Three hundred dollars—and if Kevin lost it all, it would come out of his first paycheck with the team. If he failed the Test, he'd be doing Fisher's dishes for the next month.

He set the money on the felt and watched the dealer exchange it for sixty red five-dollar chips. Another Chinese man in a matching jacket also watched the transaction from a stool set directly between the three blackjack tables. The pit boss, Kevin surmised; Micky had given him a crash course in the casino hierarchy a few days ago. Dealers were watched over by pit bosses, who were controlled by shift managers, who in turn answered to the floor manager, who kowtowed to the casino manager (the CM), who in turn bowed directly to God—or corporate headquarters. In Vegas, that translated to some faceless monster with a hundred million shareholders and almost as many lawyers. Here, in Chinatown, God was probably some drug smuggler with one eye and an ivory cane. Kevin didn't want to think about that. He was here to *play*.

As he stacked his chips in a neat pile, he used his shoulder to scratch his right ear. Two seats down from him, Martinez shivered and said, "It's colder than a witch's tit in here, Al. Don't you guys pay for heat?"

The dealer laughed, showing his black gums. Kevin took five chips from his pile and placed them on the betting circle. It was only twenty-five dollars, but it was five times his minimum unit, the proper bet for a count of thirteen. If he'd been bankrolled, he'd have twenty-five hundred on the table.

The cards came out, and Kevin drew a solid twenty against the dealer's eight. He stood, won, and adjusted the count, matching up Micky's and Martinez's cards, analyzing the depth of the shoe, calculating his index and his bet without even blinking his eyes. He leaned back on his stool, his expression smooth. He raised his bet another chip, then called for the cocktail waitress.

For the rest of the shoe, he played perfectly, keeping the count all the way to the shuffle card. Throughout, he maintained an easy banter with the dealer and the passing waitresses, joking about his luck, how his girlfriend was going to spend it all on clothes anyway. A second shoe started up, and he played through on Micky's signal. By the third shoe he was up nine hundred dollars, and the pit boss was asking him to fill out a ratings card—even Chinatown had its comp system. He used an alias, David Chow, and had no problem jotting down a fake address without interrupting his count. He grew more boisterous with each hand; he wasn't drunk, but he was playing the part, making his cheeks red by holding his breath when nobody was looking, throwing his chips out recklessly when he raised his bet, asking the dealer for help adding up his cards when the pit boss was watching.

He was putting on quite a display but, through it all, always kept the perfect count. The casino atmosphere didn't distract him; instead, he found the ambient noise bolstered his energy level. By midway through the fourth shoe, he was enjoying himself so much, he didn't notice the shadow closing in over him from behind.

He was fingering his chips when the strong arms suddenly wrapped around his chest, yanking him off his stool. He tried to shout, but a canvas bag came down over his head, muffling his voice.

He felt himself lifted off the floor and half carried, half dragged across the room. People were laughing around him—a strange reaction, he thought in the part of his mind that was still functioning. Then he heard a door open and close, and he was tossed in a corner. He hit the ground hard enough to take his breath away.

There was a moment of silence, then the canvas bag was ripped off his head. He was in some sort of a closet. The floor was damp beneath his jeans, and the air reeked of mildew.

Fisher was standing over him, a wicked smile on his face.

Kevin stared at him, shocked. "What the fuck are you doing?"

Fisher ignored his outrage. The bulked-up dropout's voice came out perfectly calm. "What's the count, Kevin."

Kevin blinked. He could still hear the laughter coming from outside the closet. It was obviously a prank—but it had scared him half to death.

"You motherfucker. I've got nearly a thousand dollars at the table—"

"Kevin," Fisher repeated. "What's the count?"

And suddenly, Kevin understood. This was part of the Test. The casino environment hadn't distracted him. The pit boss, the cocktail waitress, the dealer—none of them had taken his attention away from the cards.

So Fisher had taken it a sadistic step further. He had tried to throw Kevin's concentration by brute force.

"What's the count," Fisher demanded.

Kevin glared up at him. "Craps, you fucking ape. The count is plus seven. Now let me get my goddamn money!"

The door to the closet swung open behind Fisher, and Martinez stuck his head inside. Micky was next to him, and both of them were smiling. They had been listening from outside the whole time.

"Sorry Kev," Martinez said as Fisher helped him to his feet. "There isn't any money. This was all a mock-up. The house knows us here. They don't let us play for real."

Kevin laughed out loud. "You're kidding me."

Fisher squeezed his shoulder. "They let us use the place for our Test. Helps them keep track of the local card counters."

Kevin rubbed sweat from his eyes. This was insane—and invigorating as hell. He knew he had just gone through an initiation, of sorts. *He was one of them now.*

"Congratulations," Micky said, reaching forward to shake his hand. "And welcome aboard."

Kevin nodded. A strange feeling came over him as he looked into Micky's eyes; he felt unnerved by the fatherly sense of satisfaction he saw in the older man's gaze. Then Martinez clapped him on the back, bringing him back to the moment.

"Pack your bags, bro. We're going to Vegas."

EIGHT

Las Vegas, Present Day

I couldn't see his eyes behind the thick protective goggles, but Damon Zimonowski's lips were curled back, his teeth clenched together in an expression of pure violence. His arms were extended, his impressive six-foot-three body hunched slightly forward. I pressed my hands tight against my cushioned headphones as his finger whitened against the trigger. I could hardly believe that I was actually standing there—that this was the setting of a background interview for my book on Kevin Lewis's double life and not a scene from one of my novels.

The .357 jerked three times, the explosions rocketing through the indoor shooting range, and Damon shouted in joy. I tried to get a look at the target at the other end of the twenty-yard corridor, but I couldn't see past the Plexiglas extension that separated our two lanes.

Damon stepped out of his shooting stance and handed the .357 to a teenager in overalls, then yanked off his goggles to look at me.

"Just what the world needs," he said, grinning. "Another goddamn blackjack book."

I thought about protesting, then decided to leave it alone. I wasn't writing a blackjack book per se, but I couldn't explain that to Damon.

My meeting with the somewhat frightening Vegas denizen had been set up by Kevin Lewis—or David Lee, as Damon knew him from his days as a casino host at one of the posh monsters on the Strip. Damon was my first subject, the first name on the list Kevin had provided me as part of our bargain. For this interview, however, Kevin had made me promise not to mention the real thrust of my book, and after Damon's display with the .357, I didn't want to ruffle any feathers.

The way Kevin had described him, Damon was the perfect research subject, a mixture of old and new Vegas. After a brief stint in the marines, he'd moved here from Dallas in 1974, in search of his own version of the American Dream. He'd worked for the casinos in a dozen different capacities over the years, clawing his way up from security guard to blackjack dealer to pit boss to shift manager—ending up as a host at a high-profile Strip casino in the mid-1980s. Over the next decade he had moved among six different casinos before finally deciding to get out of the gambling business altogether. Like many other residents who had watched Vegas transform over the years, he had realized that the city was experiencing a remarkable population explosion: the opposite of Atlantic City, where the surrounding urbania declined as the casinos moved in, Vegas had been in an almost constant state of boom for the past four decades. New industries were springing up to service the rapidly growing mecca, and in the future, the hottest action wasn't necessarily going to be in the gambling pits. Damon had become a developer of sorts. He now owned a piece of the newly opened shooting range located just outside the city, as well as a small stake in a nearby supermarket.

The kid in the overalls took my headphones, and I followed Damon to a small lounge area by the front door. There was a chalkboard on the wall, with gun-club schedules scrawled across the slate in bright green letters. A watercooler gurgled beneath the board, and two potted plants curled precipitously together by a window that looked out onto the nearly empty parking lot. My rented Geo looked clownishly small next to Damon's mammoth four-wheel-drive Suburban.

"You know," Damon continued, filling a cone-shaped paper cup with water from the cooler, "Vegas is the fastest-growing city in the world, the last fucking place left on earth where a bum with no skills can make a decent living—and all anyone wants to write about is fucking blackjack."

In the ten minutes I had known him, I'd already grown used to Damon's liberal use of expletives. But under the color, he was making an interesting point. The phenomenon of Las Vegas was much more than a card story: The town's growth, financial influx, architectural fluidity, and character were all unique in human history. Where else in the world could a cocktail waitress afford a mortgage on a house and a lease on a car? Where else could a college dropout who parked cars for a living earn enough to send his kids to private school?

Kevin Lewis's story fit into this framework because it defined an integral moment in Vegas's time line: His first baby steps into his double life coincided with the relaunch of Vegas on a megascale.

"People love to gamble," I answered. "And they understand blackjack because it's simple, and it seems like it's almost fair. People believe it's the only game you actually have a chance of beating."

Damon grunted, crushing the paper cup with his meaty hand and tossing it into a wastebasket. "It's not even the biggest game in the casino anymore. Slots are more than sixty percent of the action. Blackjack was hot in the eighties and nineties, but we're moving into the era of machines."

I nodded. I had read about the advance of the machines. Now even slots were in danger of being overrun by video poker—the Internet porn of gambling games. Quick, addictive, and somehow satisfying, the machines ate money faster than a New York City rental agent. But I wasn't interested in gambling machines.

"It's the nineties I'm writing about. And not just blackjack. I'm interested in how Vegas changed, how its character was reflected in the big players of the decade."

Damon crossed his arms, shrugging. "Well, on the exterior, Vegas is always changing."

I could fill in the details on my own. From my research, I had concluded that Vegas had gone through five distinct periods since gambling was legalized with the passing of Nevada Assembly Bill 98, back in 1933. First there was the mobster era, beginning just after World War II. Inspired by their success in illegal gambling parlors in the Midwest, infamous Mafia figures such as Morris "Moe" Dalitz and Bugsy Siegel moved into town. Funded in part by two hundred and fifty million dollars of Teamster money, the mobsters built the first major casinos—such as Siegel's six-million-dollar Flamingo. The Flamingo was quickly followed by the Sands, Riviera, Dunes, and Tropicana.

In the sixties, the moderately insane tycoon Howard Hughes took over where the mobsters left off, adding an element of corporate legitimacy to the town through his business and political connections, while funding another building boom. Then, in the seventies, architectural monarch Kirk Kerkorian gave birth to the first of the huge resorts with the construction of the first MGM Grand (later becoming Bally's) in 1973. At a hundred and twenty million dollars, with twenty-one hundred rooms, the casino was the dawn of the true Vegas-styled entertainment complex and a precursor to things to come.

After a brief but failed flirtation with the idea of "family entertainment" characterized by gaudy amusement-park-styled attractions and decor, Vegas decimated the competition from Atlantic City and emerged from the recession in part by reinventing itself as the world's foremost *adult* amusement park. Luring millions of conventioneers with a state-sanctioned, lax attitude toward the sex industry, and a new focus on the consumption-oriented middle class, the city built by gangsters became America's premier vacation and corporate conference destination. At the end of the eighties and the beginning of the nineties, fueled by America's economic boom and a lust for high living, a massive influx of corporate money spawned the Vegas we know today: an over-the-top world of excess and imagination.

Beginning with Steve Wynn's Mirage, built in 1989, Vegas picked up where the MGM Grand of 1973 left off. Inaugurating a multibillion-dollar construction boom, the Mirage was a six-hundred-fifty-million-dollar trip into fantasy. From the fifty-four-foot erupting volcano out front to illusionists Siegfried and Roy's "Secret Garden" attached to the pool, the Mirage reinvented the concept of the megaresort. But the Mirage was only the beginning. On its heels came Excalibur—Camelot brought to life; the Luxor—a massive black glass pyramid that would have made Ramses feel right at home; the Hard Rock—a sex-charged L.A. rock club gone kitsch; and New York, New York—the Big Apple if it had been reimagined by Disney, with buxom cocktail waitresses instead of college kids in mouse costumes.

Culminating in the construction of the massive Bellagio and Venetian (costing $1.6 and $1.2 *billion* respectively), Vegas currently sported nineteen of the world's twenty biggest hotels, hosting over thirty million visitors a year, generating five billion dollars in gaming revenue, utilizing sixteen miles of neon tubing . . .

Etc., etc., etc.

Damon Zimonowski's simple statement pretty much covered it: *On the exterior, Vegas is always changing.* Inside, however, something about the town was still the same. It was this dichotomy that interested me, because in my mind, Kevin Lewis and his friends represented that very dichotomy—the flashy, modernized exterior concealing an inner, dark core.

"At its heart," Damon continued, "it's all about greed. We build the casinos because we want to take your money. You come here because you want to take our money. The rest is just window dressing—how we lure you in, how you justify it to yourself when you get back home."

"But it's not an even game," I said as the sound of gunfire suddenly echoed behind me. I glanced back, saw the kid in overalls standing in the last shooting stall. "The casinos make sure the system is rigged in their favor."

Damon laughed. "That's the nature of the motherfucker. It's no different than any other business. You don't open a movie theater and let people in for free. You charge 'em for the entertainment. That's what Vegas does. The house's edge is the price of the movie ticket."

I had heard this line of reasoning before, from an employee of the Nevada Gaming Commission. When you sat down to play blackjack, the casino was providing you with an entertainment service. You paid for that service by losing more than you won. People like Kevin Lewis were getting their entertainment for free—and then some.

"But the house doesn't always have an edge," I said, leading.

Damon watched as the kid in overalls reloaded. "Except with the cheaters."

"And the card counters," I said, hoping he understood the distinction. Many casino employees liked to blur the categories together. But legally, there was a difference. It had been tried and won in court numerous times. Card counters did not alter the natural outcome of the game, which was a key component of the Nevada legal definition. Nor did proficient counters employ devices to help them beat the house.

"Sure," Damon admitted. "The card counters, too. Though that's a more debatable issue."

"What do you mean?" I asked. We were getting to the goods the roundabout way.

"Most people who say they can count cards are full of shit. They end up losing more than the civilians. It takes enormous discipline, dedication, and mathematical skill. You got to be a goddamn genius to do it right."

I nodded. More gunshots exploded behind me, though I fought the urge to turn around. "But there are geniuses out there. And sometimes they *do* beat the house."

Damon rocked his impressive frame back on both heels. "I've met my fair share. You heard of Ken Uston? He was the god of 'em all. Had a team back in the seventies. Then the casinos finally wised up, kicked him out whenever they saw him. He tried suing, saying his constitutional rights were being violated. Didn't fly in Vegas."

"Card counting didn't end with Uston," I said.

"Not by a long shot. Its heyday was in the late eighties, early nineties. That's when everyone in America was obsessed with easy money. Smart kids were heading off to Wall Street, law school, whatever. Even smarter kids thought they could make more in Vegas."

This was the crux of Kevin Lewis's story. By the early nineties, greed had reached new heights, and smart kids—math majors, engineers, the Wall Street–bound—wanted a piece of the great American pie. Some of them came to Vegas.

"And it drove Vegas crazy," I finished for Damon.

He shook his head. "It's not as cut-and-dried as that. Card counters can be good for business, too. They make the civilians think the game is beatable. Some fucker writes a book about a bunch of kids who beat Vegas, and they think they can do it, too."

My face reddened. Damon wasn't working for the casinos anymore, but his comment hit pretty close to home. I wondered if it was just luck—or if somehow my mission had been compromised. I decided it was time to press the topic.

"So in their heyday, how much do you think card counters cost the casinos every year? How much can they really win?"

The kid in the overalls was on his way over. The writer in me imagined he still had the .357, but I knew I was just being dramatic.

"It's not what they win that makes the casinos nervous," Damon said. "It's the fact that they *can* win. Over time, nobody beats the house—that's the cardinal rule of Vegas. You fuck with the cardinal rule, you fuck with Vegas."

He winked at the kid in the overalls. "And sooner or later, Vegas finds a way to fuck you back."

NINE

Thirty Thousand Feet, November 1994

Somewhere over Chicago, the sky went black on the other side of the glass egg at Kevin's shoulder. He pulled his baseball cap down low over his forehead, concentrating on the cards splayed out on the seat-back tray. The steady stream of cool, stale air blowing out of the plastic nipple above his head had been keeping him awake since takeoff; he couldn't figure out how Martinez had been able to fall asleep so easily. The crazy fool was sprawled out in the seat next to him, one foot in the aisle, both hands clasped behind his head. It probably helped that he was under five-six. *These seats are made for circus folk.*

Martinez had tried to use his frequent flier miles to get them into first class, but the flight was way overbooked. America West 69—the Friday-night neon express—was usually pretty full, but this weekend was even worse than usual because of the fight. George Foreman vs. Michael Moorer, a high-profile pay-per-view event at the MGM Grand. Martinez had assured Kevin that the whole city would be jumping by Saturday night. Fights made for perfect card-counting conditions; crowds of drunk, raucous people filling the blackjack pits, high-rolling celebrities drawing everyone's attention, mammoth sports stars throwing huge money down on foolish bets—nobody was going to notice a bunch of Asian kids hovering around the tables. The same went for New Year's, Memorial Day, July Fourth—all the major Vegas holidays. Whenever the crowds came out, the card counters followed in droves.

Kevin continued dealing to himself, counting the cards without really trying. He had realized a few days ago that he no longer saw the numbers; he'd practiced so much, counting had become pure instinct. But Micky Rosa had made him promise that he'd continue dealing for at least two hours a day.

Kevin finished with the shoe, then shifted his legs to try to get more centered in the cramped seat. The heavy money belt around his waist didn't help, nor did the bulging plastic bags strapped to each of his thighs. *One hundred thousand dollars in hundreds, wadded into ten stacks of ten thousand each.* A fortune under his clothes—and a hell of an inconvenience. But since this was his first trip with the team, he had been designated "donkey boy." It was his job to see that the stash got to Vegas intact.

Along with the cash, there were another two hundred and fifty thousand dollars in chips jammed into his carry-on bag. It had been nerve-racking, shoving the bag through the X-ray machine; but Martinez had assured him that even though some chips show up on airport detectors, the Logan security people weren't smart enough to realize their worth. On the inside, a five-hundred-dollar chip looks the same as a one-dollar chip.

Altogether, it was a staggering amount of money, and about half of it belonged to Micky. According to Martinez, another quarter million dollars was waiting for them in safe-deposit boxes spread around downtown Las Vegas. He had explained that the six-hundred-thousand-dollar bankroll was about average for their team; it was hard to handle much more than a million at the tables without getting noticed, and anything less than a half a million yielded lower returns. Martinez and Fisher had griped a bit that all they could invest was a hundred thousand each; Micky and his "friends" hogged the rest, giving them the most potential for profit. But it was, after all, Micky's team.

Repositioned, Kevin closed his eyes, trying to ignore the cold air licking his cheeks. In his mind, he went over the brief conversation he'd had with Felicia before leaving for the airport. He hadn't even considered telling her the truth about where he was going. She didn't know Martinez and Fisher—although knowing them probably would have just made things worse—and she certainly didn't know anything about the blackjack team. Over the past few weeks, Kevin had covered up his practice sessions with lies about extra swim team practices and a made-up linear-algebra study group. Like Kevin's father, Felicia wouldn't have taken the time to understand that what he was doing wasn't wrong.

Kevin felt bad about the lies, but he also enjoyed the idea of living a double life. He touched one of the wads of hundred-dollar bills attached to his legs, and smiled. *I feel like James Bond.*

The airplane jerked through a spate of turbulence, and Kevin opened his eyes. Martinez was finally awake, rubbing spit from his lips as he stretched his legs under the seat in front of him. Then he elbowed Kevin and pointed at the man seated across the aisle. The guy looked to be in his mid-forties; white, little John Lennon glasses, and an oxford shirt. Kevin looked more closely and saw that he had a blackjack book open on his lap and a deck of cards in his shirt pocket.

Martinez sighed. "You see it every flight. Welcome to amateur hour. There's nothing the casinos love more than a guy who *thinks* he can count cards. The dude probably bought the book at the airport."

Kevin laughed. "At least he'll know basic strategy."

"That would be fine, as long as he stops there. But they never do. He'll bet five dollars a hand for an hour, maybe two. Then he'll see a group of low cards, and he'll think that means it's time to go crazy. He won't take into account that he's one deck into the shoe and the face cards have been raining like Niagara. He'll drop three hundred dollars by six A.M."

Kevin knew Martinez was right. The average visitor to Vegas lost three hundred dollars during a weekend. Primarily male, middle-aged, visiting for three nights; spending another three hundred dollars on food, rooms, and entertainment, in addition to three hundred for the flight. Altogether, that blackjack book would cost him nine hundred dollars.

"These weekend flights are the funniest thing," Martinez continued. "On the way out, everyone's smiling, laughing, joking. They're all thinking about the great time they're going to have and how much they're gonna win at the tables. The flight home is like a wake. Everyone comes home a loser."

"Except us," Kevin finished for him.

Martinez shrugged. "Sometimes we lose. But the longer we play, the more inevitable it is that we win. The opposite goes for the peasants."

Kevin watched the guy across the aisle remove the cards from his shirt pocket and deal them to himself. His lips were moving as he counted the numbers. Kevin shook his head. If the guy really did somehow start to win, he'd be so obvious they'd spot him in a second. And then—well, they'd ask him to leave. Wasn't that what Micky had said?

"Martinez," Kevin asked, lowering his voice. "How many times have you been asked to leave a casino?"

Martinez paused before answering. "Three, maybe four. I can't go to some of the places downtown anymore—more because of who I've been seen associating with than because of my own play."

Kevin raised his eyebrows. "Seen associating with?"

Martinez nodded. "You need to understand something, Kevin. From the moment you walk into a casino to the moment you leave, they're watching you. You've heard of the Eyes in the Sky? The fish-eye cameras hanging from the ceiling in the casino pit? Well, the truth is, there are cameras like that everywhere. In the elevators, in the restaurants, even in the hotel hallways. And there are assholes who spend all day and all night staring at TV monitors linked to those cameras, trying to see faces that they recognize."

Kevin guessed it was a bit more technical than that. He went to MIT; he knew about the computer software that police agencies were using to match faces with photos. He figured that with all the millions of dollars at stake, the casinos were using similar techniques.

"Well," Martinez continued, "the thing is, there's this book. It's put together by this detective agency hired by the casinos to catch cheaters—and card counters, who they lump in with the rest of the bastards. Plymouth Associates, the agency's called. And certain notorious card counters have found their way into the Plymouth Facebook."

Kevin exhaled. If he had thought it through, he probably wouldn't have been surprised by the idea of a detective agency hired by the casinos, or that they'd have a file on card counters. But it made things seem a bit more serious than Micky and the rest had let on.

"Is your picture in the Plymouth Book?" Kevin asked.

Martinez shook his head. "Not yet, as far as I know. Neither is Fisher's. But Micky's on the first page. And if they see any of us hanging out with Micky—well, you can bet there will be trouble."

"You mean they'll ask us to leave."

"That's right." Martinez was quiet for a moment, then turned toward Kevin. "Well, they might also try and back-room us."

Kevin pressed his lips together. This was the first he'd heard of anything that could happen to a card counter other than being asked to leave. At thirty thousand feet, moving six hundred miles an hour toward Vegas with cash all over his body—and *now* Martinez decided to tell him?

"What the fuck does that mean? 'Back-room'?"

Martinez waved a hand, Micky-style. "Calm down. It's really nothing. They try to get you to come with them to a back room, usually in the basement of the casino. It's just an intimidation thing. If you go down there—and you'd have to be a fucking idiot to go down there—they'll take your picture, make you sign something that says you won't come back to the casino. At that point, you're officially eighty-sixed; if you do return, you're legally trespassing and they can arrest you. But they never do. Basically, back-rooming is just a bluff to scare you off."

Kevin didn't like what he was hearing. He wasn't easily frightened, but he didn't want to be bullied by casino thugs. "So Micky's been back-roomed before?" he asked.

Martinez shrugged. "I don't honestly know. But other counters from MIT have been. It's no big deal. Vegas is run by major corporations. It's not the mob, like the old days. It's Hilton and Holiday Inn. You think Hilton is going to open itself up to a lawsuit for strong-arming a card counter?"

Kevin knew Martinez was right. The huge corporations had too much at risk to do anything stupid. He figured he could handle the intimidation tactics. Hell, it just added another element to the game. Another reason not to get caught.

"If they ask you to go to the back room," Martinez said, "just say no and walk away. Don't let them take your picture. Truth is, they've already got a picture of you from the ceiling camera anyway. And don't sign anything—and especially, don't give up your chips. They have no right to take your chips." Martinez folded his arms back above his head. "Oh yeah, one other thing."

"What's that?"

"Don't let some guy named Vinnie take you on any long drives out into the desert."

Three hours later, the plane banked hard to the right, starting its descent. Kevin pressed his face against the window, peering beneath the wing. He couldn't see much of anything: an ocean of sable desert, seemingly darker than the sky. After a few minutes, he began to notice a scattering of lights, tiny little pinpricks in the liquid sheet of black.

Then, suddenly, a bright glow erupted, first formless, then mushroom-shaped. In a moment, the city became visible, the amazingly bright lights of downtown feeding into the long, radiant Strip and its mammoth hotels. At one end, the newly opened, sleek, dark glass Luxor Pyramid, beaming light ten miles straight into space from a *forty-billion-candlepower* beacon attached to its peak—the most powerful spotlight in the world. Halfway down the Strip, the shimmering, emerald-green MGM Grand, its main building stretching the width of four football fields. Nearby, the Mirage, its bright red volcano spitting flames into the sky. Then the Excalibur, Caesars, Bally's—such an assault on Kevin's vision that he had to blink. An oasis of color and light, neon jewels sprouting in the middle of nowhere. *Down there,* Kevin thought, *it's all down there.*

Then he turned away from the window and started dealing to himself one last time.

TEN

Las Vegas, November 1994

Martinez had three rooms at the MGM Grand, booked under the name Peter Koy. Fisher had a bank of rooms at the Stardust under the name Gordon Chow. And Micky Rosa was checked in someplace downtown, with five rooms under three different names. Eleven rooms for eleven people, most of them suites, all of them free. But to Kevin, it didn't sound like they'd be spending much time in the rooms.

Micky explained the rules as the team gathered in a corner of the arrival gate. It was close to midnight Vegas time—three A.M. back in Boston—but all of them were energized. Maybe it was something in the air. It was a common story, real or urban myth, that the casinos pumped high levels of oxygen into their ventilation systems to keep people awake longer. Kevin wondered if McCarran Airport had a similar policy. Even the airport bristled with blinking, buzzing slot machines.

"From this point on," Micky said, addressing his monologue to Kevin, since the rest had heard it countless times, "whenever we're in public, we don't know each other. We don't use our real names, and we never mention MIT. If you need to go back to one of the rooms to rest, make sure you go alone. Once we're in the rooms, we're okay—

as far as I know, they don't put cameras in the rooms. But the hallways and elevators are definitely wired, so we have to make sure we stagger our breaks."

He paused as a group of elderly tourists in matching sweatshirts rumbled by, eyes glistening as they took in the nearby slot machines. When they were out of earshot, he continued. "We're going to play in two shifts, five of you on the floor at a time. The first shift will start at the Mirage and go until six A.M., then the second shift will go from six to eleven. We're going to avoid the day shift—that's when the more senior casino employees are on the floor. We'll resume again tomorrow night at eleven, after the fight, and go again in two shifts until eleven A.M. Sunday."

Kevin nodded with the rest of them. It was a heavy schedule, but nothing he couldn't handle. He'd get plenty of sleep during the day.

"Martinez will be the Big Player in the first shift, Fisher will BP for the second. Kevin, Kianna, Michael, and Brian will spot first, the rest will spot second. Spotters, make sure your BP can see you at all times. Try not to look at each other at all, and never work the same tables."

Kevin glanced at Kianna, who didn't seem to be listening at all. Her dark hair was tied back tightly against her neck, and there was a fair amount of skin peeking out of her low-cut top. She was wearing makeup and high heels and looked like she was going out dancing. Nobody would ever suspect that she was here to count cards.

Michael and Brian were next to her. Michael was wearing a polo shirt and slacks, as if he'd just come from the tennis court. Brian was in a ratty T-shirt and jeans with a lopsided baseball cap on his head. Neither of them seemed nervous; this had all become routine.

"If there's an emergency of any kind, spread the signal and we'll all head to the designated meeting place. Tonight let's make it the volcano outside the Mirage. And remember—no back rooms, no pictures, no signatures. The law is on our side."

Micky reached into his pocket and pulled out a plastic card, handing it to Kevin. Kevin was surprised to see his own face on the card. It was an authentic California ID under the name Oliver Chen.

"Where'd you get the picture?" Kevin asked.

"Your MIT facebook. When we get back to Boston, you can order up some credit cards to go with it as backup. All perfectly legit."

Kevin slid the card into his wallet. As he did so, he noticed that one of the plastic bags full of cash was slipping down his leg.

"Uh, Micky—" he started, but Micky seemed to understand.

"Martinez and Fisher, go with Kevin into the bathroom and split up the stash. It should be enough to cover us tonight. Tomorrow I'll retrieve the rest from the safe-deposit boxes."

He reached out with both hands, placing one on Kevin's shoulder, the other on Martinez's arm. "Guys, this is going to be a great weekend. Let's have some fun."

Something in his tone made Kevin certain that to Micky Rosa, this wasn't about fun.

This was business, pure and simple.

Removing one hundred thousand dollars from beneath his clothes in a crowded public restroom wasn't as difficult as Kevin had imagined. After locking himself in a stall, with Martinez and Fisher in stalls on either side, he lowered his pants and freed the plastic bags from his thighs. The money belt gave him a little more trouble; it had somehow twisted around to his back, and his left elbow slammed into the stall wall as he shimmied in search of the clasp.

"Take it easy in there," Martinez whispered from the next corral. "Sounds like you're giving birth to a monster."

Kevin ignored him, splitting the cash into two piles, then passing them to Fisher and Martinez. He kept five thousand for himself, the designated Spotter stash. Each of the other Spotters would get their five thousand from the chips in his duffel bag, which Micky was now carrying.

Kevin waited until Fisher and Martinez had exited the bathroom before following. He noticed that his heart was racing; even though the secrecy was probably unnecessary, it made him feel even more like a spy.

When he exited the bathroom, the others were already gone. He could still see Fisher's wide shoulders bouncing above the rush of people moving toward baggage claim but Martinez had vanished, his little form swallowed by the mob of travelers. Kevin was on his own.

It took him a good twenty minutes to find his way to the cab stand. As he waited in line, he wondered if Martinez and Fisher had taken limos, as in Atlantic City. Or had that just been part of the recruitment tactics? Here in Las Vegas, things seemed much more serious. Maybe it was the presence of Micky. *You can't fuck around when the boss is in the office.*

The taxi driver didn't seem surprised that Kevin wasn't carrying any bags, and kept him awake during the short ride to the Mirage with a sob story about two ex-wives and four ex-kids. Kevin kept the window open the whole time, letting the warm breeze pull at the collar of his shirt. He wasn't even sure what time it was anymore. The five-hour flight had deposited him in a chronological fugue state.

The cab dropped him in front of the hotel lobby, and he took a moment to stroll through the faux-tropical lagoon outside, admiring the huge, brightly lit volcano in the center. The volcano was in mideruption, red plumes of flame spraying high into the air as a crowd of tourists applauded. It was an awesome sight, one that would be repeated every fifteen minutes until midnight. Kevin wondered if it was just as impressive the tenth time around.

Would the thrill he was feeling at that moment—the moment before his first real casino play—ever wear off?

He tucked in his shirt and headed through the glass doors that led into the Mirage. An inadvertent smile moved across his face as he took in the vast atrium: Like the lagoon, it was decorated in the fashion of a tropical jungle, with thick foliage, rumbling brooks, and even the odd waterfall. The air seemed misty, unlike the dry desert air outside, and the entire place *smelled* authentic.

Surrounding the vast atrium was the Polynesian-themed casino, split into a number of different play areas, all festooned with real and plastic plant life. Kevin got his bearings and moved toward the blackjack pit to his right.

The place was jumping—as crowded as the Tropicana in Atlantic City, but with a different clientele. Women in shiny tube tops, showing ample curves and way too much skin, mingled with conventioneers in leisure suits. Groups of Japanese men, red-faced from alcohol and shouting loudly at one another, melded into junkets from the Midwest. Cowboy hats, silk suits, leather pants, gold lamé, slicked-back hair, ponytails, even the odd tuxedo—it was like no crowd Kevin had ever seen before. The energy level was incredibly high, and his ears were ringing from the noise as he reached the blackjack pit. Even though he had prepared for this, he was anxious; this place was as distracting as an amusement park.

He moved into the center of the blackjack area and began to scope the scene. The high-stakes section took up a good fifteen tables, all with minimum bets of one hundred and maximums of five thousand. It was a moderate spread, good enough but not optimum. At certain intervals, the Big Players would be playing more than one hand at a time to take full advantage of the changing count.

Shifting his gaze nonchalantly as he walked, Kevin easily picked out Brian and Michael, two tables apart. Michael, the preppy tennis jock, was chatting easily with a beautiful blonde sitting next to him. She looked like a stripper, with magnificent fake breasts and a skirt riding high up her thighs. Nobody would be noticing Michael, that was for sure.

Brian, the physics geek, was playing a different role, slumped over at the third-base position, two empty glasses in front of him, constantly rubbing his eyes like he was about to pass out. He looked like a geeky college kid left behind by his friends, too drunk to hit the clubs and too stupid to quit gambling for the night. He hardly even seemed to look at his cards; it took Kevin a second to realize he was reading the numbers from the reflection on his empty drink glasses. *A real pro.*

And if Brian was a pro, Kianna Lam was playing on a whole different level. Kevin had walked around the pit twice before he even noticed her, sitting at the first base of a crowded table set between two jungle vines. Her little body was daintily perched on her stool, her legs crossed, her hands folded neatly in her lap. Surrounding her—engulfing her, it seemed—was a group of drunk Asian businessmen. They looked to be rich Chinese, just off the plane from Hong Kong. They were giving her advice as she played, trying to impress her in a mixture of Chinese and broken English. She flirted back, covering her mouth when she laughed, responding in equally accented English. Even the dealer was smiling at her, helping her add her cards together.

Kevin shook his head, amazed. Martinez had told him that she was one of the top card counters in the world, almost as proficient as Micky. More impressive than her skill, her *act:* Asian, female, with a heavy accent and a cute figure. She could count right in front of a pit boss, and he'd never believe she was a pro.

Kevin wanted to be that good.

He set his jaw, approaching a half-empty table a few feet from a gurgling miniature waterfall. He sat down next to a bald, pudgy man in a bright green Hawaiian shirt and yellow shorts. Next to the man was a small, mousy woman with glasses and a ruffled white skirt.

The man smiled at Kevin as he sat down. "Come to join our sinking ship?"

Kevin laughed, reaching into his pocket for his cash. "That bad?"

"My wife and I have been here twenty minutes, and we're down five hundred bucks. If it gets any worse, we're going to have to hitchhike back to Chicago."

Kevin counted out twenty hundreds, setting them on the felt. The dealer—a short Latino-looking man with a mustache and overly manicured fingers—re-counted them, exchanging them for black chips. Kevin placed a single chip in the betting circle, then winked at the pudgy man and his wife.

"Maybe we'll all be hitchhiking together."

Over the next ten minutes, Kevin played out an uneventful shoe. The count never went above positive three, and stayed below zero for most of the deal. The cut depth, or *penetration,* was pretty good, however; the dealer was cutting all the way to the last deck in the shoe. Which meant that the dealer was favorable, and it was just a matter of time.

As he played, Kevin kept his eyes open for Martinez. It wasn't difficult for him while counting, since he was keeping to basic strategy and never raising or lowering his bet. Three hands into the second shoe, he caught sight of the BP. Actually, it would have been hard to miss him. He was wearing a blue crushed-velvet shirt and black leather pants. His hair was slicked back, and a gold necklace glimmered beneath his wide-open collar.

Christ, Kevin thought. He watched as Martinez strolled around the blackjack pit, seemingly oblivious to the action all around him. He passed Kevin's table twice, but the count was still too low to be worthwhile. Then, suddenly, he headed for Michael's table. He sat next to the tube-topped stripper and immediately began flirting with her as he pulled a huge wad of cash out of his back pocket. Kevin could only imagine what she was thinking. Michael, the tennis jock, was clearly out of the running.

Kevin went back to his cards, playing and counting and chatting away with the nice couple from Chicago. The shoe ran through again—and again, the depth was nearly five decks, a wonderful counting opportunity. Kevin's attention perked as the first few rounds of the next shoe came out: plenty of twos and threes, sending the running count higher and higher. Pretty soon it was in double digits, and Kevin began looking for Martinez again. Just his luck, Martinez was rising from Michael's table, scooping black and purple chips from the felt. Kevin leaned back on his stool, crossing his arms over his chest. He didn't see Martinez look his way, but suddenly the velvet fog was lurching toward his table.

The couple from Chicago stared as Martinez dropped onto the stool next to them, dumping his chips in a messy pile on the felt. "Howdy, everyone! What's shakin'?"

His voice oozed Southern California. The mousy woman moved a few inches closer to her husband. Kevin sighed loudly. "We're not doing so great. I've already blown through half of last month's *paycheck.*"

Martinez grimaced. Then he pushed a seemingly random handful of chips into his betting circle. Three blacks, two purples, six green. *One thousand four hundred and fifty dollars.* Let the Eyes in the Sky try and figure that one out. They'd never guess that this velvet-clad, crazy motherfucker knew the count was positive fifteen, with less than a third of the deck left.

"Don't worry. I bring good luck. I always bring good luck."

Martinez reached under his collar, pulled out a tacky gold medallion and kissed it. Kevin had to kick himself to keep from laughing.

Even the dealer smiled. "Where are you from?" he asked as he dealt the cards. Kevin got a king, Martinez a queen. "Los Angeles?"

Martinez swatted a hand against the felt. "What gave me away? Just flew in an hour ago. Gotta get out of town on the weekends, you know. I get enough of the industry during the week."

The next set of cards came out. Kevin drew a nine for a solid nineteen. Martinez drew another queen, a strong twenty. The dealer had a six showing. *Heaven on felt.*

"You work in Hollywood?" the mousy woman asked, excited.

Martinez grabbed another handful of chips. "Benny Kato's the name. I produce music videos. Mostly street hip-hop, you know, pow-pow-pow, 'word up,' and stuff. Hey, count this up for me, boss. I want to split these suckers."

He pushed the chips across the felt. The dealer stared at him for a moment, then started matching the chips with Martinez's bet. He set a second pile of fourteen hundred and fifty next to the first and split the two queens. Then he turned his head over one shoulder and called, rather loudly: "Splitting tens."

A grey-haired man in a slick dark suit looked over from across the pit. He took in Martinez's velvet shirt and visible gold chain, then nodded. The dealer proceeded with the deal.

Kevin's heart thudded as he watched the cards come out. Splitting tens was an unconventional move—usually, an extremely stupid move. Unless the count was high and the dealer's card low. Then it was an extremely *profitable* move. Martinez drew another face card on his first hand and a seven on his second. The dealer flipped over a ten, then drew a queen, to bust. Everyone at the table won.

Overall, Kevin was down three hundred dollars.

Martinez had just bumped up twenty-nine hundred dollars in a single hand. It wasn't luck. It wasn't gambling. His odds of winning were significantly higher than fifty-fifty.

If it was anything at all, it was *acting*.

"See," Martinez shouted. "I always bring the goddamn luck!"

He yanked his medallion out of his collar again, and offered it to the mousy woman from Chicago. She shook her head. He shrugged, then kissed it himself.

The next afternoon, Kevin came awake staring at himself. It took him a full minute to realize he hadn't gone insane: There was a mirror on the ceiling.

He was lying in a bed the size of his room back in Boston. To his right, a vast picture window overlooked the Strip. To his left, a marble hallway led to a marble bathroom with a marble Jacuzzi. Straight ahead, a set of double doors opened into a circular living room with curved leather couches, plush white carpeting, and a revolving widescreen TV.

Kevin wasn't sure what time he had finally drifted off to sleep. The only thing he knew for certain was when he had stopped playing: ten-fifteen A.M. He distinctly remembered writing the time down on his log sheet while locked in a bathroom stall at the Stardust. Along with the time, he had kept track of all his wins and losses, as well as all of his call-ins (including the count, how many spots were played, how many decks they went through, how deep the dealer's penetration, and Martinez's win-loss performance). Probably the most difficult part of a Spotter's job was to keep track of everything that went on at his table. At the end of the trip, Kevin would have to turn in his notes to Kianna, who was acting as team secretary; the old team secretary, a kid Kevin had never met, had left MIT for a job at a computer software company and no longer had time to travel with Micky's crew.

By ten fifteen, Kevin had filled both sides of his log sheet. Six different casinos, more than twenty blackjack tables, and at least a dozen call-ins. It had been exhausting, even with the five-minute breaks he took every hour, mostly spent crouching in a bathroom stall, jotting notes in the log.

Overall, Kevin was down a little over a thousand dollars. During his watch, Martinez was up fourteen thousand. Kevin had no idea how much Martinez had made with the other Spotters, but altogether it had probably been a very lucrative night.

At ten-fifteen, Martinez had given him the signal to quit—rubbing the back of his neck—and he had happily complied. They had taken separate cabs back to the hotel and carefully avoided sharing elevators up to the rooms. Kevin hadn't seen Fisher, Micky, or most of the others since the airport. Brian and Michael were staying in rooms down the hall. He wasn't sure where Martinez had slept, or if he had slept at all. Micky had strict rules against drinking or partying, even between shifts, but God only knew how Martinez spent his time in Vegas. He probably knew the town better than anyone.

Kevin stretched his arms above his head. His muscles were stiff from sitting at the tables all night, and his eyes burned from the secondhand smoke. He was also hungry; he had eaten an enormous room-service breakfast, but that was hours ago. He sat up, searching for the menu. He had just tracked it down when the double doors that separated his bedroom from the living room swung inward.

Fisher was standing in the doorway, a crooked grin on his face. He aimed a plastic bag at Kevin. "Here, catch. That's your tuition."

The bag landed on Kevin's chest. He could see stacks of bills inside. He was getting good at estimating money amounts by weight and width.

"Twenty thousand," he stated.

"Don't get too excited," Fisher said. "It's not all for you. That's the player split from last night."

Kevin whistled. Twenty thousand split eight ways was twenty-five hundred apiece. Pretty good for one night's work.

"It won't always be that high," Fisher said. "It was a particularly good night. In fact, Martinez and I think we should let you try a little Gorilla play before the fight."

Kevin sat up in the bed. Although spotting had its moments, overall it was a mental grind. The real glory was in the big betting, and Gorilla was the first step.

"Seriously? Micky thinks I'm ready?"

Fisher shrugged. "Well, actually it was more my idea. Micky likes to take things slow. But he shouldn't make all the decisions; he doesn't even play anymore, he's burned out of too many casinos. He's making a whole lot of money off of us, just sitting around by the pool."

This was the first real dissension Kevin had heard since joining the team, but he wasn't surprised it was coming from Fisher. He had an aggressive personality, and, like Martinez, hated being told what to do. Unlike Martinez, he didn't always know when to keep his feelings to himself.

Despite the hotheadedness, Kevin genuinely liked Fisher. Although recently he had spent a lot more time with Martinez, he felt closer to Fisher, who was more like him. A tough spirit from a good family who just wanted more out of life.

"Do *you* think I'm ready?" Kevin asked.

Fisher grinned. "Only one way to know for sure."

Fight night, the MGM Grand, Las Vegas.

From the moment the elevator doors slid open on the casino level, Kevin was swept up in a sea of frenetic energy. He was a molecule in a hyperenergized electromagnetic field, his brain function replaced by pure reactive adrenaline. The assault on his senses was nearly overwhelming. It was like New Year's Eve at midnight in Boston: a mob of drunken revelers packed together, all dressed in colorful, sometimes bizarre fashion, everyone shouting and pointing and rushing in random directions, buzzers and bells and bright lights and flesh, so much goddamn flesh, women in leather skirts and saran-wrap tops, men with their shirts open to the navel and too much jewelry, wannabe mobsters in pinstripes, middle-aged tourists from the Midwest, cowboys and Wall Streeters and L.A. hipsters . . .

Kevin closed his eyes, slowed his breathing, recalibrated. As in swimming, he tried to find the pinpoint of blue straight ahead. He stepped into the casino and weaved through the crowd, focusing on the blackjack tables and swarms of gamblers around them. Along the way, he liberated a Scotch from a passing waitress's tray. He took a sip, then splashed some of the pungent liquid on his shirt. He mussed up his hair, undid a few buttons, rolled one sleeve almost to the elbow. His gait slowed, his feet landing farther apart. Anyone watching would have witnessed the shift: from MIT whiz kid to drunken prep school burnout.

As he staggered through the crowd, he took stock of his counters. Kianna was at the table closest to the elevators, surrounded once again by the Hong Kong Mafia. Michael and Brian were at tables near the back of the pit. And Martinez was at a central table, sitting with three African-American men in expensive silk suits. Kevin was about to start a second pass around the casino when he saw Martinez's arms fold together.

Clutching his drink, he swept through the abnormally large crowd behind the table and wedged himself into the one remaining seat, first base. He jammed his hand into his pocket, pulled out ten thousand dollars in cash, and plopped it down on the felt. As the dealer began counting out chips, Kevin offered a wide smile to the table. "How's everyone doing tonight?"

Martinez grunted. "Getting crushed like a carton of eggs."

The three others nodded amiably, and Kevin was suddenly struck by how huge they all were. They made Martinez look like a plastic doll; their legs seemed impossibly long, disappearing beneath the table. Kevin turned his attention to their faces. A lifelong sports fan, he had no trouble recognizing two of them: Patrick Ewing and John Starks. He was at a blackjack table with three star basketball players from the New York Knicks.

No wonder so many people are gathered around the table. Kevin glanced at Martinez again, but his teammate was ignoring him; he'd already passed the count, so nothing else mattered. Not the fact that there were celebrities at the table, not the crowds standing behind them, not the pit boss who was looking over adoringly at the enormous men with deep, deep pockets.

Kevin turned his attention to the betting circles. One of the Knicks had three hundred dollars down. Starks was betting two fifty. Ewing had five hundred dollars in front of him.

Kevin placed two five-hundred-dollar chips into his circle.

The third Knick shook his head, impressed. "Hey, Big Money. That's how it's *done*." He took a handful of cigars out of his pocket and offered them to the table. Ewing and Starks each took one, Martinez declined. Kevin shrugged. *What the fuck?* He could be back in Boston, sharing a beer with Felicia at some fraternity party. Instead, he was smoking cigars with the New York Knicks.

"Thanks," he said, letting Ewing cut the tip for him with a cigar cutter. "You guys here for the fight?"

"Nothing like Vegas on Fight Night," Ewing responded.

The cards started to come out, but Kevin barely noticed them. He kept one eye on Martinez, waiting for the signal to raise or lower his bet. Otherwise, he was a Gorilla, unthinking. He had been called into a plus-twelve deck (eggs), so the odds were nicely in his favor.

Over the next hour, Kevin led the Knicks in an impressive slaughter; he racked up ten thousand dollars in profit, earning applause from the crowd by splitting tens twice and doubling down on an eight. By the time he rose from the table, the Knicks were inviting him to an after-fight party in a celebrity suite at the Mirage, and Ewing was asking him for stock tips (they had somehow gotten the impression that his father ran a billion-dollar hedge fund). Nobody was even giving Martinez a second look. He vanished into the crowd while Kevin colored up his chips.

Kevin's head spun as he stepped away from the table. This was better than he had imagined. He wished there was someone back home he could call, but the only people who would appreciate it were here with him. He checked his watch, realized it was time to shower and change for the fight. He glanced back toward the other tables to see if Kianna and the rest were already on the move.

He didn't see the Spotters, but as he was about to turn back toward the elevators, something else caught his eye. A short, stocky Indian kid was sitting at a blackjack table twenty feet away. The kid was unremarkable: dressed in khakis, betting the table minimum, patiently studying his cards. The strange thing was, Kevin recognized him. His name was Sanjay Das; he and Kevin had taken physics together two years ago. He was in Kevin's class at MIT.

Maybe it was a coincidence; maybe he was just in town to see the fight. Or maybe there was something Micky and the others hadn't told him.

Maybe Micky's team wasn't the only MIT game in town.

Kevin decided to put the thought aside for the time being. He could ask Martinez or Fisher about it when they got back to Boston. Now it was time to celebrate.

An hour later, Kevin walked down the center aisle of the MGM Grand Garden Arena, his eyes dazzled by the bright lights, pay-per-view cameras, and shouting fans. He kept checking and rechecking the seat number on his ticket; the boxing ring was getting closer and closer, and there was still no sign of his row. It seemed like he'd be sitting right on George Foreman's lap.

He was at row ten when he heard a whistle erupt from somewhere to his right.

"Hey, Big Money!"

He looked over and saw Patrick Ewing and the other Knicks waving at him. His ears rang as he stopped for a moment to shake their hands. Everyone in the rows behind craned to get a good look at him, trying to figure out who this Asian kid was: They figured he had to be someone famous, hanging out with the celebrity basketball players. Kevin took another cigar from Ewing, then bid them all good luck.

He finally found his seat—seven rows in front of theirs, right up by the ropes. With some difficulty, he found Martinez, Fisher, Micky, and the rest spread out across the front section of the arena, separated by wealthy strangers and A-list celebrities: Al Pacino, Robert De Niro, Kevin Costner, Jack Nicholson, Charlie Sheen. Somehow, in the visual cacophony that was Vegas, the MIT geeks seemed to fit in.

For a brief second Kevin locked eyes with Fisher, who raised his palms to the cavernous ceiling: *Here we are, what do you think?*

Kevin was trying to come up with a response when the lights suddenly went out. Loud music exploded from speakers embedded in the walls, and the entire arena shook as the hungry crowd leaped to its feet.

The fight was about to begin.

ELEVEN

Weston, MA, Thanksgiving 1994

There's no neon in Weston, Massachusetts.

Twenty minutes from Boston by Mercedes-Benz, Weston was an upper-middle-class enclave separated from the real world by a tree-lined stretch of the Mass Pike. The sleepy New England town was suburbia incarnate: white picket fences, yellow school buses with blinking red lights, colonial homes, lush green lawns, lemonade stands, tennis courts, basketball hoops, tree houses, porch swings, dogs on leashes, kickball and flashlight tag, public schools that looked like prep schools and prep schools that looked like Ivy League universities.

On a bright Thursday afternoon, Kevin sat next to Felicia on a porch swing, watching the leaves swirl across the back lawn of his parents' two-story colonial-style house. Though the breeze was beginning to turn cool, the crisp scent of another autumn filled Kevin with warmth. He had spent every Thanksgiving since birth in this house; his neurons were littered with ritualized memories carried by the familiar scents and sounds. Like always, his two older sisters were puttering around the kitchen with his mother: Kevin could hear them through the first-floor window, their voices carrying over the clink of plates and silverware. His father had momentarily retired to his study, with his geology books and scientific magazines. Kevin and Felicia had stolen a rare moment alone to seclude themselves on the rosewood porch that jutted out over the back lawn.

Kevin had helped his father build the magnificent, split-level porch when he was twelve years old: He remembered staring at the pile of exotic lumber that the truck had dropped off, wondering how it would ever resemble the blueprints tacked to the wall of his father's study. By the end of the summer, as the porch took form and the envious neighborhood kids began to gather for barbecues and touch football, Kevin had grown to think of his father as a suburban superhero.

It was a hard adjustment when he had exchanged his happy suburban life for a prep school surrogate family. His father had tried to explain things to him when his older sisters were likewise sent away. There was nothing more important to the elder Lewis than education; an immigrant from Hong Kong with an anglicized last name, Kevin's father had struggled his entire life to overcome a childhood bereft of opportunities. He had dedicated himself to making sure his children had nothing to overcome. In his mind, Exeter was a way of ensuring Kevin's future.

Kevin had hated leaving home, and it had taken him a few months to finally understand his father's point of view. Most of his classmates were children of obscene privilege; to succeed against them, Kevin had needed to work twice as hard. He had focused on math and science—again following in the footsteps of his sisters—because in his father's world, there was no such thing as a liberal-arts education. Math was where you were measured, math was the ruler of your potential success.

Math had given Kevin opportunities: Exeter, MIT, and now blackjack. His father was proud of him for the first two. Kevin wondered if his father could ever respect him for the third. He gently pushed off with both feet, sending the wooden two-seater swinging in a delicate arc. Felicia smiled and put her hand on top of his. "I like your sisters. They seem so grounded."

Kevin nodded. He listened to the two of them helping his mother with the dessert—something to do with apples, cinnamon, and sugary pie crust. Melissa's voice was high-pitched, singsongy; Kelly's had a deeper, more serious tone. The two were best friends, cut from a similar mold. Melissa worked for a venture-capital firm in downtown Houston. She drove a black SUV and liked to hike in the mountains. She had graduated from Yale and would soon enter Harvard Business School to continue her education. Kelly was the more fashionable of the two; she had graduated from Harvard, lived in L.A., and worked for a boutique investment bank. She wore Armani and Prada and collected East Asian art. Her hair was streaked with blond, and when she was working, she wore glasses with prescription-free lenses. Both of them had made plenty of money, putting in long hours at their respective jobs. Both would eventually get more degrees, get married, and get houses in the suburbs.

Kevin was supposed to be just like them. Kids from Weston didn't grow up to be professional card counters. They went to Harvard or Yale or MIT. The rebellious ones went to Brown, or maybe even Stanford. They became doctors and lawyers and bankers. They had families and lake houses and million-dollar mortgages. They drove Volvos and SUVs.

"Kelly reminds me of my sister," Felicia continued. "Maybe you'll meet her on Christmas. She'll be back from Paris for most of December."

Kevin nodded again, though he wasn't sure he shared her optimistic view of their future together. Over the past three weeks, he had begun to find that he had less and less to say to her. He knew it had to do with the secrets he was keeping—the weekly trips to Vegas, the aliases, the multiple credit cards, the IDs he was hiding in his desk drawers, the money he kept stashed all over his apartment, the time he spent with his new card-counting friends, the phone calls he was starting to get from casino hosts, always offering him something—a free room, a free flight, tickets to shows and fights and private parties. He wondered if telling her the truth about the blackjack team would save his relationship; more likely, it would drive her away.

Similarly, for the past few days he had thought about opening up to his dad. Kevin had never kept a secret this big from his family, and he felt like a coward for his unwillingness to explain things. He knew the secrecy was going to get more difficult over time. His life was beginning to change because of blackjack and the money that his new skill was generating.

After his first weekend in Vegas, Kevin had bought a new stereo system and a color TV. After the second weekend—and more Gorilla play—he had overhauled his wardrobe, buying some flashier outfits for Vegas and some new athletic gear. After his first experiment with the role of Big Player, he had even contemplated moving out of his shared apartment to a place of his own, but had prudently decided that would be too hard to explain.

Despite his secrecy, his parents had begun to suspect that something was going on. His mother often wondered aloud where the money was coming from for his new clothes and toys. She joked that there was a tree in the backyard from which he shook hundred-dollar bills. *She wasn't that far from the truth,* he thought.

But the more Kevin considered telling his father the truth, the more impossible it seemed. If he could somehow take his father to Vegas with him, show him that there was nothing corrupt or illicit about it, maybe he would understand. *Maybe.*

"Kevin . . ." his mother's voice drifted out from the kitchen, interrupting his thoughts. "You better get in here before your sisters eat everything in sight."

Kevin removed his hand from beneath Felicia's as he led her inside. He tried to make the motion look casual, but he thought he saw something in her eyes. A glimmer of concern, maybe a portent of the inevitable.

♠ ♥ ♦ ♣

Kevin's father was at his customary seat at the head of the dining room table. A plate of half-eaten pie was in front of him, and *The New York Times* was open on his lap, to the business section, as usual. He went through five papers a day, from *The Wall Street Journal* to *The Boston Globe.* If the TV was on, it was always CNN or the nightly news. On weekends, maybe PBS.

Kevin took the seat next to him, while Felicia excused herself to use the bathroom. He watched his father turn the pages, checking his stock portfolio. He paused to glance at Kevin and nod, then went back to the NYSE.

Part Chinese, part Caucasian, Peter Lewis was tall and fit, with thinning grey hair and a high, furrowed forehead. He hardly ever smiled, but his eyes were kind, and he almost never raised his voice. His clothing cycled between MIT, Yale, and Harvard sweatshirts—one from each of the schools his children had attended. He hoped to add more sweatshirts as the years progressed. Kevin thought he'd get two more; he'd need to have another kid if he wanted to go for three.

His father was a good match for Kevin's mother, who was just a few inches shorter, thin, with the same color hair and eyes. Unlike his father, she was always smiling, so widely it almost seemed like her round face might split in half. She was also of mixed descent; she had relatives in Ireland and Taiwan, two extremes juxtaposed in her skin: here smooth and tan, there freckled and creased, but overall exotic and attractive. Kevin could hear her still moving around the kitchen, gathering dessert plates, shooing his sisters away from what remained of the pie.

It was a rare opportunity, a moment alone with his father.

Kevin decided to test the waters: "Dad, have you ever heard of card counting?"

His father didn't look up from the newspaper. "You mean like professional poker players, who keep track of the cards?"

Kevin listened for the sound of the bathroom door. He certainly didn't want to tackle both Felicia and his father at the same time. He proceeded cautiously. "No, I mean blackjack. Some people count cards to give them an advantage."

His father turned the paper over, scanning the back page. "Foolishness. They use six decks at casinos nowadays. You can't keep track of six decks. It's not possible."

Kevin shook his head. He was surprised his father was falling for the common misconception. People thought card counting was possible only with the single-deck game, when in fact, six decks were a *better* situation for the counter. In a single deck, the dealers shuffled every few hands. If the deck went hot, you had just a moment to take advantage of the situation. With six decks, you could have ten minutes with a hot shoe.

"Dad, counters don't keep track of all the cards. It's about ratios, good cards to bad—"

"Kevin, it's a waste of time. Gamblers never win any money."

Kevin could tell from his father's tone that the conversation was over. It was a frustrating moment. Kevin understood his father's point of view—but what his father hadn't taken the time to process was that it *wasn't* gambling at all. It was more like a math or physics problem, a question with an answer—and that answer led to easy money.

In the end, Kevin decided it was just as well; Felicia was on her way back from the bathroom, and Kevin's mother was coming out of the kitchen with another plate of apple pie in her hands.

The timing wasn't right. Kevin's father wasn't ready to listen. Maybe he'd never be ready to listen.

Kevin felt strangely relieved.

TWELVE

The Double Life, 1994–95

The next six months flashed by at a thousand RPMs.

Kevin's world became a schizophrenic blend of grey reality and brightly colored fantasy. At home in Boston, he barreled through his senior year at MIT. Thankfully, most of his course requirements were already completed, so it was just a matter of coasting through a handful of engineering seminars while closing out the swim season. Splintered into that grey tapestry were his weekend excursions to Vegas with Micky and the crew: well planned, almost military-styled assaults that soon became routine but never mundane. Every third Friday night, Kevin went straight from the Infinite Corridor to the America West 69 neon express, exchanging his dorm room for a three-thousand-square-foot celebrity suite, trading dinner at the dining hall for three A.M. room-service feasts. Frat parties became Fight Nights, brews at the local bar were replaced by free champagne in crystal glasses, poured by hosts in private booths at some of the most upscale clubs in the country.

Along the way, Kevin felt himself changing. He was living two opposing lives, with two distinct sets of memories. At home, he could reminisce with Felicia about what they'd miss when they graduated: basketball games at the Garden, late nights at a pub called Crossroads, ice skating in the Boston Common. But he could also close his eyes and see the bright lights of Vegas, the high-adrenaline moments of frozen time that spun through his memory like glowing shards of shattered glass.

By Christmas, Kevin had eased into the role of Big Player. He wasn't as polished as Fisher or as theatrical as Martinez, but he had a quiet competence with the cards and a real talent for sliding in and out of a table. As Micky had said, Kevin had the *look*; no matter the situation, he never appeared out of place. He could sit at a table of conventioneers, A-list celebrities, or Hong Kong businessmen, betting twice as much as any of them without raising the attention of the pit boss. He could play in a high-stakes pit with Kevin Costner and Howard Stern, or at a five-dollar table tucked away by the slot machines, and never compromise his style of play. He learned to inhabit his aliases like a trained actor playing a role. Sometimes he was Teddy Chan, the son of a heart surgeon from Hong Kong. Other days he was Arthur Lee, an Internet millionaire from Silicon Valley. One weekend he was Davis Ellard, whose family owned supermarkets across Asia. The next trip he was Albert Kwok, the nephew of the richest landowner in Malaysia.

By mid-December, his wallet was full of photo IDs and credit cards. He created nine distinct aliases and acquired nine different casino hosts, some of them at the very same casinos. When he hit the Stardust, there was pink champagne waiting in a wraparound corner suite. At the MGM Grand, a tray of filet mignon was parked by the wide-screen TV. At Caesars, they kept a pony keg of Sam Adams chilled in his bedroom, to remind him of the fully stocked bar at the villa that his imaginary billionaire father kept outside of Rome.

But the comps were only half the story. For Kevin, the real thrill was in the game itself. Working the system, turning the math into money, keeping the count without breaking character. Much of the system was a grind: playing thousands of hands in a single weekend, keeping meticulous track of wins and losses, knowing when to get up from a table and when to start burning the cards. But to be really good, Kevin had to reach a level of sophistication as practiced as the technique of a professional athlete. Turning his rudimentary skills into expertise was the most difficult task Kevin had ever performed. Anyone could learn to count, but only a true master could earn Micky Rosa's respect.

When Kevin finally became an expert at all levels of counting, including shuffle tracking and card cutting—the two tricks he had watched Martinez and Fisher perform back in Atlantic City that first weekend—he felt a real sense of accomplishment, measurably more satisfying than when he aced an engineering midterm. The highs and lows in Vegas far outweighed the swells and ebbs at home, and the counting moments that stood out—good and bad—defined that period of his life.

Four A.M., a tropical corner of the Mirage.

Kianna was sitting at a half-empty table, tapping her bright red nails to the tune of a Jimmy Buffett ballad rolling in through the tropical bushes. Her hair was piled on top of her head and held up with white ivory chopsticks. Her eyes were overly made up, and they never seemed to focus on the cards. Two drunken college kids were hitting on her from second and third base, drawing smiles but nothing more. When one of them complimented her silk blouse, she demurely crossed her arms over her chest. Kevin moved in for the kill.

The dealer looked as bleary-eyed as the college kids, struggling through the zombie shift. He barely noticed as Kevin placed seventeen hundred dollars in two betting circles, playing the remaining table by himself. The count stayed good, and by midway through the shoe, Kevin had chased away one of the college kids and was playing three hands of ten thousand dollars each. Even Kianna was sweating, little droplets forming above her almond eyes. But Kevin stayed cool, absentmindedly touching the goatee he had grown the week before. Albert Kwok liked facial hair. He was even considering adding sideburns to the look.

Kevin won two hands and lost the third. The count stayed good, and he rode another three hands at ten thousand. He hit a blackjack and two twenties. *Thirty-five thousand in a single round.* Now the count was back near zero. Kevin scooped up his money and headed for the bar. Martinez passed him at the edge of the pit. Their eyes never met, but the role of BP had shifted for the third time that night.

Right under the Eyes in the Sky.

Two weeks later, back at the MGM Grand. The high-stakes pit was filled with a raucous crowd, mostly VIPs invited out for a club opening at a nearby posh hotel. The harsh scent of spilled alcohol melded with the thick smog from a dozen Havana cigars that was making the air shimmer.

Kevin was about to take a break and get something to eat when he was called into a positive-fourteen deck by Michael, dressed in Nike sweats and shiny new tennis shoes. Kevin was already up eight thousand dollars on the weekend; he was picturing the new snowboard he was going to buy when he got home, an imported model from Switzerland that would be perfect for cutting up the slopes over Christmas break. He figured one more run at the cards would net him a new snowsuit to go with the board.

He slid into the table cocky, spreading out two hands of fifteen hundred to start. He felt invincible, and the rising count only bolstered his confidence. After three rounds, he had moved up to two hands of ten thousand dollars each. He could feel the crowd gathered behind him, and hear them whispering to one another: *Who is this guy? Do you see how much he's betting?*

His heart thumped as he drew an eleven and a pair of nines against the dealer's five. It was the most beautiful two hands he'd seen since he'd started gambling. He doubled the eleven, raising that hand's bet to twenty thousand dollars. He drew a seven, making a hard eighteen, a decent hand. Then he split the nines—ten thousand dollars more on the table—and drew a two on one, an eight on the other. To hushed gasps from behind, he doubled the first hand, drawing an eight. He left the last hand alone.

Now he had fifty thousand dollars on the table and three good hands: an eighteen, a nineteen, and a seventeen against the dealer's five. The odds were enormously in his favor. He leaned back, a big smile on his face.

Then his stomach dropped as the dealer turned over his bottom card to reveal a six. The dealer flipped the next card, a ten, for a twenty-one. Kevin's ears rang as the dealer swept his fifty thousand dollars off the table.

"My God," someone said from behind him. Kevin clenched his teeth. He could hear Michael breathing heavily next to him. He thought about getting up, but the count was still in double digits. And now the deal was even further into the deck.

His hands were shaking as he moved three stacks of ten thousand dollars into three playing circles.

The dealer dealt Kevin another powerful eleven, an ugly fourteen, and a pair of sevens, then pulled the worst card in the deck, a six.

Kevin took a deep breath. "Here we go again," he said, as the crowd behind him pressed even closer.

He doubled down the first hand, adding ten thousand more. He drew a nine for a solid twenty, a wonderful hand. He left the fourteen alone and split the sevens. He got a ten on each, two seventeens. Now he once again had fifty thousand dollars on the table, betting on a twenty, a fourteen, and two seventeens. He would wipe out the memory of the last hand in a single stroke.

The dealer flipped his bottom card, revealing a queen. He now had a sixteen, the worst possible hand. Kevin was actually smiling again as the dealer drew his next card. Then the entire crowd groaned.

A *five.* The dealer flipped a goddamn five, for another twenty-one. On a positive-fourteen deck, Kevin had lost one hundred thousand dollars in two hands.

He sat there, frozen, watching the dealer sweep away his money. Then he rose and stumbled through the crowd. By the time he reached the elevators that led upstairs to his suite, his face had gone numb. He used his key card to access the VIP floor.

After exiting the elevator, he stumbled down the hallway to his room. He lay down on the plush shag carpet, arms outstretched. He stared at the ceiling. *A hundred thousand dollars in two hands.*

Overall, the team was still way up on the month. But it was a painful lesson to learn all at once. No matter the count, the cards could go bad. Over time, winning was inevitable, a matter of pure math. But in the short run, the game could go either way. Even math left room for luck.

It was a good twenty minutes before Kevin felt strong enough to rise from the floor and search for the room-service menu.

New Year's Eve 1994, Bally's on the Strip. Kevin counted down the last ten seconds of the year with Michael Sloan and a table of electronics salesmen from Iowa, cheering along with them as multicolored balloons floated past the huge crystal chandeliers that hung from the cavernous ceiling. Although Kevin knew the site of the lavish casino had been host to the most devastating tragedy in Vegas history—a fire in 1980 that killed eighty-seven people and injured seven hundred others—he had experienced nothing but good fortune at the blackjack tables. The room was perfect for team play: a spacious area the size of a football field, with countless felts, comfortable cushioned chairs, and good visual angles for signals. Kevin and Martinez had been tag-teaming all night, bouncing from Michael to Brian to Kianna with ease. As the horns blared and the champagne flowed, Kevin won three hands of two thousand dollars, followed by two hands of twenty-five hundred. He was spreading out another five grand in two piles when a woman slid into the chair next to him and asked if she could play one of the open circles. Kevin was about to say something obnoxious—he was checked in to Bally's under the guise of Elvin Shaw, a prickish rich kid from a wealthy Manhattan family—when he noticed the look on Michael's face two seats down. *Pure, unadulterated lust.*

He glanced at the woman, trying not to be too obvious. She was tall, with long auburn hair, smoke-colored eyes, and high cheekbones. She was wearing a silk halter top that barely contained her unnaturally round breasts, and a sliver of tan abdomen was showing above her tight leather pants. She was the epitome of the Vegas girl, the sort of woman you saw on the arm of a celebrity in the high-stakes pits or whisking through a VIP line at a trendy nightclub. Women like her did not exist in Boston, and even if they did, they wouldn't have socialized with whiz kids from MIT.

Kevin felt his face growing warm as he made room for her at the table. He had just celebrated Felicia's birthday two days before—followed by a heated argument concerning his plans to "visit his high school buddies in San Diego" over New Year's. But as he looked at this woman, Felicia was the last thing on his mind.

One of the electronics salesmen whistled, harvesting a quick glare from those smoldering eyes. Then Michael cleared his throat. "Having a happy New Year?" he offered lamely.

The woman completely ignored him, putting a single twenty-five-dollar chip in her betting circle. Kevin smiled to himself, feeling a bit more confident. *This is going to be fun.*

He moved five thousand dollars—the table limit—into his betting circle. The woman pretended not to look, but he could tell by the goose bumps on her tanned arms that she was impressed. The nearest salesman—a stubby man with a puggish face—was less subtle.

"Hey kid, don't blow your whole allowance on one hand."

Kevin laughed noisily, back in character. "You know my generation. If I don't lose it here, I'm just going to spend it on hookers and coke."

The cards started to come out, and Kevin played as aggressively as he could. He pushed the bet as long as the count was high, doubling and splitting as often as possible. He was a peacock—posturing, throwing money like crazy to get the woman's attention—and it was working. By the end of the shoe they had struck up a conversation, broken into snippets between five-thousand-dollar hands. Her name was Teri Pollack, and she was twenty-two years old. She had grown up in Southern California and still lived in L.A. As Kevin had already guessed, she made her living off of her looks: she was a rookie cheerleader with the Rams.

If Kevin hadn't spent the evening playing five-thousand-dollar hands, he might never have had the courage to ask a professional cheerleader for her phone number; but tonight he wasn't Kevin Lewis. As the electronics salesmen watched in awe, she wrote her number on a cocktail napkin and stuck it in Kevin's shirt pocket.

When she left the table, it felt like all the air had been sucked out of the casino. Kevin sat out the last few deals of a positive shoe, but he was certain Michael wasn't going to hold it against him in his spotting report. Opportunities like Teri Pollack didn't come around often. At MIT they didn't come around at all.

Kevin knew she was probably interested in him only because it was New Year's Eve in Vegas and he was betting five thousand dollars a hand. But he didn't care. This was now as much a part of who he was as his engineering pedigree.

He was so overwhelmed by his good fortune that he didn't notice the man in the dark grey suit approaching from the other side of the blackjack pit. When he finally caught sight of Michael's hands rising to his head, it was too late.

Kevin started to gather his chips as the man came up behind him and put an arm on his shoulder.

"Mr. Shaw, could I have a word with you?"

Kevin rose from his seat and took a step back from the table. The man was tall, with dark hair and a thin brown mustache. A name tag on his lapel identified him as one of Bally's shift managers, a Mr. David Cross.

Kevin reminded himself to stay in character. He took a hundred-dollar chip from his pile and tossed it to the dealer as a tip. Then he jammed the rest of his stake—a little over seventy thousand dollars, mostly in five-thousand-dollar denominations—into his pockets and turned to the shift manager.

"Sorry, Dave. Can't chat now. I turn back into a pumpkin at two A.M."

"Well, then, I'll make it brief. We can't let you play blackjack here anymore."

Kevin fought to remain calm. This was his first official barring. He had gone through the moment a dozen times in his head, but this was for real. Still, as shocking as the moment was, it wasn't exactly *intimidating*. Kevin looked the shift manager over, taking in his cheesy mustache and off-the-rack suit. He looked like a high school English teacher. In Kevin's imagination, the barring casino officials had always been burly men with bent noses. This guy wasn't a threat. He was a nuisance.

"Why the hell not?" Kevin said, rather loudly. The table in front of him had gone silent, and the salesmen were all watching with blank looks on their faces.

"Because you're too good for us," the shift manager said. He was smirking as he said it. Kevin felt anger building up inside him—but he remembered what Micky had told him. *If they ask you to leave, you leave*. Still, it seemed so unfair, so un-American. He hadn't cheated. He had used his brain to beat the deck.

He had also made twenty thousand dollars and gotten the phone number of a Rams cheerleader. All in all, a good run.

Fuck it, Kevin said to himself. He shrugged, then brushed past the shift manager, heading toward the front door. "I never liked this casino anyway. Smells too much like smoke."

Kevin was smiling as he reached the glass front doors that led to the garishly lit moving walkway connecting the casino to the Strip. Martinez and Micky hadn't lied to him; getting barred from a casino was no big deal. Card counters had the law on their side, and there was nothing the casinos could do about it. Vegas was a juicy oyster, and Kevin was going to suck the motherfucker dry.

He stepped outside onto the moving walkway, dazzled by the neon-lit canopy up above. If he had glanced back over his shoulder, he might have seen a tall, angular man with weathered cheeks, silver hair, and narrow ice-blue eyes watching him from just inside the glass doors.

THIRTEEN

Chicago, May 1995

"So this is how it's got to be. You've thought this through, and this is how you feel," Felicia said.

It was between the end of spring and the beginning of summer, and Felicia was standing awkwardly in a barren corner of the Delta Air Lines terminal at Logan Airport, her hands hanging stiffly at her sides. Kevin tried to think of something that would take the terrible, dejected look off of her face, but he couldn't bear to string her along anymore. He ran his hands down the sides of his charcoal Armani suit, reminding himself of the life he was choosing.

"I'm sorry. It's the mature decision, Felicia. We're graduating in a few weeks, and we're both moving away. I think we owe this to each other."

It was bullshit, but in the past year Kevin had become a master of bullshit. Although it had taken him a few weeks to realize it, Kevin had resolved to end things with Felicia the minute Teri Pollack had sat down next to him at the blackjack table.

"We could make it work," Felicia tried. She simply didn't understand; she was holding him back from a life he *wanted* to live. He reached for his briefcase, praying that they'd call his flight before this got any uglier.

"You'll be going to medical school in San Francisco," he responded. "And I'll probably be trading stocks in Chicago."

He'd had two interviews with the Bartlett Group, a boutique investment-banking firm located on the west side of the city. He'd applied to appease his parents, who were still getting over his disinterest in medicine and graduate school. He didn't really want to go into banking, either, but he knew he couldn't hang around Boston like Martinez and Fisher. He wasn't ready to make blackjack his full-time profession—a subject that had caused a few heated arguments with Fisher, who was beginning to take things more seriously after their stellar profits over the last six months. Micky had finally stepped in, suggesting that Kevin's job in Chicago would put him closer to Vegas and act as good cover material for a number of his aliases. Martinez had stayed out of the argument altogether. His allegiance was with Fisher, but he wasn't the sort to push his own views on anyone else.

Fisher's concerns were unnecessary; Kevin had no intention of curtailing his involvement with the team. The past three trips to Vegas had been the best weekends of his life. He'd spent most of his free time with Teri, using his comps at the various casinos to sweep her off her feet. Anywhere else, he would have felt too insecure to try to impress a woman like her. But in Vegas, he was the BP, with the keys to the city. He had standing reservations at the fanciest restaurants and front-row tickets to all the sold-out shows. The only thing holding him back from truly inhabiting his new lifestyle was Felicia—and graduation was a perfect excuse to cut her loose.

"I'm sorry," he said, as his flight to Chicago finally came over the PA system. "I know we'll stay friends."

Felicia gave him a look that nearly tore him in half, then tempered it with a hug. He could feel her trembling in his arms.

"Good luck with your third round," she said, before numbly walking away.

Kevin watched her go. Then he gathered up his briefcase and

headed for his gate. He admonished himself for the knots in his stomach. He was doing the right thing. He shouldn't have even let her come to the airport with him. Her presence had only forced him to compound his lies.

The truth was, there was no third-round interview. He was on his way to Chicago to meet Martinez, Fisher, and the rest of the team.

During his last interview trip, he'd discovered a riverboat casino parked on the Fox River in Elgin, Illinois, just forty minutes outside of Chicago. After a quick scouting session on his own, he'd invited the rest of the team to check it out. Micky had approved the layout, and they had added the stop to their playlist. It was a good break from Vegas, especially as they entered the slow gambling season. Aside from the odd arena event and July Fourth, the crowds avoided the desert oasis during the summer.

It was a good time to take the team on the road.

The Grand Victoria Casino was the most spacious gaming facility in the state of Illinois—and one of the stranger venues Kevin had come across since he'd started playing cards. Designed to mimic a nineteenth-century paddle wheeler, the steamboat looked like a cross between an amusement-park exhibit and a set in a lavish but slightly B-grade Hollywood movie. Adorned with bright lights and wood trim, the boat had been built on an ambitious scale; guests were corralled through an eighty-thousand-square-foot pavilion on the way to the casino, passing beneath a fifty-five-foot ceiling sporting an eight-foot-tall clock. The paddleboat boasted more than ten thousand visitors per day—a fact made even more impressive considering the boat's capacity was only twelve hundred. That meant the Grand Victoria was almost always running at capacity. With twenty-six blackjack felts spread across the open rectangular deck of the boat, it was an excellent card-counting arena, with just the right balance of camouflaging crowds and easy table access. Furthermore, in Micky's words, the Grand Victoria was a casino willing to "take the action." Although the table limits were only two thousand dollars a hand, nobody was going to bother them for putting down the high bets. Certain casinos in downtown Vegas—and all over Atlantic City—"sweated the action," sending a pit boss to breathe over a player's shoulder when the big bets were coming down.

Kevin's team met at Buckinghams Steak House, the complex's only upscale eatery, decorated to look like a Victorian-era parlor room. Micky handed out assignments; as in Vegas, he was going to sit out, letting Kevin, Martinez, and Fisher run the show. Kianna and the rest seemed happy to remain in spotting positions—maybe it was the responsibility of carrying large amounts of cash, maybe it was just a function of their personalities—so they would spread out across the floor, covering nearly half of the tables all night long. Martinez took the first shift and Kevin the second, while Fisher would wait until early morning to play cleanup. That meant Kevin would hit the floor as BP around two A.M. Unlike in Vegas, the BPs would not spot when they were waiting for their shift. The venue was too close-knit; a player who suddenly mutated from a minimum-betting-table squatter to a roaming rich kid would draw notice here.

Kevin, Micky, and Fisher remained at a corner table at Buckinghams as the rest of the team headed into the casino. Micky passed out cigars—Havanas given to him by one of the other unnamed investors, a real estate tycoon Kevin would never meet—and the three of them shared Vegas war stories. Micky never spoke about his life before blackjack; it was as if he had been reborn on the Strip with the discovery of his true calling. He spoke reverently about card counting: To him, it was both a business and a religion. Even though he couldn't really play anymore, he spent most of his free time practicing the art and making innovations.

While Micky talked, Kevin watched his waving hands as well as Fisher's cool expression. It was obvious that tension was growing between the elder manager and the lead team player. Kevin wondered if it was just about money; Micky's large investment put an artificial cap on how much Fisher and the rest could earn. Still, there could be more to the story. Kevin knew very little about Micky's history with the team. He had recruited Fisher and Martinez and taught them to play, but whatever else went on behind the scenes was still shrouded in mystery.

Micky's stories about the old days stirred Kevin's imagination and fueled his respect for the old guard of card counting. Micky had made millions during the golden age of blackjack—the late seventies and early eighties, when the casinos were just beginning to recognize the risk that counters posed. The dangers counters faced were much more palpable then as well; Micky's stories were littered with tales of violent backroom experiences and run-ins with Neanderthal security personnel. Although the worst that had ever happened to Micky was getting roughed up in the parking lot of a downtown hotel, other counters had had fingers broken and even worse: There were rumors of card counters disappearing after long rides into the desert. Of course, Micky assured him that it was different now. Casinos would never risk their valuable gaming licenses by being involved with such brutal activities. But Micky had certainly *earned* every penny of his fortune.

Still, as he looked at Fisher's dark expression, Kevin was beginning to think that it would soon be time for a changing of the guard. He hoped it would be a smooth transition; he liked to think of the team as a pleasantly dysfunctional family. If Micky was forced into retirement, couldn't he still play the father figure?

They'd moved from cigars to dessert by the time Martinez strolled through the restaurant, a wide smile on his face.

"We're up big," he said, sliding into the booth next to Kevin. "The dealers and pit bosses are fucking clueless here. They're dealing so deep I can see the floor." He unzipped his pants—right at the table—and pulled a plastic bag full of cash out of his underwear.

Kevin grimaced as he accepted the warm bag and removed the stacks of bills. "I sure as hell don't want to know where you carry the chips."

By three A.M., everyone at the Grand Victoria knew the name Barry Chow. The rumors were spreading with each hand Kevin won. A junket of overly made-up secretaries at the roulette table by the entrance had heard he was the son of a rich plastic surgeon from L.A.—the doctor who had done Pamela Anderson and Cher—on vacation from a rich kid's rehab in some small town in Indiana. The old men in bowling shirts playing the slot machines were convinced his dad owned Sony, even though his last name sounded Chinese and he spoke perfect English. The dealers, mostly transplants from Chicago by way of a dealer school in Vegas, didn't care who his father was—just that he was tipping black chips. And the pit bosses, mostly frustrated middle-aged men trying to work their way out of the bush leagues, were in love with his action; maybe he was winning this time around, but at two thousand dollars a hand, he'd be welcomed back any day of the week. He was the biggest thing to hit the paddleboat since Michael Jordan stopped by two months before. And even Jordan didn't bet like Barry Chow.

Kevin was having the time of his life. He was the center of attention, all alone at a table that Kianna had just abandoned, surrounded by a huge crowd of onlookers. He was playing all eight betting circles at once, taking full advantage of a plus-nineteen count. Kianna had helped him burn out a sea of low cards—hitting over and over again through an ugly run until the count started to turn—and now the shoe was bursting with color. Kings, queens, jacks, and aces, springing out with each flick of the dealer's wrist.

It was fucking beautiful. On the last round of the shoe, Kevin hit the limit with each of his eight hands, putting two thousand dollars in purple chips in each betting circle. He drew seven twenties and an eighteen against the dealer's seven. The dealer flipped his hole card, revealing a ten—and Kevin won all eight of his hands. The dealer started to pay him off, then realized that his rack was empty. He didn't have enough to cover Kevin's win.

The poor man shrugged sheepishly and called out to the pit boss: "We need a fill over here!"

His words were met with a crackle of applause from the crowd. The pit boss scurried to find the chips. Kevin felt like an addict on a cocaine high. He leaned back, kicked his feet up onto the table—*right on the goddamn felt*—and waited for them to pay him off. He knew he looked like the most arrogant prick in the world, but he didn't care. Hubris had no place in a card counter's vocabulary. There was plenty of time for humility back in Boston, where in a few weeks Kevin would walk down an aisle in a black robe to accept his diploma.

Kevin Lewis was graduating with honors from MIT and going to work for an investment-banking firm. He was quiet and humble and loyal to the people who knew him. He came from a good family and had just broken up with a wonderful girl.

Barry Chow had his feet up on a blackjack table in Elgin, Illinois, and was waiting to get paid.

Barry Chow was king of the goddamn paddleboat.

FOURTEEN

Boston, June 1995

The team meeting took place at two A.M. in the back room of a bar on Beacon Street, just a few blocks from the Mass. Ave. Bridge and still within view of MIT's main campus. The meeting had been called by Fisher, but Micky was presiding over the gathering as usual, camped at the head of a round wooden table weighed down by overflowing pitchers of Sam Adams. Kevin sat next to Martinez, who was absentmindedly shuffling and reshuffling a deck of cards while watching the Red Sox on the small TV above the door. Fisher was positioned between Kianna and Michael, the three of them sharing a heaping order of chicken wings piled inside a cone-shaped roll of wax paper. Brian and the rest were on the opposite curve of the table, four sets of eyes entranced by a buxom waitress who was presently wiping down the liquor cabinet that took up most of the far wall.

As Fisher spoke, Kevin watched Micky's face. His expression was indeterminate, obscured by the Coke-bottle glasses and excruciating teeth.

"The bottom line," Fisher started, his voice conspiratorially low, "is that we're not taking full advantage of our system. We've had an incredible run, but we can do even better. Now that we've got three competent BPs, we should be fielding a much bigger team."

Kevin had expected something like this. Fisher had been growing more and more frustrated with the limits on the profits he could earn. Over the past eight months, the team had produced an astonishing 25 percent profit on their investment. But Fisher and Martinez had been limited in their stake to a couple hundred thousand each. The bulk of the profits had gone to Micky and his silent partners.

Adding more members to the team could increase both their profit margins and their investment cap. Fisher and Martinez could each invest more in the team if they had enough Spotters to play three BPs simultaneously. And Kevin, too, could begin to enjoy a bigger payday; the day after his graduation, Fisher had invited him to become a small-scale investor. Kevin had around fifty thousand dollars saved up from the year. He had considered putting a down payment on an apartment in Chicago, but he could earn twice as much investing the money in the team—and at much less risk. Meanwhile, he'd be able to pay rent on a two-bedroom palace with what he made each weekend in player wages.

"I don't think any of us would argue with the idea of more profit," Kianna said, daintily fingering a chicken wing, "but we've got a pretty good, close-knit team. I wouldn't want to risk what we've got to chase after a few more dollars."

Fisher shook his head. "Expanding the team doesn't have to put us at risk. We just need to be selective about who we bring in."

Martinez grinned as he fanned his cards out in front of him. "Look how well Kevin's worked out. In a few more weeks, we'll have him completely potty-trained."

Kevin rolled his eyes. Micky cleared his throat. "I agree with Fisher that we could stand a little expansion. A few new players would allow us to run all three shifts simultaneously. The key is, we have to choose people we can trust, and people who fit our profile."

Fisher looked like he had swallowed something bitter. Kevin guessed that he was hoping for a much bigger expansion—maybe even a doubling of the team. But he was still deferring to Micky on leadership decisions. Kevin wondered how much longer that would last.

"What exactly is our 'profile'?" Kevin asked.

Martinez took the ball. "Non-Caucasian, for one thing. Twenty-year-old white kids with million-dollar bankrolls raise a lot of suspicion. Asian, Greek, Persian—the kind of kids you see parking their BMWs outside of the Armani Café on Newbury Street, that's who we're looking for."

"You don't think white people have money?" Michael said, jabbing at Martinez with a chicken wing.

"Some do, but they don't throw it away in the casinos. Gambling is an Asian obsession. And nobody lets their kids run as wild as rich Persians and Greeks. Walk around any casino, the people throwing down purple chips are almost always dark-skinned. Card counters, on the other hand, are usually balding white men with glasses. We can use one stereotype to trump another."

Kevin knew Martinez was right. Nobody gambled like the rich Chinese and Japanese tourists from Hong Kong and Tokyo. And a twenty-year-old white million-dollar player stood out like a torch in a casino. Casino personnel had a very simplistic view of the world. An Arab with a million-dollar bankroll was the son of a sheik. An Asian kid betting a thousand dollars a hand was the heir to the Sony Corporation. A woman in a pretty dress could *never* be a card counter.

"It's true," Micky added. "One of the best card counters I've ever met is African-American. Wears the gaudiest pimp outfits I've ever seen. Bright blue suits, shirts with ruffles, that sort of thing. He plays alone, bets like wild—raising and lowering from five dollars to five thousand, right under the pit boss's nose. And nobody ever suspects him of anything, because the casinos simply don't believe that a black man can count cards. Their own racism turns around and bites them right in the ass."

"So we've got our assignment," Fisher said, resuming control of the meeting. "We're looking for a few new recruits, preferably far from the regular stereotype. They need to work well in a team setting. And most important, we need to find people we can trust."

Kevin wondered if the same sort of meeting had taken place before his recruitment to the team. Fisher was right; trust was a huge issue. Even the Spotters were responsible for five thousand dollars a weekend. It would be simple to report a loss at the tables and pocket any amount of money. A few weeks earlier, Micky had run a computer analysis on each individual's play, to make sure the reported wins and losses fell within the expected deviations based on perfect basic strategy. The purpose of the analysis had been to test the team's efficiency, but it could have just as easily been to double-check the Spotters' reports. Kevin hoped it never came to that: They needed to be able to trust one another like a family, even if sometimes they didn't act like one.

Martinez set his deck of cards down on the table. "Anyone got any suggestions?"

Kevin sat back, thinking. One name immediately came to mind.

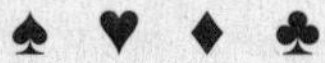

The poker game was in full swing by the time Kevin and Fisher descended to the basement of the three-story frat house. Located two blocks down Beacon from the bar where they had just finished their meeting, the vaguely Victorian building had a certain dilapidated charm: paint peeling in all the right places, bathrooms with exposed fixtures and cracked porcelain tiles, bedrooms with beads for doors and carpets hanging from the walls. The Back Bay address was the frat house of choice among MIT's jock population, home to most of the varsity teams. Kevin had rushed and pledged there his freshman year but had spent less time on Greek life as an upperclassman. As a freshman and sophomore, he had enjoyed his fair share of bacchanalian evenings. At MIT, there was no place better to meet eager young women, bused right to the building's front steps from the nearby all-girl colleges. The bus was lovingly renamed the "fuck truck," and the girls supposedly came in search of the least socially inept segment of the MIT population. Usually, they went home empty-handed.

The basement of the frat house was minimalist at best: a rectangular box with visible hardwood floors, a fully stocked bar along one wall, a regulation-size pool table, and a velvet-lined poker table in an alcove beneath a pair of dartboards. Even though the school year had ended, the basement was crowded. College-age kids—mostly male—were lined up at the bar, filling pitchers from the kegs of cheap beer. Others crowded around the pool table, playing a drinking game that involved placing beer-filled plastic cups near all six pockets. As Kevin and Fisher skirted the table, a team of lacrosse players upended one of the beers with a poorly aimed cue ball and ended up downing everything on the table. Kevin shook his head, remembering the many times he had passed out in a corner of this basement, his clothes and skin stinking of beer. *College.*

They reached the poker alcove and came to a stop behind the table. There were seven players seated in a circle, most smoking cigars and drinking from mugs emblazoned with the fraternity seal. A short African-American tennis player with too much facial hair was dealing the cards faceup, halfway into a hand of seven-card stud. There was a large pile of chips in the center of the table, and smaller piles before six of the seven players. Only one of the frat kids seemed to be on the winning side of the cards; a pile twice the size of the pot was stacked in neat towers in front of the last player—who also seemed to be drawing into a nifty full house, queen high.

Kevin tapped Fisher's shoulder, gesturing toward the kid with the lucky hand. The kid was extremely tall—over six-five—with spiky dark hair and an athletic, stretched-out frame. His face was narrow, his eyes a little too close together. His features looked Slavic, his size partially obscuring his lineage—half Chinese, like both Fisher and Kevin.

"Andrew Tay," Kevin whispered. "He's a sophomore, just joined the swim team. He was also an all-American baseball player in high school—"

"Stop," Fisher grunted. "You're turning me on."

"Just watch him play," Kevin responded.

Tay barely looked at his cards as the deal continued. He threw out his bets haphazardly, carrying on conversations with the other players while they tried to focus on their hands. Pretty soon the others started to drop out, frightened by his strong visible hand. Just before the last card of the game was dealt, the playing field had dwindled to Tay and one other player, who was also drawing into a full house—but this time, king high.

Instead of folding, Tay pushed a large stack of chips into the center of the table. He smiled at the other player, daring him to match the bet. His confidence was unnerving; Kevin could see the other player weakening with each passing second. Finally, he folded, unwilling to take the chance that his last card would give him the full house. Tay scooped up his winnings and began to stack them in his neat towers.

"He's pretty good," Fisher said.

"He's better than that. Rumor has it he's paying off his student loans playing in games all over the city. At the frat house, it's just friendly, nickel-and-dime chips. Otherwise they wouldn't let him play."

"If he's a pro—"

Kevin shook his head. "He hasn't been to Vegas since he was ten years old. Don't let his size fool you, he's just a kid, real small-town. He grew up in the hicks outside of Detroit. But he's crazy smart. He'll be Phi Beta Kappa next year, electrical engineering. He works in the robot lab in his free time."

Fisher was impressed. "He's got the math, and he's got the look. Can we trust him?"

Kevin nodded. Tay looked up to him like a younger brother—his loyalty bordered on idolization. He'd never think of crossing Kevin, and he'd jump at the chance of joining the blackjack team. Tay had told Kevin all about his childhood: His earliest memories involved lying on the ground playing craps with his father, a man who had kept his family afloat during the Vietnam War by rolling dice on the lower deck of an aircraft carrier. Tay had grown up around gambling. Every spring, the Chinese side of his family would caravan to Vegas. His size had enabled him to hit the tables with a fake ID at the age of fourteen.

"That's one down," Fisher said, decided. "We'll bring him to the Infinite Corridor tomorrow night."

"So now we just need to find two more," Kevin responded.

Fisher cocked his square head. "I think I might know a perfect pair. They don't fit the casino profile—but they don't fit our profile, either. They don't fit any profile. I'm not sure Micky's going to like them, because they don't go to MIT. But they're as smart as any of us. And they sure as hell know how to work as a team."

Kevin realized who he was talking about, and a wide smile broke across his face. It was a wild idea.

The casinos would never know what hit them.

FIFTEEN

Foxwoods Casino, Present Day

She was wearing a tight black leather miniskirt and high-heeled shoes. Her shoulder-length red hair flared out around her elevated cheekbones and angled chin, framing her confident Nordic features. Her body was sharp like her jaw, more corners than curves, and her thin frame couldn't have weighed more than ninety pounds. But the look in her blue eyes was a warning: Don't judge a girl by the length of her skirt or the color of her hair. *This bitch will rip you to shreds.*

I sat down next to her at the blackjack table. The dealer had just finished shuffling and was rolling the deck back into the shoe. There was only one other player at the table, an elderly woman in a bright pink jumpsuit. She could have been wearing a neon flamingo on her head and the dealer wouldn't have noticed: His gaze was pinned to the redhead with the razor-edge chin.

"Christ," the redhead commented as he started to deal the cards. "How long have I been sitting here? I wish my husband would finish playing craps so I can the get the hell back to Manhattan."

She brushed her chips with her hand, the enormous diamond on her ring finger flashing brilliantly above her bright red fingernails. The dealer sighed, his attention returning to the cards. *Another high-class arm charm, blowing time at the blackjack table while her husband rolls the dice.*

The dealer never would have guessed that in fact Jill Taylor was a tough fledgling corporate consultant at one of the top firms in the country. That she had graduated with honors from MIT undergrad and Harvard Business School, and lived by herself in a million-dollar town house in Hartford, Connecticut. That, at twenty-seven, she was recently divorced from an advertising executive who no longer wanted to compete with her professional drive, her firebrand personality, her unyielding "need for speed."

The dealer definitely never would have guessed that she and her husband had once been one of the premier card-counting couples in Vegas history.

Her act had him completely fooled. She could get away with anything at his table—and over the next hour, I watched her count cards with an expert's ease, while raising and lowering her bet with a rich woman's disdain. Even when she moved into the thousand-dollar-per-bet range, the pit boss never came over to look. On her own, she was a formidable presence in the gaming pit. I could only imagine what she and her husband had been like on Kevin's team.

When she finally cashed out her chips, she was up more than ten thousand dollars. I waited a few minutes for her to clear the gambling area before following her toward our arranged meeting spot. It was slow going: As usual, the casino was surging with visitors from all over the Northeast. It was an amazing thing to comprehend, considering that the place was located in the middle of nowhere.

The largest casino in the world wasn't in Las Vegas or Atlantic City. It squatted, monstrously, in a forest deep in the heart of Connecticut. From outside, it had the appearance of a many storied, pastel-colored spaceship that had fortuitously crash-landed on American Indian land. Foxwoods Resort and Casino had been built on a massive scale: The main complex totaled 4.7 million square feet, with 315,000 of them dedicated to gaming. The casino boasted 350 table games and more than 5,800 slot machines spread through five distinct gambling areas. Its 11,500 employees serviced an estimated 50,000 guests daily—an incredible accomplishment considering that the entire Pequot Indian tribe which had built the casino numbered a mere 300 members.

As far as I could tell, I didn't pass any Pequot as I made my way to the Golden Dragon, a kitschy Chinese restaurant in the heart of the casino. Most of the guests looked like they had driven in from the suburban towns that surrounded Boston, places like Revere and Sudbury and Waltham, where hair spray and wide polyester collars were still heavily in vogue. I did, however, observe a giant Lucite statue of an American Indian standing proudly in the center of the building's main atrium: *You can take the casino out of Vegas, but you can't take the Vegas out of the casino.*

Jill was waiting for me at a table in the back corner of the restaurant. She was picking at a plate of beef dumplings with a pair of polished wooden chopsticks. She didn't look up as I sat down, nor did she seem interested in trading pleasantries. Even though we hadn't seen each other in years, she wasn't going to waste time with small talk. Casual chatter might have fit with some of the characters she had played in the casinos, but in real life, Jill was one of the most directed people I had ever met. When she was at MIT and I was at Harvard—we both graduated the same year—we had been acquaintances but not friends. It was only years later that I learned to see through her hard exterior to the complex woman underneath. Even so, I never would have guessed that, like Kevin Lewis, she had lived a double life. Jill was the one who had first introduced me to Kevin, but she hadn't revealed his secret to me, allowing him to offer the story himself. When he finally told me that Jill and her husband had been two of his recruits, I realized that it made perfect sense. Jill was the last person you'd expect to find counting cards, which made her perfect for the team.

"So you're really going to write the damn thing," she said, jabbing a dumpling right through the heart. "You're going to make a lot of people nervous."

I watched her brush red hair out of her eyes. "What sort of people?"

"The casinos, first of all. The whole idea of card counting makes them nauseous. They like people to *think* that blackjack can be beat—it gets them to the tables. But they don't want people to *know* that blackjack really can be beat. Because then they'd have to admit to all the un-American things they have to do to keep the game in their favor."

She wielded the dumpling at me like a medieval weapon. "And the card counters won't be happy with you, either. You're going to give away a lot of their secrets. And you're going to popularize the notion of team play, which will make it even more difficult to pull off."

"I have to admit," I responded, "I never would have pegged you for a defender of something like card counting."

Jill smiled at me. "It took me a while to come over to the dark side. When Kevin and Fisher first presented the idea to Dylan, I wasn't thrilled. We had just gotten married, and I was in my first year of business school. I didn't know Fisher. He and Dylan had met through a rotisserie football league—you know, where you create virtual football teams and bet on the outcomes. The football league was bad enough; with blackjack, I was afraid Dylan was going to get us involved in something illegal. But I looked into it thoroughly. I'm told the law is pretty clear: As long as you don't alter the outcome of the game, or use a mechanical device such as a calculator or a computer, the worst they can legally do is throw you out."

"Still—" I started.

"I know. Straitlaced, conservative, hard-assed business girl running around Vegas with a bunch of overeducated anarchists. But I found the thrill of the game almost as addictive as the field of consulting. The idea of going up against a huge corporation, finding ways to beat them in their own arena—it was a real high."

I nodded. I had heard this from everyone on the team. They all saw themselves as little Davids going up against a giant, neon Goliath. Except in their version, David got rich off the battle.

"And the money—"

"Was the only real problem for me," she interrupted. It was an annoying habit, most likely the result of her business training and her hyper personality. "This was before the CTRs came around—the cash transaction reports. Nowadays, when you withdraw more than ten thousand dollars, the casinos fill out a form and report it to the IRS. Back then we walked out with as much cash as we could carry, and nobody got so much as a postcard. I made it very clear to Dylan that I wouldn't be a part of it if there was any tax evasion going on. Profits from gambling are income and have to be reported. I wasn't going to sacrifice my career for Micky Rosa."

"It must be hard to deal with so much cash," I said.

"If you don't want anyone to know where it's coming from, sure. It's nearly impossible to get large amounts of cash back into the system. You can't deposit it into a bank. For a while, we looked into setting up some sort of limited-liability corporation. You know, have everyone buy shares and draw an income. But it became too complicated. I decided it was much easier just to declare it as gambling proceeds."

I bent closer to her as a Chinese waiter swept by our table, carrying a pot of tea. "What about the others? Did they declare the money, too?"

Jill shrugged. The look on her face told me to change the line of questioning. I didn't really want to know the answer—I wasn't out to get anyone in trouble. I was pretty sure Kevin had played it as straight as possible. The IRS had made sure of that on at least one occasion. But I wasn't nearly as sure about the rest. I decided to leave it alone, for now.

"What about the lifestyle? You don't seem the Vegas type."

Jill blinked. "What, you don't think I'd look good in a rubber tube top? Seriously, I found the atmosphere pretty stimulating. I liked being able to play a different role—especially while I was slogging through business school."

She twirled one of the chopsticks, remembering. "I was able to flit around from table to table, and nobody ever paid me any attention. In the daytime, I'd dress in my beach clothes, like I'd just come from the pool. At night I'd dress like this—short skirts, fuck-me heels."

Another waiter looked over, then blushed when Jill stared him down.

"I act like I'm scared to play," she continued. "I always mention that my husband's playing craps—it's strange for a woman to play alone unless she's some old Japanese broad."

"And what about your friends back in Boston," I broke in, speaking quickly so she wouldn't interrupt me. "How did you keep it a secret from them?"

"Harvard Business School was pretty competitive; people kept secrets from each other as part of their daily routine. I do remember one story that was pretty funny. I was working for the summer at a consulting firm in town. A group of us flew out to Puerto Rico for a project, and they put us up in a hotel that had a casino. One night, after we finished a presentation, my boss was so worried about the casino, he actually escorted me back to my room. He thought I'd get accosted by the sort of 'element' that hung out around the card tables."

I laughed, picturing a stiff-lipped corporate type worrying about Jill Taylor. She shook her head, red hair flying everywhere.

"Of course, I snuck out in the middle of the night and played a few hands."

There was sheer joy in her tone. The bug had obviously bitten deep. "Were your experiences with the team pretty positive?"

She started poking at the dumplings again. "There were certainly some personality conflicts. I can be a tough little bitch. And at first Martinez was the worst sort of chauvinist. He didn't believe that a woman could ever count as well as a man. To be fair, I didn't help things by arguing throughout my testing period. I always thought he was fucking with me, just to make me look bad. But he was just being a tough teacher. I eventually—*eventually*—learned to respect him."

"Once the team hit Vegas," I prodded, "things smoothed out?"

"At first," she said. "There was so much money coming in, we had nothing to fight about. The first six months were like a dream. We took card counting to a whole new level."

Her eyes were bright as she recalled the high life, the incredible Vegas weekends I'd already heard so much about. But there was something else in her voice, something foreboding. I was going to say something but decided to let her get there herself.

She tapped her red fingernails against the tablecloth. "The brighter you burn, the hotter it gets, right?"

I wasn't sure what she meant. Through my interviews with all of the elements, the story was unfolding for me just as it had in real life, and I was fighting the urge to jump ahead. Jill Taylor had already been there. I could tell from her voice—she didn't want to go back.

"Dylan and I used to joke that we'd get divorced over this," she finally said. "Now he lives in the South of France with his new girlfriend. I'm a consultant in Hartford. And neither one of us has been back to Vegas in five years."

SIXTEEN

July 1995 to October 1995

Andrew Tay was absurdly tall for a card counter. At six-five, he towered over everyone else at the table, and if he back-spotted his way into a shoe, he almost had to squint to see the cards. It was impossible for him to vanish into a crowd, and he couldn't wander unnoticed through an airport. If someone was looking for him, they'd find him—in a club, in a bar, in a crowded casino.

Likewise, Jill and Dylan Taylor stood out in the average Vegas crowd. They were upwardly mobile professionals: Jill was enrolled in the most elite business school in the country, while Dylan drew a six-figure salary from one of the highest profile advertising agencies in Boston. They traveled like newlyweds, staying in honeymoon suites and eating in five-star restaurants. People remembered them—because of her fiery halo of red hair, because of his buttoned-down look and serious manner, because pretty couples stood out in a crowd.

And yet, somehow, these three additions enabled the MIT blackjack team to catapult their card counting to a higher dimension.

Beginning the weekend of July 4, 1995, Kevin was assigned the three new recruits as his permanent squad. Micky Rosa's team was now divided into three separate groups able to work simultaneously, each with three Spotters and a BP. Usually split among three different casinos, the teams worked eight-hour shifts—playing as many as fifteen hundred big-money hands a night. Calculating a profit of up to 10 percent per hand, and an average bet in the thousand-dollar range, the team was capable of generating a hundred and fifty thousand dollars a night for its investors. On many weekends, the team did much better than that, as they learned to maximize each member's strengths and take advantage of the disparate personalities.

Because of his height, Andrew Tay couldn't blend in. But he could signal like no other Spotter in the business. Kevin could stand thirty yards away, pretending to hover around a roulette wheel or a clamorous game of craps, and still have no problem registering a call-in from his towering teammate. And no pit boss in his right mind would ever suspect that the flashy, arrogant Asian kid with the big bankroll had any connection to the sloppily attired, oversized frat boy who'd been playing the minimum all night long. Tay's negatives as a counter had to do with his age, not his size: He was still very much a kid, prone to showing his emotions. He never made mistakes with the cards, but he was notoriously paranoid; he'd signal that he was getting "heat" so often that Kevin had to stop taking him seriously.

Dylan Taylor was on the opposite end of the personality spectrum. At twenty-six—the oldest member of the group besides Micky—he had been an accounting major at Babson. Before going into advertising, he had worked at a PR firm where he met Jill, a summer intern, for the first time. He was of average build and height, with meticulously coiffed blond curls and a conservative style of dress. In his white oxford shirt, blue blazer, and khaki pants hemmed perfectly above his shiny leather loafers, he approached the blackjack tables like a Young Republican. He played flawlessly, and his Spotter notes were so good that Kianna immediately offered him the position of team secretary. He took the office extremely seriously, creating detailed player charts after each weekend excursion, calculating expected gains and losses and analyzing how the players stacked up.

Meanwhile, his wife burned up the tables with her fierce personality and unavoidable sex appeal. Kevin wondered from the start how the couple ever ended up together. Where Dylan was meticulously calculated in all he said or did, she liked to launch herself into every situation with the ferocity of a pit bull. Kevin had watched her tear apart dealers and players alike—not to mention Martinez and Fisher—when she felt a need to assert herself.

Despite their differences, the couple never seemed to fight—at least not in public. They shared a room and ate almost every meal together. Though Jill was often a bit hard to take, Kevin was developing a close friendship with Dylan. Unlike Fisher and Martinez, Dylan had a life outside of blackjack. He went back to his advertising firm every Monday and saw blackjack as a lucrative hobby, not a lifestyle. Although Kevin wasn't satisfied with his banking job in Chicago—he found it stifling and not nearly intellectual enough to inspire him—he still resisted the idea of making blackjack his full-time occupation.

Even so, his weekends overshadowed his weekdays. That first July Fourth fully opened his eyes to the true potential of what they were doing. All three teams played like well-oiled machines, and the cards fell even better than expected. On Sunday morning, Kevin found himself relaxing by the Mirage pool, waiting for Teri Pollack to meet him for brunch. On the ground next to his lounge chair sat a duffel bag, partially unzipped. His team had finished gambling for the weekend a few hours earlier, and Kevin was going to deliver the bag to Micky at the buffet line at the Rio Hotel. He had tried getting the zipper to close all the way, but the bag was overfilled, stacks of purple chips barely contained by the bulging material. Kevin wasn't sure, but he guessed there was somewhere on the order of nine hundred and fifty thousand dollars in the bag, more than half of it pure profit from the weekend. As he lugged it through the casino, the only thought crossing his mind was that they needed to get a better duffel.

Kevin's cavalier attitude toward the money was unavoidable.

Because of his new position as one of the team's investors, there was so much cash coming in by the end of the summer that he didn't know where to put it all. When he dug through his laundry basket at his apartment in Chicago, he'd find stacks of hundred-dollar bills at the bottom—as much as a hundred thousand dollars held together by tight rubber bands. When he reorganized his CD collection, he uncovered a garbage bag full of purple chips hidden behind one of his stereo speakers: enough to pay his rent for the next five years. When he went to restaurants with friends or colleagues, he always paid with hundred-dollar bills; not to show off but to get rid of the damn things.

He was making far more money in Vegas than at his banking job. And he was having far more fun. The routine had become second nature: Fly in Friday night, play hard until Sunday morning, then party like a rock star until the return flight—usually the red-eye back to Chicago early Monday morning. Up until football season, Teri would fly into Vegas to meet him, usually arriving late Saturday night and joining him at one of the various Strip hotels Sunday morning. They'd spend half the day in bed, then hit the pool, a swank restaurant, and a posh nightclub. Teri would take him to the airport, kiss him good-bye, and a few weeks later it would start all over again.

With the new additions to the team, Kevin shifted into the role of teacher, and along with the responsibility came a certain swagger. Separated from Martinez and Fisher, he was top dog, and he strolled through the casinos like he was invincible. Once in a while he even brought Teri with him—something Micky never would have condoned—and let her carry some of the cash. He became a fixture at certain casinos—the Stardust, the MGM Grand, the Mirage—and many of the pit bosses thought of him as a friend. None of them knew who he really was, but they knew he was rich and liked to make big bets. And on Sunday nights he liked to party.

Labor Day weekend, end of 1995, he found himself escorted to a private booth in a newly opened club at the Hard Rock Hotel. Surrounded by strippers and starlets from L.A., Teri on his arm, Jill and Dylan one booth over but never making eye contact, and Tay on the dance floor, his head bouncing high over the crowd, Kevin watched the flickering lights and wondered if life could possibly get any better. He had seventy thousand dollars in a money belt around his waist and another quarter million back in his room. Card counting was the key that had unlocked the casino's coffers, and there was no reason to think the party ever had to end.

The next morning, as Kevin nursed a hangover while standing in the taxi line at O'Hare Airport, he impulsively decided it was time to quit his job. He didn't know what he was going to do next, but Vegas allowed him the freedom to seek out the life he wanted to live. He didn't have to make blackjack his profession; but it could cushion him between jobs.

The weekend before he moved back to Boston, the entire team came out to Chicago to help him pack and throw him a coming-home party. More important, they came to hit the Grand Victoria riverboat in full force, because Vegas was in the downtime between Labor Day and New Year's Eve.

By nine P.M. they had managed to get all twelve playing members of the team on board the boat at the same time. Kevin had been designated BP for the evening, and the eleven others were spread out across the blackjack area, covering much of the casino. Kevin went from one hot deck to another with almost no time in between; he'd barely rise from Dylan's table before catching a call-in from Tay, then find himself passed from Tay to Jill, then to Martinez and Kianna and Brian. Soon his pockets were bulging with chips, and he had lost track of his winnings. He took a quick bathroom break, locking himself in one of the stalls. Then he stacked the chips on the toilet-paper holder, careful not to drop any on the floor. They were positively killing the Grand Victoria—at least ninety thousand dollars in the past four hours. Kevin was riding high as he returned to the casino floor, and was immediately called in to Fisher's table, a positive-twelve shoe. He was about to push a thousand dollars' worth of chips onto the table when he froze, suddenly staring at a blackjack table twenty yards away.

Sitting in the third-base position was a short, stocky Indian kid in a light blue shirt and khaki pants. It was the same classmate he had seen in Vegas his first weekend with the team, so long ago. Sanjay Das, from his sophomore physics class at MIT.

Vegas might have been a coincidence—but this was a riverboat in Elgin, Illinois. Furthermore, as Kevin shifted his gaze past Sanjay to the next table, he saw another familiar face: a Japanese kid with thick glasses and a plaid shirt—Sanjay Das's roommate. Kevin shook his head, blown completely out of character. He could tell that Fisher was watching him out of the corner of his eye, so he touched his ear, giving the signal that he needed to talk. Then he quietly gathered his chips and headed back to the bathroom.

He waited for Fisher to enter behind him, then went to one of the urinals in the far corner of the room. Fisher stood next to him, waiting for him to speak. Kevin made sure no one else was in earshot, then cleared his throat.

"Five tables down from us—the Indian kid at third base. I know him. He's from MIT."

Fisher didn't seem surprised, but a bitter look crossed his face. "That's right. And he's not the only one. There are at least seven others with him."

Kevin stared at him, bewildered. "Another team?"

Fisher nodded. His lips were curled back at the corners. "I saw them when we first came in. I was going to tell you, but decided to wait until we got back to Boston."

"There's more than one MIT team?" Kevin asked again. Even so, how could they have discovered the Grand Victoria? Even Martinez had never heard of it before Kevin went for his interviews in Chicago.

"That's right. Actually, they've been around a bit longer than us. We call 'em the Amphibians. They call us the Reptiles—because we came from them. Which suits us, because we're next on the evolutionary chain."

"Micky," Kevin realized. "He's got money with the Amphibians too."

Fisher slapped a hand against the cement wall above his urinal. "That's right. He couldn't resist bringing them out here to hit the riverboat. Doesn't matter that this was our turf—or that we're risking burning this place down with nearly twenty counters in the room at the same time."

Kevin didn't like Fisher's tone, or where his friend was obviously heading.

"Listen," Fisher continued. "I respect Micky more than you know. But he's not a player anymore. He's a dinosaur, man. His time came and went. Now he's making money off of all of us, and we simply don't need him anymore."

Kevin exhaled. He had seen this coming for a long time. Now that they had brought in new talent, and unlocked new potential for profit, Micky and his investors were the only thing standing in the way. Fisher wasn't going to be satisfied with partial control and partial profits. He wanted the lion's share. And Kevin was beginning to see things his way. He was the one working the floor—why shouldn't he reap a larger portion of the benefits?

"You know what happens to dinosaurs," Fisher said, flushing the urinal with the palm of his hand.

"They run amok in amusement parks?" Kevin said, aiming for levity.

Fisher didn't crack a smile. He was dead serious. "Dinosaurs go extinct. If they don't do it on their own—someone has to help them along."

SEVENTEEN

Boston, Halloween 1995

Vegas had Fight Night. New Orleans had Mardi Gras. Boston had Halloween.

Thousands of college students howling through the streets, dressed in costumes that were usually more about skin than scare. Glowing jack-o'-lanterns and dangling plastic skeletons leading the way to overflowing campus keg parties, Ivy League masquerade formals, and brewery-sponsored bar celebrations. Crowds of witches, ghosts, Victoria's Secret–garbed fairies, and the odd *Star Wars* character roaming throughout the Back Bay, most of them too inebriated to feel self-conscious about how ridiculous they looked. When the bars and parties finally shut down a little after two in the morning, drunken hordes of bizarre Brothers Grimm characters poured back onto Boylston and Newbury, in search of the rarest creature of all—a vacant taxicab.

"Like a Salvador Dalí painting come to life," Kevin mumbled as he followed Fisher and Martinez up the front steps to Micky Rosa's apartment building at the base of Beacon Hill. October had been a particularly balmy month, and this evening was no exception. Most of the costumed girls they had passed had been dressed as genies or schoolgirls, showing even more skin than usual. Kevin was reminded of the outfit Teri had worn the last time he saw her in Vegas: a backless rhinestone shirt and tight leather pants. This was just about the only night of the year that she would fit in around Boston. Truth was, Kevin could not imagine her outside of Vegas. Or, more accurately, he couldn't imagine himself *with* her outside of Vegas.

They reached the front door to the building, and Fisher searched for the bell. The building was a converted five-story town house, split into three separate condos. Micky owned the top two floors—impressive, considering this was one of the most expensive parts of town, a charming mix of old and new wealth within easy walking distance of both the Commons and the Charles.

Since they had called ahead, Micky was expecting them. He buzzed them inside and sent the elevator down to pick them up. He was waiting for them in the hallway and ushered them into his living room with a wide smile.

Though the apartment was obviously expensive, the decor was right in tune with Micky's disheveled appearance. Mountains of books were spread over the hardwood floor, and the shelves that ran along the far wall were so cluttered they buckled in the middle like they were about to collapse. There were two poorly matched couches facing each other in the center of the room, and a torn, aging leather easy chair tucked into a corner.

As Kevin followed Fisher and Martinez to one of the couches, he noticed that most of the books were about card counting and Las Vegas, and most of the items on the shelves had to do with blackjack: dozens of unopened decks of cards, actual Vegas shoes, memento chips from various Strip hotels, even a pair of dealer uniforms that Kevin recognized from the Mirage. It was obvious from just a quick glance at the way Micky lived that his world revolved around blackjack. That only made what was about to happen more difficult.

Micky offered the three of them drinks—which they declined. Then he sat across from them and waited for Fisher to start. Fisher seemed to be searching for the right words, then shrugged and just let it out all at once.

To Kevin's surprise, Micky took the news fairly well. He listened carefully as Fisher explained the situation to him: The team no longer wanted or needed his money. Although everyone appreciated what he had done for them so far, it was time for the team to take care of itself.

When Fisher was finished, Micky leaned back on his couch, crossing one leg over the other. He turned from Fisher to Martinez, then settled his gaze on Kevin, the youngest of the three. "So you've all agreed on this."

He wasn't smiling anymore, but his tone was still amicable. Kevin had expected anger or, at the least, disappointment. But Micky seemed to have seen this coming. That didn't make Kevin feel any better. Micky had taught him how to count cards. He had been Kevin's surrogate father in Vegas, and things were going to be very different without him.

"We took a vote," Fisher plowed forward. "It was unanimous."

It hadn't been anywhere near as simple as that. The team meeting the night before had lasted more than seven hours. The opposition to Fisher's decision had come mainly from Kianna, who believed that Micky was the soul of the MIT blackjack team. The argument had turned heated, even personal—Fisher accused her of letting an emotional attachment to Micky cloud her judgment about the team. Micky was a father figure for Kianna as well, and, Fisher had intimated, maybe something more. She had not denied the accusation; instead, she had pointed out what many of them were thinking. Micky knew more about card counting than anyone on the team. Things were going well at the moment, but what if the atmosphere changed?

In the end, she had succumbed to Fisher's persistence. They were giving away too much of their hard-earned money. And there was nothing to fear from the casinos. Not that Micky could protect them—he couldn't even set foot on the gambling floor.

"If that's your decision," Micky said, showing his palms. "That's how it will have to be. I'll notify my investors tomorrow morning. I guess the stock market will have to be good enough from now on."

He laughed, the sound revealing a little pain at the edges. Despite his demeanor, this obviously wasn't easy for him. He had built this team from the ground up. Kevin reminded himself that Micky still had the Amphibians. Hell, for all he knew, Micky had a dozen teams running around Vegas. He'd be okay in the end.

"I hope we can all remain friends," Micky said, as Martinez and Kevin nodded. "Maybe help each other out now and then. I know that things are going extremely well right now, but let me give you guys some advice. Don't let yourselves get too comfortable. Remember everything I taught you. Every time you walk into a casino, they're watching. Every time you cash in a chip, they're taking notes. Sooner or later, they're going to start asking questions. And things *will* change."

Kevin felt a chill in the room. It was the first time Micky had ever said anything so negative about their future prospects. Kevin could see that his words had also affected Martinez, whose cheeks had gone taut. But Fisher still wore a bitter expression. He was finished with Micky and was ready to move on.

"One last thing," Micky said, as the three of them rose from the couch. "The most important decision a card counter ever has to make is the decision to walk away. From a bad table, from a negative shoe, from an unfriendly casino. It was the one thing I was never very good at."

He shook each of their hands, pausing in front of Fisher.

"Good luck," Micky said quietly. "Let's hope the cards keep falling our way."

EIGHTEEN

Boston, November 1995

With Micky gone from the picture, the "other" figure on Kevin's IRS forms was growing at an amazing rate. At Fisher's urging, he increased his investment to a quarter million dollars—almost all of it earnings from his first year and a half as a card counter. Kianna, Mike, and Brian all made heavy investments in the team, and even Dylan and Jill were permitted to make a small investment, more to keep them happy than because the team needed the money. Martinez and Fisher provided the bulk of the stash, more than four hundred thousand dollars apiece. Andrew Tay continued to spot for dollars, but he wasn't complaining. How many sophomores were earning five thousand dollars a weekend?

The split with Micky had little effect on the team's performance over the next six months. The cards did continue to fall in their favor, and they had stellar weekends beginning with New Year's and running all the way to Memorial Day. Kevin saw less of Teri during this period—football was in full swing, and she was traveling with the Rams most weekends—but he was so busy planning trips for the team that he wouldn't have had much time for her, anyway. The logistics of bringing twelve people to Vegas who weren't supposed to know one another, along with over a million dollars in cash and chips, was a problem challenging enough for any engineering major.

As the newest—and largest—member on the team, Andrew Tay became the "donkey boy," carrying most of the stash taped to his body. In this role, his paranoia came in handy; he carried the bags of money as if they were filled with unstable explosives, and worked his way through airport security with a drug smuggler's intensity.

Fisher took over for Micky from the moment they arrived in Vegas; he gave a shortened version of Micky's speech, then made out the assignments that he and Martinez had prepared the night before. Kevin stuck with his squad—Tay, Dylan, and Jill—and usually rotated among the Mirage, the Stardust, and the MGM Grand. He knew most of the pit bosses by name and became familiar with a good percentage of the dealers. A few of them might have noticed that he was unusually lucky at the tables; but amid the swarms of big-money gamblers who hit Vegas on the big weekends, good luck wasn't enough to raise anyone's suspicions. Sooner or later, they assumed, a big gambler would give it all back. That was the nature of the disease.

Most of the Vegas excursions went smoothly; in fact, only one incident marred an almost perfect record of highly profitable play.

It happened the Saturday of Memorial Day weekend, sometime past midnight. Kevin and his squad were working the tables at the MGM Grand when Kevin noticed one of the Amphibians—Sanjay Das's Japanese roommate—sitting at the same table as Tay. There was nothing worse than two card counters working the same table. From the Eyes in the Sky, the matched play would look ridiculous, like a comedy skit played out in cards. Kevin didn't know if Micky was behind the similar schedule, or if the Amphibians were also working on their own, but he wasn't going to let them fuck up his weekend. Tonight the MGM Grand was *his* turf.

Even though Tay hadn't called him in, he sat down at the table right next to the Japanese kid and threw down an insignificant bet.

Then he started in on the kid, talking in a loud, drunken voice: "Man, I've been playing cards for six, seven hours. That's like four hundred hands, and you should see how many sixes and sevens and nines I got, and I have so much trouble adding 'em up, seven plus six and six plus eight, and hey, what have you got there, a five and a nine, is that fourteen or what?"

The Japanese counter stared at him, his face reddening. He was getting rattled, probably losing the count. Kevin continued throwing numbers lodged in incomprehensible babble, until finally the kid got up from the table and started to walk away. Kevin rose, following him straight into the bathroom. When the kid lined up at one of the urinals, Kevin slid in next to him.

"Hey, jackass," Kevin started. This wasn't Boston, this was Vegas, and in Vegas, Kevin didn't mince words. "We were here first."

The kid looked at him. "Excuse me?"

"You know who I am. So take your team and find some other place to play. We both stay here, we're going to burn each other out."

The kid mulled it over. Then he shrugged. "I never liked the buffet here anyway."

He left without flushing—and took his team with him.

Back in the casino, Kevin made an executive decision and decided to shut things down early. If Tay had been compromised by working the same table as the Amphibian, there was a chance he'd get caught in the surveillance fallout, and there was no reason to take the risk. They'd already made enough to carry them all the way through the summer.

That Sunday night, they had a blowout party in a celebrity suite at the Stardust. Kevin did so many shots of tequila that he lost count and ended up challenging Tay to a wrestling match on the living room floor. In the scuffle they knocked over a coffee table, upending one of the duffel bags. Chips and cash flew everywhere, littering the shag carpet. Kevin lay on his back laughing, scooping huge handfuls of hundred-dollar bills and tossing them into the air. He closed his eyes, his head swirling, as he bathed in a cool green rain of Benjamins.

The quiet summer gave way to a clarion fall.

The second week of October, Martinez got wind of a new casino in southwestern Connecticut. Constructed in the same vein as Foxwoods, which had opened a few years earlier, the Mohegan Sun was the newest addition to the panoply of Indian casinos sprouting up in wooded areas across the country, built on a massive scale to lure suburbanites who couldn't quite justify the flight to Vegas. Back when Micky was in charge of the team, they had avoided Indian casinos for the simple reason that the reservations were considered independent legal entities; there was no way to guarantee a player's rights like in Vegas. If the tribal council suddenly decided that card counting was illegal, things could get ugly pretty fast. Nobody wanted to end up languishing in an Indian jail.

But the Mohegan Sun seemed too good to resist. Martinez had heard through contacts at MIT that the Amphibians had hit the casino its opening weekend—just a week earlier—and positively killed the place. The Amphibians had taken a quarter million dollars from the Indians, who hadn't had any idea what had hit them. They simply weren't prepared for card counters: From what Martinez had heard, the place was full of inexperienced dealers and pit bosses. They were dealing almost to the bottom of the deck, giving easy access to the last card on the rollover, and were completely unprepared for a card-counting assault. Their pit bosses probably couldn't even recognize amateur back-spotters, let alone the MIT pros.

Kevin, Fisher, and Martinez took a straw vote, and the decision was made. They would hit the Mohegan the following weekend. Only Jill dissented, warning that if something went wrong, they could get themselves into a legal mess. But the team was riding so high from the past six months that not even the fear of an Indian jail could dissuade them.

The Mohegan lived up to the hype: Although smaller than Foxwoods, it was charmingly designed with tribal-inspired interiors—plenty of exposed wood, hanging plants, and artificial sunlight, a stark contrast to the smoggy atmosphere of most Vegas casinos. The Casino of the Earth was enormous—the fourth largest in the U.S.—with over 180,000 square feet of gaming area and more than 190 tables.

Because of the casino's size, Fisher and Martinez suggested that the entire team play together, like they had in Chicago. Kevin and Martinez would take turns as BP, and Fisher would spot and monitor the casino personnel in case anything went wrong. If he sensed trouble, he would give a signal and they would all head outside to the parking lot.

They rented two vans with drivers to bring them into Connecticut early Friday night. The ride took about two hours, with an extra forty minutes tacked on by a short stop at a strip club in Hartford, where a "friend" of Martinez's from Vegas was dancing for the weekend. When they arrived at the casino, they immediately split up and headed for the tables; they weren't checking in to the hotel or breaking for food. They would work straight through the night and get the hell out of there. Fisher called it a surgical strike.

By two A.M. they were up a hundred thousand dollars. By four, they were closing in on the Amphibians' take, with more than two hundred and thirty thousand dollars in purple chips filling a duffel bag slung over Andrew Tay's shoulder. At five, Kevin was BP with a stake of over a million dollars in chips, nearly a third of it sheer profit. On the final play of the night, he had six hands of five thousand dollars apiece spread out across an empty table, Fisher watching from ten feet away. After doubling and splitting, Kevin ended up with eight hands of five thousand, and won every hand. He nonchalantly glanced back at Fisher to signal that it was time to quit—when he noticed that Fisher had gone pale. He turned back to see a pit boss approaching from the other end of the casino.

Christ. The stoop-shouldered, balding pit boss didn't look Indian, but he carried with him the weight of the entire Mohegan tribe. Kevin had visions of his team scalped and strung up in the trees surrounding the casino. Then he noticed that the bald man was smiling and had a clipboard in his hands. What's more, he didn't have any security in tow.

"Mr. Chiu," he said, using Kevin's alias of the moment. "We've been watching you all night."

Kevin's stomach turned upside down, and he began looking for the exits. "Why is that?"

"Because you're exactly the sort of person we want to feel at home here at the Mohegan Sun. Are you aware of our comps program?"

Kevin shook his head because he had momentarily lost the ability to speak.

"At the Mohegan," the man continued, "you can use your comp points to purchase wonderful gifts from our casino treasure chest. And Mr. Chiu—you've generated an amazing amount of comp points."

He showed Kevin the clipboard. At the top of the sheet of computer paper was a large number corresponding to Kevin's average bet and the amount of hours he had played. The rest of the page was filled with items Kevin could purchase using the comp points—everything from microwave ovens to a Harley-Davidson motorcycle. Kevin blinked, then forced a look of calm on his face. "You're running a great casino here," he said, as he began to go down the list.

That evening the team left the Mohegan Sun with three hundred and thirty thousand dollars in profit. Kevin ended up stocking his new apartment—courtesy of the Mohegan Sun comp program—with a brand-new wide-screen TV, a Sony stereo, two VCRs, a cordless phone, a Sony camcorder, six Walkmen, and a rice cooker.

Although Kevin didn't find out until years later, a few weeks after his team killed the Casino of the Earth, the Mohegan Sun got the accounting numbers for their first two weekends of play—and discovered a horrid discrepancy at the blackjack tables. Realizing they had been the victims of a card-counting coup, they immediately instituted changes to their gaming rules. First and foremost, they outlawed mid-shoe entry; if you wanted to sit down at one of their tables, you had to wait for the dealer to shuffle. At the same time, they retrained all their dealers to place the cut card at three decks, shuffling well before the running count became useful. Card counting became impossible at the Mohegan Sun—the place was effectively "burned down" by the two MIT teams. If Kevin had known about the changes that came as a direct result of his team's play, he might have wondered how the Vegas casinos were going to react when they eventually recognized the threat rising out of the underbelly of MIT. They had already tried changing their blackjack rules once before, and had met with disastrous results. No doubt they'd have to figure out some other way to discourage the MIT card counters.

But Kevin was oblivious to the changes at the Mohegan Sun. He only knew that he had earned enough money to pay a year's rent in a single night.

The team followed up its rout of the Mohegan with an incredible holiday season in Vegas. They earned a staggering 80 percent return on their investments by the end of February and continued pounding out profits right into the following summer. Micky Rosa's warning faded away as the team grew richer with each passing month. To be sure, there were more than a handful of losing weekends; sometimes the cards did not fall their way. And at one point, Dylan ran an analysis on Brian's play, after a long losing streak that was costing them close to five thousand dollars every night he spotted. But the losses fell within the expected variances, and Dylan didn't see any reason for them to worry. Brian would start winning again soon enough—and the wins would more than make up for the losses.

At the beginning of the summer, Kevin decided it was time to start working again. He was tired of trying to describe his imaginary occupation to family and friends outside the card-counting community, and he was beginning to feel too marginalized by his weekend-based lifestyle. Teri—whom he still saw on a regular basis—didn't understand his urge to do something more productive with his free time. She didn't think there was anything more productive than earning money, and the team was certainly doing that. But Kevin needed more.

He used his engineering background to land a position in the business development department of a small start-up in Boston. The job allowed him some control of his own schedule and wouldn't interfere with his Vegas weekends. Even so, Fisher was unhappy with Kevin's decision and made no secret of his feelings. One drunken Sunday evening at the Hard Rock, he questioned Kevin's loyalty to the art of counting, and they nearly came to blows. But in the end, Fisher apologized, explaining that he was just afraid Kevin would lose his "edge" if he became a nine-to-fiver. Kevin assured him that would never happen. He had stayed with the team because he couldn't be satisfied by a nine-to-five life. What he didn't tell Fisher was that he couldn't be satisfied with the gambler's lifestyle either—he needed a combination of the two.

The start-up's atmosphere fit well with Kevin's personality—and he quickly moved up the ranks of the company, earning stock options and a salary that almost compared to his Vegas take. Between the two, he was making more than his father had ever made in his life, and he was only twenty-four years old.

For his twenty-fifth birthday, he used his host connections to get the entire team front-row tickets to the fight of the season: Mike Tyson vs. Evander Holyfield at the MGM Grand. Fisher and Martinez were touched by the gesture—payback for that very first weekend when they took him to Atlantic City and introduced him to their way of life. Fisher decided it would be a banner weekend for the team. They would gather the biggest stake they'd ever attempted, letting everyone on the team invest at once. It was a risky venture—more than two million dollars in play at the same time—but they were emboldened by the past two years of success. Micky's warning aside, it didn't seem like there was anything to fear.

It was a Fight Night like no other: Kevin had never seen the MGM Grand so crowded, and by seven P.M. on Saturday, the people were packed so close, it was almost impossible to move through the gambling area. Kevin and Fisher agreed that they needed to postpone play until later that night. The team headed off to their separate rooms,

Ten minutes before fight time, Kevin began experiencing the first signs of a bout of food poisoning—intense stomach pains, nausea, the works. Realizing that there was no way he could make the fight, he used the hotel phone to call an eight-hundred number Fisher had set up in case of emergencies, and left a message that he would meet the team in the casino when he felt better. Normally, he would try and struggle through the pain to see Tyson and Holyfield, but since he hadn't gotten any sleep the night before, his body was already working on fumes. It was disappointing—but there would be other fights. Tyson wasn't going anywhere, as far as Kevin knew.

Kevin lay down on the vast king-size bed for a short nap. The stomach pains subsided around eleven-thirty, and he took a quick shower, got dressed, and headed downstairs.

When the elevators opened on the casino floor, he was met with a strange sight. The entire place was empty. The crowds had vanished, and the only people he saw meandering between the slot machines were dressed in the MGM Grand security uniforms.

He moved toward the blackjack pit. Right in the center of the gambling area, one of the tables was lying on its side. Yellow police tape was wrapped around the table, and Kevin could see piles of different-colored chips strewn across the floor.

He stood there, staring in utter shock, until a floor manager passed by.

"Eddie," Kevin asked. "What the hell's going on?"

The man stopped, recognizing him immediately. "You weren't at the fight, Mr. Fung?"

Kevin shook his head. "Looks like things got out of hand."

"Sure did. Tyson bit off Holyfield's ear! Damnedest thing I ever saw. A riot broke out. Then someone fired a handgun out here in the casino. Everyone started stampeding. Turned over one of the blackjack tables, chips flying everywhere. People started grabbing the chips, and we had to evacuate the place. Shut the whole casino down for the night."

Kevin whistled. He wondered how much money a place like the MGM Grand was going to lose, closing down for the night. "How much did people steal?" Kevin asked, looking at all the black and purple chips spread out across the floor.

"Don't know, but we got some of them on tape. Someone upstairs told me he saw a friend of Dominique Wilkins, the basketball star, scooping up purples. Crazy stuff. We're having a meeting later tonight. Don't know what's going to happen for sure, but I hear that the last time something like this went down, they changed the five-hundred-dollar chips and up, so the thieves couldn't exchange them for cash. Of course, that won't affect our prized guests such as yourself—I can vouch for whatever chips you've got lying around your room."

Kevin nodded, but inside he was on fire. It wasn't the few chips in his room he was worried about. *Overall, the team had over two hundred thousand dollars in MGM chips.* Added to the fact that the entire team was playing under aliases, that could make for a tricky situation. No one other than professional card counters kept that much money in chips. If they tried to exchange them for the new chips, there would certainly be an investigation. Their aliases would break down, and hell would break loose.

Fuck. Kevin quickly went back up to his room and called the eight-hundred number again. Fisher called back ten minutes later and told him to meet at the Paradise, one of their emergency rendezvous.

The bouncer at the door to the Club Paradise Gentleman's Club was built like a mountain. His huge frame was stuffed into a two-thousand-dollar pinstriped suit, crafted out of enough material to blanket half of Nevada. He was African-American, with a crew cut and multiple tattoos running up the back of his neck. The rumor was that he had played football for a number of NFL teams before a car accident left him with a limp and a job at the hottest high-class strip club in Nevada.

A wide smile broke across his face as Kevin got out of the MGM Grand limo—provided free of charge by his host, of course. Kevin had a hundred-dollar bill in the palm of his hand as he moved past the velvet rope outside the club, ensuring that the smile would be just as wide the next time Kevin frequented the Paradise.

The bouncer passed him off to the club manager just inside the door. Another hundred-dollar bill got another smile, and Kevin was led through the dark entrance area of the club toward the VIP booths near the back.

The air was thick with the mingled scents of cigar smoke and expensive perfume. There were leather couches and chairs spread throughout the main area of the club, a dimly lit rabbit warren of alcoves and raised sections surrounding two stages. The club was crowded, the chairs and couches occupied by well-dressed men, predominately middle-aged. Kevin recognized a few celebrities thrown into the mix, many of them frequent guests to the Paradise: James Caan, Jack Nicholson, Dennis Rodman. The Paradise was a favorite with the Hollywood and sports world A-list, and a passing glance at the women dancing on both stages and throughout the club explained why.

Mostly blond, tall, and well endowed, the women of the Paradise were the best on the Strip. Some of them had graced the pages of *Playboy* and *Penthouse,* some were headliners at the expensive clubs in New York, L.A., and points in between. Others were models who had, for whatever reason, given up runway careers and gotten breast jobs. Most were under the age of twenty-five, many as young as eighteen. All were exquisite physical specimens as well as skilled dancers—without a doubt, the cream of the strip-club crop. They came to the Paradise because they could make as much as three thousand dollars a night, and sometimes much more if they danced for a big enough celebrity or a rich enough Japanese businessman.

When Kevin reached the VIP area, he thanked the manager and made his way to his customary table on his own. Fisher and Martinez were already there, and a half-dozen colorful drinks were spread out across the tablecloth. A beautiful blonde was seated on Martinez's lap, gyrating as he whispered into her ear. Her bra was resting on Fisher's thigh, and her staggeringly large breasts glowed in the flashing lights from the VIP stage.

Kevin dropped into a leather seat next to Fisher and gestured toward Martinez. "Seems like you guys have recovered from the excitement pretty well."

Fisher nodded. "You missed a hell of a scene. Tyson went nuts, then the crowd went nuts, then someone started shooting. Christ, I thought we were going to get trampled. Martinez and I hid behind the slot machines until they closed the casino. The others got out right away and headed over to the Mirage."

The dancer finished her dance and reached for her bra. Martinez introduced her to Kevin. "This is Barbie. No kidding. She's from Dallas."

Kevin smiled as he shook her hand. Truth was, he'd met her before. Along with Fisher, Martinez, and Tay, he had spent a fair amount of time at the Paradise. Some nights he went through a couple thousand dollars on lap dances, other nights he just sat in the back and nursed a few drinks, but he found the dark anonymity of the place calming. The visuals were pretty good as well.

Barbie put her top back on and headed off toward the VIP stage. As she climbed up to the silver dancing pole in the middle of the raised platform, Martinez leaned in close to Fisher.

"It's settled," he said. "She'll bring some of her friends over to our room tonight to work out the details."

Kevin stared at the two of them. "What the fuck are you two doing? We've got an emergency here. The MGM Grand is going to change all its high chips. We're sitting on two hundred thousand dollars in worthless plastic. And you're arranging a goddamn orgy?"

Martinez grinned. Fisher gripped Kevin's leg. "Relax, you fucking Mormon. We're not arranging an orgy. We're solving our problem."

Kevin swatted his thick hand away. His stomach still hurt from earlier, and he wasn't in the mood to play games. "Who's solving our problem? You and Barbie?"

"That's right," Martinez responded. "Kevin, who carries around multiple thousand dollar chips, other than professional gamblers?"

Kevin suddenly realized why Fisher had told him to meet at the Paradise. He leaned back in the leather chair. It was fucking brilliant.

"High-class strippers," Kevin said, impressed.

Celebrities, gamblers, and businessmen all had similar routines:

Win or lose, they hit the strip clubs shortly after hitting the tables. When they were winning, they came to spread their good fortune. When they lost, they came to drown their sorrows in alcohol and silicone. They paid for their drinks in cash, but they often tipped with chips. The strippers didn't mind—it was all money to them.

"Barbie's going to get six of her friends to help," Fisher said. "Each one will exchange fifteen to twenty thousand of our chips for us. The rest we can handle ourselves—ten to twenty thousand each."

"And how much is this going to cost us?" Kevin asked.

Martinez shrugged. "A lot of lap dances. It will cut into our bottom line a bit, but nothing we can't handle."

"Can we trust these girls?" Kevin didn't like the idea of bringing in total strangers to help them out. Especially girls who were notoriously opportunistic.

"They're businesswomen," Fisher said. "And this is business. They've got no reason to turn us in. The casino isn't paying them—we are."

Kevin pursed his lips. It was a great plan. The MGM Grand wouldn't question girls who looked like Barbie. Either they were high-class strippers or high-class whores. Either way, it wouldn't be surprising for them to show up with thousands of dollars in MGM Grand chips. And Fisher was right, these weren't the sort of trashy girls you saw at airport strip clubs. These women made a few thousand dollars a night. If they weren't entirely trustworthy, they were certainly predictable.

"A few of them might walk off with some of our cash," Martinez admitted. "But overall I think we'll make out okay. And we won't give ourselves away. That's the important point."

Kevin nodded. A few thousand dollars one way or the other didn't matter, as long as they didn't sacrifice the system. "You guys are pretty smart for college dropouts," he said.

Martinez laughed. "We know how Vegas works, Kevin. It's all

about greasing the right wheels. Lubing the system in all the right places, so it doesn't grind down on top of you. This place is designed for people like us. People who know how to play the game."

Martinez was right. In the past two years, they had become experts at the game. They knew Vegas better than anyone—better than the dealers, the pit bosses, even the casino managers—better than anyone except maybe the strippers. Kevin began to relax, watching Barbie slither up and down the silver pole.

NINETEEN

Las Vegas, Present Day

The music was a throbbing mix of hip-hop and Top Forty, the bass turned up so loud the floor seemed to heave with each synthesized beat. Daggers of bright light from a half-dozen disco balls sliced through the strangely misted air, illuminating slivers of nude flesh everywhere I looked. When the overhead lights blinked on for a brief moment as the clock struck three A.M., an image straight out of Caligula's fantasies was seared permanently into my memory: a sea of undulating skin rippling and rubbing and writhing as far as my eyes could see.

To call Las Vegas's Crazy Horse Too a strip club would be misleading—both to the connoisseurs of the form and to those who abhor the very idea of nude flesh for cash. Built, consciously or unconsciously, to resemble a Roman orgy at the twilight of the Empire, complete with faux marble pillars smudged with cheap makeup and deeply pocketed chairs that resembled poorly upholstered thrones, the CH2 was quite possibly the most decadent place I'd ever been.

It was a Thursday night, and I was seated at the back wall, just a few "thrones" down from the pillared entrance to the Emperor's Room, a dark alcove that acted as the club's VIP area. As usual this time of year, the CH2 was packed—roughly two hundred men of various ages milled about the two connected halls, most searching for an empty spot to settle down. Navigating through this mob of testosterone were a hundred and fifty women garbed in bikinis, lingerie, G-strings, and a few indescribable outfits that amounted to little more than carefully balanced scarves. The women were a multicultural mix of physical styles, from the surgically enhanced blond bombshell to the petite Southeast Asian geisha. Most of the dancers seemed to be in their early twenties, though there were more than a handful that didn't look a day over nineteen. But the dancers themselves—though of exceptional quality—weren't the main draw of the CH2: The appeal was its personalized brand of lap dance. Or, more accurately described by the bouncer at the front door, "a Vegas-style *friction* dance."

At the moment, the customers on either side of me were getting close-up demonstrations of the CH2's charms. To my right, a lithe Russian woman with cropped dark hair, perky round breasts, and a black leather thong had both legs wrapped around my neighbor's waist. She had his head cupped in her hands, and was rubbing her breasts against his cheeks as she jerked her lower body up and down against his crotch. To my left, a short Japanese girl with dyed blond hair and a silk kimono—cut away to reveal a truly spectacular feat of mammarian structural engineering—had turned herself completely upside down, engaging in an erotic handstand worthy of the next Summer Olympics. Her hands were flat on the floor, her body twisting like a drunken serpent, while her thighs clenched tight around the shocked face of a middle-aged real estate agent from somewhere in the Midwest. These two dances were not exceptions but the rule. In some darkened corners, the lock of bodies was so libidinous, I felt like I could get arrested just for watching. This was a side of Vegas that made it the most popular bachelor party destination in the history of mankind; an oasis of sexual freedom represented on one end of the spectrum by the topless showgirls who performed in some of the major casinos, and on the other by the whorehouses just outside the Las Vegas city limits. Prostitution itself was not legal in Las Vegas; you had to travel forty minutes to indulge legally in the oldest profession. But for many, the CH2 was the next best thing.

I was trying my best not to watch the Japanese gymnast or the Russian turbo-thruster when a tall blonde in a black silk teddy walked right in front of me. She put her hands on her hips, pushing her ample chest forward, and gave me a pouty red smile. "You look like you could use some company."

I started to stammer that I was waiting for someone when she dropped roughly onto my lap. Her perfume was overpowering, a mix of flowers and citrus, and her breasts were like pillows against the side of my head. She leaned close to my ear. "I'm April. Kevin Lewis said you wanted to interview me for some book."

I raised my eyebrows, surprised. From Kevin's description, I had been expecting someone older to meet me at the designated spot. April looked to be about twenty-five, with wide blue eyes and a smooth, girlish face. She wasn't the hardened man-eater I would have envisioned, knowing her background. She had spent the past six years as an exotic dancer here in Vegas, first at the Paradise and, now that she was past her prime in stripper's terms, at the CH2. For most of that span she had also worked as a high-priced escort, contracting herself out to various hosts at the posh Strip casinos. In other words, April had been another perk available to the high rollers—along with the champagne, the filet mignon, and the celebrity suites.

I introduced myself and asked if there was somewhere quiet we could talk. April smiled, then took my hand and led me to the entrance to the Emperor's Room. It wasn't what I had in mind, but April didn't leave any room for argument. She wasn't hard on the outside, but inside she knew how to play the game.

It cost me three hundred dollars for an hour of her time, and a twenty-dollar tip to the VIP bouncer for an isolated couch in the back of the dark alcove. A waitress in a tight bustier brought us champagne and two glasses, and April waited for me to pour. While I fumbled with the bottle, she reached behind her back and undid her teddy.

"Hold on," I said, "you don't have to do that. I'm just here for research."

"Sure you are." She laughed as if she'd heard that line before. "Relax. I just want us to blend in. They have strict rules here about fraternizing with the customers. You don't want me to get into trouble, do you?"

The teddy came off.

"So how did you meet Kevin?" I asked, trying to focus on the champagne. I knew the answer to my question—Kevin had related the story to me in great detail—but I was curious to hear it from her side.

"I picked him up at the Hard Rock," she said simply. Then she smiled. "He was sitting at a high-roller table in the Peacock Lounge. Purple chips stacked almost to his chin. Loud, obnoxious, spilling booze all over the felt. Just another asshole throwing his money away."

April swirled her champagne with a finger. "I waited until he got up from the table, then moved up next to him. I asked if he wanted to buy me a drink. He completely lost his shit. The loud, obnoxious boozer turned into a shy, geeky kid. I saw right through him, and he knew it."

I nodded. Kevin could play casino personnel, but when it came to a beautiful woman like April, he was all MIT. April was one of the few people in Vegas in whom Kevin had confided. They had connected right from the start, perhaps because of their similarities. In a way, they were both leading double lives.

"We became friends. He used to come see me at the Paradise. I also knew his girlfriend at the time—Teri Pollack—from the party circuit. Cute girl, great body. She could have made a lot of money if she'd wanted to."

I wasn't sure if she was talking about stripping or something more. Kevin had told me that April was a very open person, that nothing was really out of bounds. I decided to see if he was right.

"How much money can a girl make?"

"Depends what she's willing to do. At the Paradise, I took home a couple thousand dollars a night. When I was making house calls, I could earn five hundred to three thousand dollars an hour. Now I'm making a lot less, but I can still handle my mortgage and my car payments."

She didn't seem embarrassed by the open admissions about her past and her present; maybe it was the anonymity of the Emperor's Room, maybe it was the fact she was topless and sitting on my lap, or maybe it was just that this was Vegas after three A.M. It was a poorly kept secret that Las Vegas had one of the country's most permissive attitudes about the sex industry. Anyone with a phone book and an itchy dialing finger could find a *legal* escort willing to negotiate *illegal* "extras." If that wasn't good enough, the city was crawling with swingers clubs and after-hours establishments where any entrepreneurial conventioneer could find his favorite flavor of vice. Vegas hadn't earned the nickname "Sin City" because of Siegfried and Roy.

"Were most of your customers high rollers? I mean the house calls."

She sipped her champagne, leaving a half-moon lipstick smear on the glass. "I had a business association with a few of the hosts at some of the major casinos. When someone who could afford it came into town and wanted a blonde, they called me. Celebrities, athletes, high-rolling gamblers. The same people who hung out at the Paradise after the fights—the ones who couldn't be satisfied with a lap dance."

Vegas had an underside that everyone suspected but never really got to see in action. Somewhere down the line, Kevin and his friends had come right up against that darker side. Though April's experiences as a stripper and a call girl had nothing to do with card counting, she represented the part of Vegas you didn't read about in the guidebooks.

"Do you like Vegas?" I asked.

She paused, surprised by the question. Then she shrugged. "I like money. In the real world, I'd be working behind a register. Even though I can't make the lineup at the Paradise anymore, I can make a great living bouncing around this shit-hole. Where else could a girl like me afford a house and a car?"

Her face hadn't changed, but I could finally hear evidence of the harshness I had expected. Maybe it was the fact that at twenty-five, she was already considered old in her line of work. Or maybe it was just me, an outsider asking questions that could only lead to clichéd answers.

"You could work at one of the casinos," I said. "From what I hear, they're always hiring."

She refilled her champagne, her naked breasts jostling as she maneuvered the bottle. "This place is no different than the casinos. We're all a bunch of liars, just like them."

I tried to shift beneath her weight. My legs were starting to cramp. "What do you mean?"

She waved her arms toward the smoked-glass wall that separated the Emperor's Room from the rest of the club. "All the girls are so friendly and smiling and happy to see you. They dance and dazzle and tell jokes while they take your money. Inside, they hate your guts. Each and every one of them. They think you're a sucker and a mark."

The vitriol was out of place on her girlish face.

"The casinos are exactly the same. They give you glitz and flash and glamour. But inside, beneath the smiling faces, they hate you. They know you're a greedy bastard, and they use it to get at your money. They lure you in and rob you blind. And they laugh at you when you leave, every one of them. They laugh and try to figure out ways to get you to come back."

She downed her champagne and put the glass on the floor next to the couch. She put her hands on my shoulders and looked me right in the eyes as her toned body started to undulate against my lap.

"At least here, you get something for your money. At the casinos, they'd milk you dry and leave you outside on the sidewalk, if they could."

I wanted to stop her, but it was beyond my control. Instead, I gave her the only response I could think of—the company line. "At the casinos, you have a chance of going home a winner."

She shook her head, her mane of blond hair dancing over my face. "Don't be naive. Nobody wins in Las Vegas. Kevin Lewis knows that better than anyone."

TWENTY

Las Vegas, Fall 1997

Over the next two months, Kevin didn't give much thought to the minor loss of revenues that resulted from the MGM Grand debacle; he was far too busy with his job back in Boston to worry about a few thousand dollars of "lap dance money." His start-up had begun to take off, and he was traveling three days a week to meet with clients all over the country. To Fisher's dismay, Kevin put Vegas on the back burner, figuring that the late part of the summer was the slow counting season anyway. It felt surprisingly good to live a normal life, even for a short period of time. He still spoke to Teri on the phone once a week, but the more time he spent away from Vegas, the more obvious it was that they had nothing between them *besides* Vegas.

When Fisher and the team began making the game plan for Labor Day weekend, Kevin actually considered postponing his return to counting for a while longer. But two nights before the team left for Vegas, the memories started pouring back—the feel of the money in his hands, the beautiful face cards streaming past, the champagne breakfasts and filet mignon feasts—and he dug back into the laundry basket for his portion of the stake. The life was too irresistible. A veteran at twenty-five; card counting was deeply in his blood.

To Kevin's surprise, the first venue on his squad's weekend playlist was one of the newer Vegas megaresorts—New York, New York. The casino was definitely not a favorite among professional card counters, though it was certainly one of the great "wonders" of Las Vegas, an architectural phenomenon designed to make every visitor's jaw drop. The mini-replica of New York City was like a guidebook gone three-dimensional: Tourists wandered from a replica of Grand Central Station at one entrance to the Brooklyn Bridge at another, passing by a one-third-size Statue of Liberty, as well as detailed representations of Greenwich Village, Wall Street, and even Times Square. The casino itself looked like the back lot of a Hollywood movie studio, the Gotham decor so authentic that it seemed like you could smell fresh bagels and bialys above the customary scent of cigarettes and cheap perfume.

But like the city itself, New York, New York was a transportation nightmare. So many tourists came just to gawk that the narrow pathways winding through the resort were jammed in a constant state of pedestrian gridlock. It was hard enough to gamble there on your own; team play was nearly impossible, a task of elbows and shoulders to force a pathway from table to table.

Still, Fisher wanted Kevin's squad to give the tourist trap a shot. It was all part of an effort to spread their team's play across a wider variety of casinos, in the hopes of lessening the risk of burning out any individual hot spot. Fisher felt that Kevin had played the MGM Grand, the Stardust, and the Mirage so heavily in the past year, there was a growing chance that someone in one of the surveillance rooms would finally begin to put things together.

Kevin thought Fisher was being needlessly paranoid. He hadn't experienced any problems since his first barring back at Bally's, and he had made friends with most of the pit bosses at his favorite haunts.

Still, he deferred to his teammate's wishes. Fisher was more experienced—and liked to play the big boss. He was already chafing at Kevin's increased interest in a stable life back in Boston. If a change in scenery would make Fisher happy, Kevin was willing to comply.

It took a good thirty minutes for Kevin's Spotters to situate themselves in the main gambling area. Dylan and Jill found seats closest to the Brooklyn Bridge entrance, while Tay was nearer to the Statue of Liberty. Kevin began his rounds, aggressively pushing his way through the throngs of people. He often lost sight of Dylan and Jill, but he could usually see Tay's head above the crowd.

Partially because of the limited range of movement, he went down a quick seven thousand dollars in the first hour of play. His mood ebbed lower and lower as he was jostled by the tourists, and inside, he was cursing Fisher for making him play this amusement park. Overhead, he could hear the faux Coney Island roller coaster whizzing around the upper part of the casino; the screams of the riders made his head throb. He wanted to get back to the relative calm of the Mirage or the Stardust. Even the MGM Grand was better than this.

He caught sight of Jill through a crack in the surge of people, and saw that her arms were crossed over her chest. Either she was trying to keep the mob of people behind her table from looking down her low-cut blouse, or she was calling him in to a hot deck. He ambled over, missing at least two hands before finally reaching the table.

He slid in between Jill and an overweight man in a Hawaiian shirt and baggy shorts. The rest of the table was full, most of the players dressed in equally colorful and equally tasteless clothes.

Jill passed him the count—"I sure hope my sister remembers to feed my cat"—a solid plus nine. He started at a minimum bet of seven hundred dollars and quickly followed the cards up to two thousand a hand.

In ten minutes he won seventeen thousand dollars, erasing his loss for the evening and lightening his mood. Maybe New York, New

York wasn't so bad after all. After he was done for the evening, he'd be able to get himself one heck of a deli sandwich.

Out of the corner of his eye, he suddenly realized that Jill had her hand deep in her red hair. *Shit.* He looked around, trying to see the danger, when a barrel-chested man in a dark suit stepped out from behind the dealer and leaned over Kevin's shoulder.

"Mr. Chow, a word, please?"

Kevin could tell from his tone that there wasn't going to be any offer of comp prizes. He breathed deep, reminding himself to stay calm. He'd been through this before.

He scooped up his chips and shoved them in his pockets. "Actually, I was on my way out. That goddamn roller coaster is driving me nuts."

He stood, but the man was blocking his way to the closest exit. The guy's name tag said ALFRED, SHIFT MANAGER. His eye sockets were surrounded by saggy dark bags—bloodhound eyes. Definitely old Vegas, definitely experienced.

"Mr. Chow, we don't want you coming back. You are no longer permitted to play blackjack at our casino."

To top it all off, he actually had a Brooklyn accent. Kevin could feel all the other players at the table looking at him, a few of them wide-eyed. Only Jill seemed to be concentrating on her cards.

"That's fine," Kevin said, his stomach tight. "If you don't want my action, I'll leave."

"There's a few questions we'd like to ask you before you go. If you'd kindly come with me downstairs—"

Kevin stepped around him and started for the door. He was trying hard not to panic. It was his first brush with the real possibility of being back-roomed. He didn't see any security personnel nearby, but he wasn't going to wait around for them to show up. As he pushed through the press of people, Alfred stayed one step behind him.

"Sir. Sir! Sir!"

Kevin kept moving. People all around were staring at him. Alfred hadn't touched him, hadn't made a move to physically detain him, but he wasn't going away. He followed all the way to the exit, stopping only when Kevin stepped through the glass doors to the sidewalk. Kevin kept going for ten more yards before glancing back. The man was staring at him through the glass with those bloodhound eyes. Next to him was another man, tall, gangly, with weathered cheeks, narrow, ice-blue eyes, and silver hair. Kevin stared at the two of them for a full beat, his breath coming in short bursts. Then he turned and jogged down the strip.

At that very moment a few blocks away, Martinez was fast asleep in a king-size bed in another major Strip casino's largest celebrity suite, his arms wrapped around the narrow waist of a twenty-one-year-old college student he had met two hours earlier. Her name was Betty or Amy or Andy, definitely something with a Y, and she was visiting Vegas for the first time as part of her sister's bachelorette party. Martinez had met her at one of the blackjack tables, impressing her with his five-thousand-dollar bets and his bright red silk shirt with alligator-shaped buttons. Since his squad had run up an impressive eighty-thousand-dollar profit in the first four hours of play, he had called the night early, taking Cindy or Mindy or Libby upstairs to "show her the view from the celebrity floor."

He had intended for her to be gone by three A.M. so he could head back down to the casino, but things had gotten pretty heated pretty fast. Exhausted, he had forgotten to set the alarm. He didn't even hear his two-way emergency beeper going off in the living room of the suite. The team had been outfitted with the beepers—complete with digital screens for abbreviated communication—after the riot at the MGM Grand, but Martinez hadn't gotten used to keeping the thing with him at all times, as Fisher had urged them to do. So he was blissfully unaware of Kevin's traumatic evening.

If he had heard the beeper, he might have been better prepared for what happened next. He might have been ready for the sounds of deep male voices coming from out in the hallway, or the scraping of a key in the lock. He might have woken up before the door to the suite crashed open.

Instead, it was the girl who awoke first. Her scream ripped into Martinez's skull, and he sat straight up, his eyes wild.

There were three burly men wearing light blue security uniforms standing in the doorway to his bedroom.

"What the fuck?" he managed.

"Get dressed," the biggest of the three men said. He had frizzy hair and long sideburns. He must have weighed close to three hundred pounds. He looked like he owned at least one pickup truck. "The casino manager wants to talk to you downstairs."

The girl wrapped the blanket around herself and leaped out of the bed, leaving Martinez lying stark naked on the mattress. His face turned bright red as he scrambled for his clothes.

"This is fucking ridiculous. You have no right to come in here. I'm a guest of this hotel."

"Not anymore," the mountainous security guard said.

Ten minutes later Martinez was led by private elevator to a basement room two floors beneath the casino. The room was little more than a twenty-by-twenty cell, with cinder-block walls, a low ceiling, and a heavy wooden door. There were only two pieces of furniture in the room: a steel desk and a matching metal chair, both darkened with age. There were no pictures on the walls, no plants in the corners, no signs of life. Martinez guessed the place had not been designed by the same architect who had planned the lavish casino upstairs.

The three security guards left Martinez in the room by himself, locking the door behind them. Martinez immediately checked the knob—no luck. After the immediate shock of the room invasion had worn off, he had regained much of his composure. He'd never been back-roomed before, but he knew the drill. It was a game, and as long as he played carefully, he'd be all right.

After twenty minutes, the door opened, and a man Martinez recognized from the casino floor entered, followed by the security guard with the sideburns. The casino manager was in his mid-fifties, with iron-grey hair and thick, watery lips. He had grandfatherly eyes but an angry jaw, an ugly juxtaposition. He was wearing a tailored grey suit and had a Polaroid camera in his hands.

He handed the Polaroid to Sideburns, and pointed toward the cinder-block wall.

"Mr. Gomez," he said, using Martinez's alias of the moment. "Please stand up against the wall."

Martinez shook his head. "No, I don't think so. In fact, I'd like to leave now."

Sideburns jabbed a finger in his direction. "Get up against the fucking wall!"

Martinez stood his ground. He spoke calmly, determined. "No. I said I'd like to leave now. Are you holding me against my will?"

His language was carefully chosen. He had heard enough stories from Micky to know how this worked. He also knew that he was finished at the casino. They didn't bring in the casino manager unless they were sure. Pit bosses, security guards, even shift managers were trivial nuisances. Casino Managers represented the casino itself.

The CM rubbed a hand against his thick lips. "We have the right to hold individuals suspected of cheating or committing other crimes at our casino."

"Are you accusing me of cheating?" Martinez countered. He felt his face getting flushed. His fear was turning into anger. He didn't like the way this middle-aged fuck was pushing him around. And he certainly didn't like the way Sideburns was glaring at him, taunting him with the Polaroid like it was some sort of weapon. Fuck, they must already have hundreds of pictures of him from the Eye in the Sky.

"No," the CM admitted. "But I do have a report that maybe you pushed one of our security guards. Isn't that right, Jimmy?"

Jimmy the Sideburns nodded, grinning. Martinez couldn't believe this shit. It was like something out of a bad movie.

"Fuck this! You want to call the police, call them. Otherwise you let me out of here or I'm calling my lawyer."

The air in the room went taut as the CM mulled it over. Martinez knew they wouldn't call the police. The one thing all casinos abhorred was publicity they couldn't control. They had nothing palpable to charge him with. In fact, neither the CM nor the security guards had even mentioned card counting. They couldn't hold him, because that would be akin to kidnapping and would open them up to a serious lawsuit. They had no legal choice but to let him go.

"All right, you little punk," the CM mumbled. "But you listen to me. You are hereby notified that you are no longer welcome at this casino. If you step foot in the door, you'll be trespassing, and we will fucking arrest you. You got that?"

Jimmy the Sideburns reluctantly opened the door, but Martinez took his time leaving the room. The guard stayed with him all the way to the front entrance of the casino, where his bags were waiting for him, hastily thrown together. Luckily, most of his chips were with Michael, his squad's donkey boy. But his silk shirts were all balled together, and one of them was missing a sleeve.

Martinez spat as he dragged his bags toward the Strip.

Kevin wanted to take the next flight back to Boston. He was thoroughly shaken by the aggressiveness of his barring, and especially by Martinez's story. He couldn't believe they had taken Martinez right out of his room. Jill and Dylan didn't think they had done anything illegal—it was their hotel, maids entered hotel rooms all the time—but they were concerned about Martinez's backroom experience. If they had wanted to arrest him on some trumped-up charge such as attacking a security officer, they could have caused quite a hassle. Jill agreed with Kevin that they should call the weekend short.

But Martinez and Fisher both wanted to stay one more night. Martinez was more angry than scared, and Fisher was more concerned with figuring out how badly the team had been "made." They didn't know whether the two barrings were related or coincidental. And since only Kevin and Martinez had been kicked out—all of the Spotters left singly once they got the signal to evacuate—it was possible that the team hadn't been compromised. It was strange that Kevin had been barred from a casino he hadn't gambled at before—obviously, there was some level of collusion going on behind the scenes. Kevin described the man with the silver hair and weathered cheeks he'd seen standing next to the shift manager, and Fisher wondered if the guy was one of the private investigators Micky had warned them about. If so, they were in bigger trouble than just two barrings; the Plymouth Agency supposedly worked for many of the casinos in town, sharing information on suspected cheaters and counters with pit bosses up and down the Strip.

"There's only one way to find out for sure," Fisher said as they conspired over breakfast at a dive a half mile from the nearest casino. "We finish out the weekend and see what happens."

In the end, Kevin and Jill decided to give Fisher what he wanted. The team was too young to consider themselves dinosaurs—there had to be hundreds more casinos that would still accept their action.

Kevin and Martinez both checked in to the Rio under assumed names: Billy Lo and Andy Sanchez. The Rio was set a short but reassuring quarter mile off the strip. A brightly colored, hugely popular casino with a festive, masquerade-style atmosphere, the Rio drew a young, mostly suburbanite crowd. The casino was set in the center of a "village" filled with shops and restaurants, and periodically assaulted by mock Mardi Gras floats suspended from the ceiling above the gaming area, complete with costumed performers lip-synching Motown songs. Like New York, New York, the Rio was not a gambler's first choice; the cacophony could turn the most centered player schizophrenic. But it was a good respite from the MIT team's regular haunts.

After dumping their bags in separate suites on the VIP floor, Kevin and Martinez flipped a coin, and Kevin won the role of BP for the evening. Both of their squads were going to spot, while Fisher's team sat out the session, enjoying some quality time at the Paradise. They'd stay in close beeper and phone contact, calling the eight-hundred number at regular intervals with updates on how the play was progressing.

At around midnight, Martinez and the Spotters spread out through the carnival-themed casino, taking positions at the tables. Kevin checked his bulging pockets, feeling the heft of the purple chips at his disposal. They had over one hundred thousand dollars in Rio chips from past play, so Kevin wouldn't need to resort to cash unless he hit a big losing streak.

He walked between the tables, his eyes scanning the colorful casino. Almost immediately he saw Martinez signaling him, an oven-hot deck. Kevin ambled toward the table—then noticed that a pit boss was standing only a few feet from the dealer. The pit boss—stocky, with thick glasses and a double chin—didn't seem to be paying any attention, but Kevin felt his adrenaline rising just the same. He was battle-scarred by the night before. He chided himself for acting like Tay, scared of every casino employee who passed by. He had to get over his fears if he was going to be of any use to the team.

He sat down at the table and shoved a handful of chips into the betting circle. Suddenly, the pit boss looked up, saw him, and stepped right next to the dealer. He reached down with thick fingers and pushed Kevin's chips back out of the circle. "Your money's no good here."

Kevin stared at him. He could hear his heart in his ears, and he could feel Martinez shifting uncomfortably in the seat next to him.

"Why not?" Kevin finally asked.

"I think you know why not, Mr. Chow."

Kevin blinked. Chow was the name he had used at New York, New York. His neck burned as he got the sudden urge to look up toward the cameras in the ceiling. He imagined that all the lenses were trained on his face, matching his picture with a file some fucking PI had given them.

Kevin got up, took his chips, and backed away from the table. The pit boss held up a hand.

"One moment, Mr. Chow. I'd like to ask you a few questions—"

Kevin turned and quickly headed toward the elevators. He didn't look back to see if Martinez had left the table as well, but he hoped his friend had enough sense to get the hell out of there. He reached the elevators and hit the button for the VIP floor. He didn't like heading up into the hotel, but he had to retrieve his bag. If he left it in the room, he'd probably never see it again—or the fifty thousand dollars in chips he had stashed inside.

As he rode upward, he glanced at the fishbowl camera in a corner of the elevator ceiling. He knew they were watching him. He wondered if security guards would be waiting in the hallway on his floor, or in his room. Sweat beaded across his back.

The hallway was empty, and he moved quickly to his suite. He pulled the door open carefully, but there were no signs of any security inside. He rushed to the bedroom and hastily packed his bags. Then he headed back to the elevator. He had almost made it to the main floor when his beeper went off, causing him to jump a full two inches off the floor. He yanked it out from under his belt and looked at the digital screen. The words blinked across in slow motion:

GET THE HELL OUT OF THERE.

Kevin clenched his teeth. *What the fuck do you think I'm doing?*

FASTER.

There was a blank moment, then the digital words continued.

TRIED CALLING YOUR ROOM. FRONT DESK SAID ALREADY CHECKED OUT.

Christ. Had the front desk simply made a mistake? Or had the casino checked him out while the pit boss was barring him? If Kevin wasn't a registered guest anymore—he wasn't certain, but he thought that might mean he had no legal right to be in the hotel. He was safer in the casino—still private property, though somewhat protected as an area open to the public. But walking around the hallways of the hotel, he could legally be considered trespassing, even without a previous warning.

Thankfully, the elevator was already decelerating as it reached the casino floor. Kevin put away his beeper and burst out into the village, nearly crashing headfirst into a masquerade performer with red and purple plumes sprouting from his head. Kevin pushed past him and raced toward the exit. He kept his head down, hoping that the cameras would lose him in the crowds of shoppers. But just as he neared the glass exit he heard a loud shout aimed his way:

"Mr. Chow! Just a word!"

He didn't stop moving. He could hear footsteps behind him but he barreled forward. He hit the exit and raced outside onto the sidewalk. He didn't stop to look for a cab or think about how absurd he looked: a terrified Asian kid running along the highway toward the Strip, his duffel bag clenched tight against his chest.

TWENTY-ONE

Boston, Fall 1997

By the time Teri arrived in Vegas that Sunday afternoon, Kevin was back in Boston licking his wounds. He had finally calmed down by the fourth hour of the early-morning flight—with help from Martinez and Fisher, who had a less frantic take on the situation. Certainly, something had changed that weekend in Vegas. At least a handful of the casinos were passing around pictures of them, perhaps through a PI firm such as Plymouth, and a couple of their aliases had been compromised. But the team itself still seemed undetected. None of the Spotters had been rousted, and Fisher hadn't met with any trouble. Even after Kevin had been kicked out of the Rio, Martinez had managed to play a few more hands before walking out on his own volition. There was no reason to panic—they just needed to be more careful, and more prepared.

They would no longer stay in the hotel where they gambled. It was too dangerous returning to their rooms to retrieve their bags, and after what had happened to Martinez, nobody felt safe sleeping in the same place they plied their trade. They would also keep a better look-out for approaching pit bosses and casino personnel—usually identifiable by their suits and name tags—so that the BPs could get moving before the confrontation took place.

Kevin wanted to avoid Vegas altogether, at least for the next few months. Even though he realized in retrospect that he'd probably been in less danger than he had thought, the race through the Rio had thoroughly disturbed him. But Fisher and Martinez immediately nixed that idea. Kevin had a job outside of counting; they relied on the cards to pay rent. If they were going to continue as a team, they had to get right back on the horse. The three barrings were a frightening development, but they didn't change the overall profitability of the team. Even if they burned out all their favorite gambling spots, there were many more casinos to hit.

In an effort to mollify Kevin's fears and rebuild the team's confidence, Fisher suggested they hit Chicago the following weekend. Kevin acquiesced, actually smiling as he thought about the quaint paddleboat on the Fox River. Maybe Fisher was right. Maybe a visit to the Grand Victoria was the perfect thing to set his mind at ease.

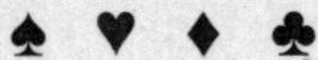

Of the team, only Jill and Dylan opted to skip the weekend jaunt to Chicago. Unknown to Kevin at the time, the couple had gotten into a heated argument the night Kevin had been kicked out of New York, New York. Dylan had thought the barring was no big deal, but Jill was concerned that the team wasn't taking the casino's response seriously enough. She saw card counting as an exciting hobby, but not something that was worth any amount of risk, no matter how vague. She had a career to think about; even a trumped-up charge was enough to put her in a bad light when applying for jobs at conservative corporate firms.

Dylan, usually the more traditional of the two, thought she was overreacting. He wanted to join the team in Chicago but wouldn't leave Jill alone at home for the weekend. In the end, he decided to give the weekend a miss.

Arriving at Buckinghams Steak House late Friday night, Kevin felt the old surge of adrenaline. As Fisher laid out the weekend plan, Kevin dealt himself cards at the table, forcing any remaining fears out of his body. This was his home turf, a casino he had been tearing up for over a year. Nobody could touch him here.

Kevin drew the first shift as BP, and the team slowly worked its way onto the paddleboat. Kevin began wandering among the tables, waving at the pit bosses and dealers he knew by name. Everyone smiled when they saw him, and he began to feel more and more at ease. Tonight he was Jackie Wong, the son of a neurosurgeon from Manhattan. He was rich, arrogant, and always grinning.

He sat down at Kianna's table and opened up with a thousand-dollar bet. The cards kept getting hotter, and he worked his way into a groove, moving up to the two-thousand-dollar limit. Pretty soon he had three hands out, and he had almost forgotten about the Rio and New York, New York.

Then Kianna jerked her hand toward her head, spilling her drink all over the table in the process. Kevin looked up in time to see, walking toward him, one of the pit bosses he knew from his very first trip to the casino. The man's name was Robert Steiner, and he had once even invited Kevin to invest in a noncasino-related business he had started. Short, balding, with wide blue eyes and chubby round shoulders, he was a family man with two kids getting ready to head to college and a wife who dealt cards during the day shift.

Kevin was already out of his seat and moving away from the table when Steiner reached him. He smiled as affably as possible, reaching out to shake the pit boss's hand. Steiner shook back, but his grip was limp, and he had a confused look on his face. "Jackie, we've got a little problem."

Kevin tried to remain cocky, in character. "Am I taking too much of your money? You know I'll blow it all back at the craps table."

Steiner looked pained. "We can't have you hopping from table to table anymore."

Kevin raised his eyebrows. He couldn't believe he'd been pegged as a card counter here, in Chicago. If they didn't want him moving around, they thought he was either back-counting the shoes or working with teammates. Steiner was breaking it to him gently because he was a friend, but Kevin was effectively on his way to being barred.

"This is crazy," Kevin said, feigning indignance. "I've been playing here for years."

"Maybe it's the guys you're hanging out with. Maybe they're the problem, not you."

Kevin swallowed, his throat dry. "What are you talking about? I came here alone."

Steiner pointed past Kevin's shoulder at Fisher, who was sitting at a table at the edge of the gaming area, pretending to focus on his cards. "You don't know that guy?"

Kevin glanced at Fisher, then back at Steiner. "Never seen him before. Why would you think that?"

Steiner scanned the crowd, spotted Martinez standing next to a table by the entrance. "What about him?"

Now Kevin's fingers were twitching at his sides. "What the hell is going on, Rob? You know me. I always play alone."

Steiner shrugged. His tone was rapidly shifting from reluctant to annoyed. "Maybe it's some sort of mistake. But they made the call upstairs. You can't hop tables anymore. But just between you and me, I think it's time for you and your friends to pack up and get the hell out of here."

Kevin stood there for a full beat, trying to think of something to say. Then he turned and headed for the exit.

Kevin made the long-distance call from the airport. Martinez and Fisher listened from just outside the booth, serious looks on their faces. Kevin waited for the connection, then lowered his voice.

"Hi, I'm calling from Rob Steiner's office at the Grand Victoria Casino in Illinois. I just have a few questions I need answered concerning our account."

There was a brief pause on the other end, then a cheery woman's voice responded. "Of course, Mr. Steiner. Jack will be right with you—"

Kevin slammed the phone down and turned toward Fisher and Martinez. "It's official. We're fucked."

The number he had dialed had connected him to the head offices of the Plymouth Associates in Las Vegas. Evidently, the Grand Victoria had hired them to protect their casino. Plymouth specialized in cheaters, thieves, and card counters. Lately, it seemed like the agency was also specializing in tracking down kids from MIT.

"It could still be a coincidence," Fisher offered. "Plymouth works for everybody nowadays. And we *have* been hitting the Grand Victoria pretty hard. It's a small boat, and we're the biggest winners they've ever seen. Maybe we just burned them out."

Kevin shook his head. "It's connected to what happened in Vegas. They know our faces. Steiner pointed both of you out."

"But he didn't say anything about our Spotters," Martinez broke in. "We've all bet big at the Grand Victoria. Of course they've got our pictures on file. They don't know about the team."

Kevin mulled it over. Martinez had a point. "Not yet. But if they've been watching us—"

"Come on," Fisher grunted. "You sound like that big fuck Tay. Maybe they've got a video camera hidden in my ass to watch me take my next crap. Kevin, we're small potatoes. They kick us out because we win, it's as simple as that. We've just got to be smarter."

Kevin didn't like his cavalier attitude. Fisher had kicked out Micky, the one person who had experience with this sort of situation. Instead of taking the reins and trying to figure out what had happened, Fisher just wanted to plow forward—despite the risks.

"We're playing with fire," Kevin said, moving away from the phone. "We've been hit four times in one week."

Fisher looked away, disgusted. Kevin felt like smacking sense into the fool. Martinez stepped between them, putting a hand on Kevin's shoulder.

"I agree that something's going on. But what do you want to do, give up? All counters get barred eventually. As long as the team survives, we're still okay. And they haven't figured out the team—which means they haven't figured out our system."

Kevin let the words sink in. The truth was, despite his concerns, he wanted to believe Martinez. He *wanted* to keep playing. He certainly didn't want to be pushed around by some private investigative agency or a handful of casino lapdogs. He hadn't been brought up to quit that easily.

"We're smarter than they are," Martinez continued. "We quit when we want to quit, not when they tell us to."

Kevin nodded, looking at Fisher.

Fisher grinned back at him. "What do you say, Kev? Let's go to the counter and book our goddamn tickets for Super Bowl weekend."

Kevin chose the MGM Grand because it was the casino where he had first played the role of the BP, the Vegas casino where he felt most comfortable. The casino was wide and roomy, with high ceilings and plenty of easy access to the exits, as long as you knew where you were going. Like every other casino in town, the MGM Grand filled to capacity during Super Bowl weekend, even though the sports books at some of the other hotels were geared more toward the serious sport gamblers. But the MGM Grand, from its giant green lion entrance to its ornate domed casino ceiling, had the appeal of size without the constraint of abusive expense.

He checked in under a favorite alias: Ken Davis, a Microsoft employee from Seattle. Not only did he show a credit card and Washington ID at the desk, he let his Microsoft business card fall out of his wallet as he filled out the registration form. He had gotten the card from an old classmate, in exchange for the phone number of a particularly "friendly" dancer who had moved from the Paradise to one of the local Seattle clubs.

Fisher and Martinez had checked in to their own Vegas favorites: the Stardust and Caesars, respectively. The goal was to complete a short six-hour shift, then meet up at the Paradise to discuss their progress. If everything was going okay, they'd return to the casinos for another six hours of play.

Thankfully, Jill and Dylan seemed to have worked out their problems and were stationed at tables in the MGM's vast gaming area. Tay was playing the loud drunk in a crowded corner of the high-stakes lounge, making friends with most of the cocktail waitresses and enemies of all the high-stakes players.

Kevin started the night at Dylan's table, moving quickly through a positive-fourteen deck. He was up ten thousand dollars when Jill called him in to another double-digit situation. Soon he was over thirty thousand dollars in profit, and everything seemed to be moving along at a smooth pace. He had cheery conversations with two pit bosses who knew him from previous visits; one even invited him to a private party in the celeb suite of an NFL quarterback watching Sunday's game with a handful of high-rolling friends.

Everything was going so well, in fact, that Kevin hardly reacted when Tay suddenly walked by, signaling for him to follow. He waited for Tay to disappear into the bathroom before joining him, somewhat annoyed at the break in play.

He found Tay at the last urinal, and sidled up next to him. There were other people in the bathroom, so Tay spoke in a near whisper—difficult to hear, considering that he was a good four inches taller than Kevin.

"There's something fucked up going on at my table."

Kevin sighed, assuming it was just more of Tay's paranoia. "You're betting the minimum, right?"

"Of course," Tay said. His breath smelled of alcohol, but he wasn't drunk. Another advantage of his size was that he could order drinks all night and never let it affect his play. *It would take a keg and an IV to get him off his game.* "But about twenty minutes ago, this guy sat down at third base. He's wearing a cowboy hat and a jeans jacket—and I think there's a plastic earpiece in his right ear."

Kevin glanced at him. "It's probably a hearing aid."

"I don't think they'd let you wear a fucking hearing aid in a casino," Tay countered. "He's got to work for the bastards. I think he's watching me and talking to someone through a mike."

Kevin zipped his pants and hit the flusher with his palm. "That's ridiculous. You're seeing things."

"Yeah, I know, I'm a paranoid fuck. But I'm telling you, the cowboy's got an earpiece."

Kevin wanted to dismiss it as bullshit, but after everything that had happened, he decided to check it out. "Go over to the bar and get a drink. I'll take a look and join you in a few minutes."

He gave Tay time to clear out, then reentered the casino. He meandered over to the high-stakes area, nodding at a few friendly dealers along the way. When he reached Tay's old table, he slowed, checking out the players. He saw the man with the cowboy hat at third base, chatting with a woman with frizzy dark hair sitting next to him. The man looked to be in his mid-forties, with matching jeans and jacket and dark brown cowboy boots. He looked like a hick from Texas, not a casino employee or a private eye. Kevin stepped closer, searching for any sign of an earpiece. The guy's ears looked clean. Either he'd put the earpiece away or, more likely, Tay was imagining things.

Kevin skirted the table and exited the high-stakes area on the other side. He made his way to the bar near the edge of the MGM's main gambling area and spotted Tay towering over one of the stools. To Kevin's surprise, Tay wasn't alone. He was in deep conversation with a woman in a short leather skirt and a see-through white top, tied off to reveal a sliver of flat, tan stomach. The woman had curly blond hair and fantastic legs. She had a hand balanced gently on Tay's thigh, and she was laughing at everything he was saying. Kevin could tell from Tay's expression that he thought he had just hit Vegas gold.

Kevin was about to give his Spotter some room to operate when the woman leaned forward, gave Tay a kiss on the cheek, and moved away from the bar. Kevin waited until she had turned the corner before approaching. "I'm impressed," he said. "That was some quick work."

Tay blushed. "I think I'm in love. Her name's Kimberly. She's fantastic. And she's also from Boston."

Kevin's eyebrows came together. "You told her where you're from?"

Tay shook his head. "You think I'm an idiot? No, she approached me. Told me she was from Boston, visiting Vegas for the first time. She wanted some tips on playing blackjack."

Warning bells were going off in Kevin's head. Women who looked like that didn't play blackjack. They played roulette and slots. "What did you tell her?"

"Just the basics," Tay said. "Then she asked me where I was staying and if I had any friends here who wanted to meet up with her friends tomorrow night."

Tay's excitement was tapering as he analyzed Kevin's expression. "A bit suspicious, now that you fucking killed my buzz. And I thought I was just getting lucky."

Maybe it was Kevin's turn to be paranoid, but he didn't like the feeling that was building in his chest. "Wait here," he said.

He moved quickly around the bar, following the path the woman had taken a few minutes ago. He pushed through a crowd of sports fans in NFL jackets, then navigated around two craps tables to the edge of the gaming area. He finally caught sight of the curly-haired woman near the elevators that led to the tower rooms. She was in the midst of an intense conversation with a tall, spindly man with silver hair. When the man looked up, Kevin recognized his weathered cheeks and narrow blue eyes.

Kevin quickly faded back into the casino. His breath was coming fast, and his cheeks felt hot. It was the same guy who had watched him from behind the glass entrance to New York, New York. The woman must have been working with him—flirting with Tay to seduce information out of him.

There was no way it was a coincidence.

The MIT team had been *made*.

TWENTY-TWO

Las Vegas, Present Day

I was standing in the center of a narcissist's fantasy.

My face stared back at me from twenty television screens, piled on top of one another in rows five across. When I smiled, I smiled twenty times, my teeth burning as bright as an unshaded bulb.

"It's quite horrifying," I said, and the man seated at the computer terminal in the far corner of the room laughed. The sound was a little too high-pitched, like a balloon squeezed to let the air out. The man looked like a balloon, too, his body built in round concentric spheres, from his oversize globular head to his jiggling, bulbous torso. He had round glasses and a round bald spot surrounded by a round crown of thinning brown hair.

"It gets better," the balloon man said. "Move around."

I took a step forward. There was a quiet whirring sound from above, and the images on the screens shifted imperceptibly, then resumed. My face still stared back at me in real time. Every twitch was my own, every bead of sweat tracked times twenty.

"Impressive," I said, craning my neck to look at the ceiling. I could barely see the cameras, each about the size of a roll of film. Most of them were hidden behind smoke-colored hemispheres of plastic—the fish eyes I'd seen in elevators and casinos all over Vegas. Others were uncovered, so I could watch their smooth three hundred and sixty degrees of controlled rotation. I took another step, and the cameras followed me, writhing like slick black maggots sniffing for meat.

"These are just the demonstration models," the rotund man said. "The newer versions can zoom in so close, I could count your fillings or read the time off your watch. And they move a lot quicker than these. We can track you walking across the casino, passing the image from camera to camera; into the elevator, down the hall, and eventually right into your room."

I shivered at the thought. Or maybe it was the air-conditioning. The windowless "showroom" was ten degrees cooler than the rest of the ranch-style home located thirty miles outside of Vegas, on the outskirts of one of the many "planned communities" that seemed to be sprouting up all over the desert. I didn't know whether the frigid air had something to do with all of the high-tech equipment in the room, or if it was just another quirk of the round man's personality. He was one of the strangest people I had met in the course of my research, and I had spent the better part of three months in Vegas seeking out colorful interview subjects.

Then again, perhaps nobody in the city was more colorful than Jake Eldridge. A transplant to Vegas who had made the journey from somewhere on the East Coast more than ten years before, he reminded me of the awkward, super-brilliant engineering students who wandered the hallways of the physics labs back at Harvard and MIT: shoulders permanently hunched, lips curled in a tentative smirk, hygiene and sartorial skills highly questionable. He had greeted me at the door to his home in a puke-green sweater and cargo pants. On the way to his showroom, I had been forced to navigate a minefield of discarded pizza boxes, junk-food wrappers, and empty soda cans. Only the showroom itself had been kept in pristine condition, the smooth cement floor and walls glistening white, the steel shelves lining the far wall carefully compartmentalized—items, both recognizable and seemingly alien, lined up meticulously.

It was obvious that the showroom was the focal point of Eldridge's life. As he had explained to me while he powered up the video displays stacked directly across from the steel shelves, the room combined both his past training and his present interests—his own double life.

Though Eldridge himself left most of the details to my imagination, I had gathered this much from my conversations with Kevin Lewis before contacting the engineer in his cookie-cutter home in the desert: Eldridge had received a PhD from a prestigious university in the East, concentrating in electrical engineering and computer programming. He had worked for a short time at Raytheon, developing onboard radar systems for cruise missiles. At some point, he had grown disenchanted with that way of life and had moved out west. He had worked for a number of casinos as a computer expert, beginning as a high-level programmer and slowly moving into the surveillance arena, accelerating up the security totem pole as the large Strip casinos became more and more interested in the new high-tech gadgets designed to protect their gambling interests. Two years before our meeting, Eldridge had decided to set off on his own, creating an independent surveillance company that would one day design and install entire security systems in any casino willing to foot his substantial bill.

Kevin had warned me that Eldridge would be a difficult interview. He was both strange and secretive: I would not be allowed to quote him word for word, use his real name, or reveal any details about his company or his clients. Kevin had met him at, of all places, MIT—a conference sponsored by the engineering department on developments in video technology. Eldridge wouldn't tell me any details about his life, but Kevin assured me he'd be an invaluable resource on the secretive world of casino surveillance. Looking at the minuscule cameras tracking me around the showroom, I didn't doubt this was true.

"And cameras like these are watching you when you gamble?" I asked. "This is the Eye in the Sky?"

"In the old days," Eldridge said, punching keys on his keyboard, "there was a two-way mirror that used to run the length of the casino ceiling. Above that were a bunch of metal catwalks. Security guys would walk up and down the catwalks with binoculars, gazing down at the players."

"You're kidding," I said, trying to walk out from under the pincushion of camera lenses. Eldridge kept them trained on me no matter where I moved.

"Nowadays, the major hotels have more than a thousand cameras like these set up all over the place. Everything that happens in a casino is videotaped and beamed over to a command post somewhere on the premises."

I had seen pictures of the command centers of some major Strip casinos, and they were quite impressive—like an air-traffic-control station. Considering the amount of money that moved through a casino on an average day, it made sense.

"And most of the cameras are hidden in plastic bubbles like the ones on the ceiling?"

Eldridge nodded, his many chins bouncing against one another. He hit another key, and the cameras stopped following me, freezing the image on the screens.

"The nipples? Yeah, you'll see a lot of those all over Vegas. But many of the cameras are also hidden behind colored one-way glass and false ceiling tiles, that sort of thing. They become part of the decor. And they're switched around every few days to keep the cheats from finding ways to avoid them."

"Sounds like a sophisticated surveillance system. It's a wonder anyone tries to cheat anymore at all."

Eldridge cackled. "The cheaters are pretty damn sophisticated themselves. I heard a story about one dude who actually marked cards with radioactive isotopes. He had a Geiger counter strapped to his knees. Others have tried fiber-optic cameras in sleeves, buttons, lapels. Others have used red-filtered contact lenses to spot marked cards. But you've got to be crazy to use any sort of cheating device in a casino. You can get ten years in prison. And they're bound to catch you. Especially if you've got a record or have been spotted before."

I walked closer to the shelves, eyeing some of the electronic devices in front of me. I recognized portable transmitters, wireless bugs, and directional boom mikes.

"Why is that?"

"Because guys like me are out here developing the next level of sophisticated recognition tools. Many of the casinos are already using facial-recognition software. I'm sure you've heard of it. Developed at MIT. Converts a fluid video image of a person's face into mathematical data by turning physical facial landmarks into an algorithm. This data is compared to images stored in a massive shared database, in search of a match."

I remembered reading about an experiment at the Super Bowl a couple of years before, when something akin to this technology was used to scan the crowd. The pictures were then matched up with criminal databases, and a number of "hits" were recorded. I hadn't realized the casinos were already using this software.

"The software is getting incredibly sophisticated," Eldridge continued. "Now the cameras only need a twenty-five-degree angle for a head shot and can capture as many as twelve faces at a time."

"How long has this been going on?" I asked, thinking about Kevin and his team. Their trouble had begun in late 1997, early 1998.

"At least a few years. But this is just the tip of the iceberg. Pretty soon they'll be scanning every face that comes through the front doors, and matching them with even bigger databases. They'll know if you're a high roller or a frequent guest or a wanted criminal or a cheat. They'll know how you like your room made up and how you want your eggs in the morning. If you've been to their casino before, they'll know you by your face. If you haven't, they'll know you from their shared database. Because more and more, the casinos work together."

"Sounds a lot like Big Brother," I commented.

Eldridge smiled. "It's Big Brother's Bigger Brother. And the technology is just getting better. After facial recognition we'll move on to thermography. Everyone's face gives off a distinct heat image. Then there's gait, how a person walks. As identifiable as a fingerprint. And ears. Ears are even better than fingerprints, because they're easier to spot and harder to fake. The casinos are going to be fighting this war with everything they've got."

"And they're not working alone," I added. "They also hire private investigative firms to do the dirty work."

He shook his head. "The PIs are just the middlemen. They provide the data—the digital facebooks of everyone who's ever been evicted from a casino before. Cheaters and thieves who've been caught on camera, either inside the casino, in the hotel, or on their way out to the parking lot. Sometimes the PIs go even further to get those pictures in the book: They track the suspects as long as the casinos are willing to pay them, digging as deep as the perceived danger makes it worthwhile. But the casinos themselves catch these scumbags in the act. They use high-tech systems like mine to gather the evidence to make sure the cheaters never get inside the treasure chest again."

"So the casinos are monitoring everyone who steps through the front doors," I mused. "But who's monitoring the casinos?"

Eldridge shrugged. Then he hit a key, and all the cameras trained on me.

TWENTY-THREE

Boston, Valentine's Day 1998

Emotions ran high in the darkened classroom as the team waited for Martinez and Fisher to show up. It was after eleven, and Fisher had called the meeting from Logan Airport via a pay phone. The pair had been gone all week, and not even Kevin knew where they had been or why they had gathered the team in the all-too-familiar classroom at MIT. Since Super Bowl weekend, the twelve conspirators had pretty much avoided one another. The team was in disarray, their future as a profitable venture utterly uncertain.

In Kevin's mind, there was little to discuss. Somehow the team had been compromised. They could still gamble at a number of casinos—the MGM grand, the Stardust, Caesars, among others—but the enemy was closing in fast. When Kevin shut his eyes, he could see the man with the weathered cheeks and narrow blue eyes. The image had followed him all the way back to Boston, all the way to the safe haven of his apartment in the South End. In his head, the man had become a specter, a symbol of the unknown enemy tracking them, spreading their pictures all over the gambling world.

"We need to cool off for a while," Michael said, facing the semicircle of chairs set up in the middle of the room. Only Jill and Dylan were seated away from the rest of the group, right under the shuttered windows. Both of their faces were taut, as if they had just come from an evening of arguments. Strange, considering it was Valentine's Day, and they were the only two people in the room who had anything resembling a meaningful relationship.

Kevin hadn't spoken to Teri in weeks. Since both of his last two trips to Vegas had been cut short, he had not seen her in over a month. He had thought about calling her that afternoon but decided he had little to say to her. She was part of his Vegas high life; now that he had been handed a heavy dose of reality, she didn't seem to fit into his world anymore.

"I think we just need to switch up the team a bit," Kianna offered. Like Fisher, she always wanted to push forward; she didn't care about risk. Her family had immigrated from Taiwan when she was only three years old, and she had been raised in a Chinese ghetto in California. She wasn't a stranger to difficult times. "Maybe bring in some new players. They can't have pictures of everybody at MIT."

"I still don't get how they nailed me," Tay broke in. He was wearing shorts and a sweatshirt though it was thirty degrees outside, and even during the day, the sky had turned gunmetal grey. "I hadn't even called Kevin in yet. I never raised my bet and purposefully fucked up basic strategy a few times when the pit boss was watching."

"They knew who you were before you sat down at the table," Jill said. She sounded angry, but it was hard to tell where the anger was being directed. "That means they might have files on all of us. And you know how these shitheads think. They lump card counters in with cheaters. To them, we're all criminals, and that's how they treat us."

"But nothing they do can hold up in court," Dylan countered. "They'll never even bring the police into it, because they've got nothing to charge us with."

"They don't need to charge us," Jill shot back. "They just put us on a list of undesirables, and we're guilty by association. Pretty soon we'll be getting trespassed from places we've never been before. Hey, it's been fun. But I just don't think it's worth the risk anymore."

The room went silent, everyone shifting uncomfortably. She had put it out in the open—maybe the game really was over. It was exciting when the risks were all theoretical; now they were real, and it was becoming more than a game. Nobody had been hurt yet. But maybe they had just been lucky.

"Now, this is a grim scene. Reminds me of my freshman organic chemistry class."

Fisher was standing in the doorway. His face was surprisingly tan for the middle of winter. He had a heavy duffel bag over his right shoulder. Kevin could tell from the bulges that it wasn't filled with money or chips.

"Ladies and gentlemen," Fisher said, with a flourish. "May I present, direct from Los Angeles: THE FAT MAN!"

He stepped aside, and in walked a ridiculous sight. Garbed in a bright red jumpsuit, folds of flab hanging from his chin, neck, arms, and bare legs, his cheeks inflated, even his lips swollen to twice their normal size—

"Holy shit," Jill swore. "Martinez, you look like a damn tomato."

It was the eyes and hair that gave him away. Aside from those distinguishing features, the prosthetic fat and bodily stuffing actually did a pretty good job of transforming him from a hundred-and-thirty-pound waif to a three-hundred-pound gargantuan.

A burst of applause filled the room as Martinez took a measured bow. "Of course, this is just the demonstration model," he said. "I wouldn't wear the fat suit in Vegas. It would certainly hamper my success with the ladies. But you get the general idea."

"Over the past few days," Fisher tag-teamed in, "we've been out in L.A. meeting with a top Hollywood makeup artist. For a small fortune, we've purchased some of the highest-quality disguises—prosthetics, wigs, hair coloring, skin dye—available on the market."

"They can't throw us out," Martinez said, "if they don't see us coming. Maybe they know some of our faces, some of our assumed names. Both of these are things we can change."

Kevin felt a smile crawl across his face. It wasn't just the sight of Martinez in the fat suit. It was the very outrageousness of Martinez and Fisher's plan. Makeup and wigs and prosthetic disguises—it was taking the system to a whole new plane. As card counters, they were already experienced actors and experts in character camouflage. Weren't makeup and costumes the next logical step?

"You guys are crazy," he said. But inside, he was wondering—why not give it a try? What did they have to lose? Their dignity? He watched Martinez twirl in the doorway, rolls of fat jiggling beneath his clothes.

The only real indignity was in giving up without a fight.

TWENTY-FOUR

Las Vegas, President's Day 1998

Three A.M., deep in the heart of the Pyramid.

Like New York, New York, the Luxor was a miraculous mixture of modern architecture and Vegas showmanship. Built in 1993, the thirty-story black glass pyramid housed the biggest atrium in the world—big enough to accommodate nine 747s stacked one on top of the other. Decorated with Egyptian obelisks, sandstone walls, and hieroglyphic-covered tapestries, the casino was another wonder of the city: tourist-oriented but spacious enough to provide a good gambling environment.

Situated in the center of the vast atrium, Kevin smiled at a waitress dressed like a porn-queen Cleopatra, as she leaned over his shoulder to deposit a vodka tonic with a precisely tailored lemon twist. She smiled back at him, showing even more enthusiasm when he tossed her a hundred-dollar tip. She didn't seem to be bothered by his sleek black ponytail, his ridiculous goatee, or the spiderweb of acne scars that spread across his forehead. He was sitting at one of the Luxor's high-roller tables, playing blackjack with purple chips. That was all that the Queen of the Nile needed to know.

Kevin didn't need to glance down the table at Dylan to see that he, too, was infused with good humor. His hair bright red, his face beaming beneath carefully applied blush, he looked five years too young to know anything about card counting, back rooms, or suspicious pit bosses. He certainly didn't look like an advertising executive with developing marital troubles. And his wife, seated five tables away, could have passed for a dowdy college librarian: hair tied back in a bun, thick glasses balanced over deeply wrinkled eyes, a blouse that might have been crafted from finely aged burlap. It might have seemed to the untrained eye that if Dylan was sharing his flight home with anyone in the gaming area, it would most likely be the platinum blond in the room—the six-foot-five hunched-over drunk with multiple earrings and visible tattoos who was at the other end of the blackjack pit, nervously pawing his dwindling pile of hundred-dollar chips.

Kevin pushed two thousand dollars into the betting circle, winking at the dealer. The fifty thousand dollars he had already won that night would make up for his childhood acne and his poor taste in hair.

Fisher had been right; Vegas could still be beat. There had been no heat from the pit bosses, and no sign of the gangly man with weathered skin, blue eyes, and silver hair. *The bloodhounds had lost their scent.*

If Martinez and the others were having as much luck as Kevin's squad—newly disguised, reborn under new names and new backgrounds—they could erase the last two months' losses in a single weekend.

Halfway down the Strip, Martinez had to blink to make sure he wasn't seeing things. The five hands spread out in front of him were something straight out of a dream, the kind where you woke up cursing that it wasn't real, that things like this *never* happened in real life.

He read the cards again, carefully, speaking in heavily accented English so the entire table could hear: "Brackjack. Brackjack. Brackjack. Twenty. Twenty."

He clapped his hands together, jabbering loudly in Japanese. The woman next to him hugged his shoulder, then joined the rest of the table in a round of applause. In ten minutes, the little Japanese man with the dark skin, thin mustache, and baby-blue suit had won sixty thousand dollars, drawing an incredible five "brackjacks." The pit boss had been over three times to offer him comps such as a free stay in one of Caesars luxury suites, tickets to a variety of sold-out shows, and dinner passes to all the casino's top restaurants. But the poor foreigner's English was so bad, all he did was nod vigorously: "Brackjack. Brackjack."

He bowed again and again as he finally rose from the table, shoveling chips into his bulging pockets. The only player who didn't congratulate him as he moved by was the angry little Asian woman with streaks of grey hair and mottled skin at third base who was meticulously counting and recounting her tiny pile of black chips.

Kianna would play out the next shoe, then make her way to the designated meeting spot across the street from the hotel. If there were no reported problems from any of the squads, the Spotters would return to the tables for a second shift, and the happy Japanese man would be back in action.

Back in the moment, Martinez strolled out of Caesars into the warm night air. Once outside, he lost himself in the crowd moving down the Strip. He paused for a moment at a stoplight, adjusting the mustache at the edges, making sure it was still tightly applied to his face. His skull hurt from the crown of tightly woven dark hair that added depth to his own, and he was sweating profusely beneath the cheap polyester suit. But he knew the overall effect was convincing. He could have boarded an airplane to Tokyo without raising a Japan Airlines stewardess's eyebrow.

He continued down the Strip until he reached the entrance to the home-base casino where both he and Fisher had gotten rooms under the names Nobuo Toyama and Leonard Wu. Once inside the main casino, he headed straight to the elevators that led to his room. He had twenty minutes to kill before he had to join the rest of the group at the meeting point, and he wanted to check his makeup and relieve his polyester pockets of some of the inflated stash.

He reached his suite on the VIP floor and used his card key on the double doors. Once inside, he bolted the doors behind him and went straight for the closet. His duffel bag was stuffed in a corner beneath two polyester jackets as atrocious as the one he wore. He pulled the duffel bag out into the middle of the room and unzipped it. It contained about four hundred thousand dollars, mostly in cash. Martinez began taking handfuls of chips out of his pockets and adding them to the stash. He had almost gotten his pockets down to a more reasonable bulge when there was a sudden knock on the double doors.

Martinez looked up, startled. There was a second knock, more insistent.

"Mr. Toyama. This is hotel security. We'd like a word with you."

Martinez's head spun. He looked down at the open duffel and the stacks of hundred-dollar bills. *Fuck.*

Fuck fuck fuck.

"Mr. Toyama, we know you're in there. We just watched you walk through the casino on our camera. Please open the door."

The lock clicked open, and someone applied a shoulder from outside. Luckily, the dead bolt held. But Martinez knew it was just a matter of time. He glanced at the large picture windows overlooking the casino's swimming pool. He could hear fireworks in the distance below, and bright flashes sprang up into the night. He was fifteen floors up. He had a sudden image of himself crashing through the window, swan-diving toward the pool.

"Mr. Toyama, don't make us bust down the door."

Martinez clenched his teeth. He grabbed the duffel bag in both hands and rushed through the suite, searching for a hiding place. There was a closet in the bedroom, but it was the first place they'd look. He entered the bathroom, his shoes skidding against the marble floor. Then he pulled back the lace curtain, revealing the enormous marble bathtub.

"Mr. Toyama! Open this goddamn door!"

Martinez climbed into the bathtub and lay down on the bottom. He clenched the duffel tight against his chest and waited for the inevitable.

A minute later, there was a loud crash, the splintering of wood. Heavy footsteps moved through the suite. Martinez heard the closet door swing open. Then the footsteps moved into the bathroom.

The curtain was yanked aside. Martinez looked up and saw three angry faces staring down at him.

"I guess this looks pretty strange," he said.

One of the men grabbed him by the shoulders and yanked him up out of the tub. Another pulled the duffel bag out of his grip and ripped the zipper open. The third man—dressed in a dark grey suit, unlike the others who were in the pale blue uniforms of security guards—pointed to the marble floor.

The man with the duffel turned it upside down, shaking vigorously. A rain of cash and chips clattered against the floor. The first guy let Martinez go and got down on his knees, sifting through the pile. He ignored the hundred-dollar bills, concentrating on the chips. After a few minutes he looked up at his boss and shook his head.

"Nothing from our casino."

Martinez stared at the three of them. They had no right to go through his money. Even if they had found their casino's chips, they had no legal way to confiscate them. Maybe the brutish security guards and the Neanderthal pit boss didn't know much about the law. Or maybe they just didn't care.

The pit boss stepped forward, his face inches from Martinez. "You think you're fooling anyone with that idiotic mustache?" He jabbed a thick finger into Martinez's chest. "You got five minutes to get out of our hotel, college boy. And tell your friends—if we ever catch any of you in here again, you're going to wish you never set foot out of Boston."

Martinez nodded, stunned. Somehow they had seen right through his disguise. His sense of bravado was entirely gone. He could smell whiskey on the pit boss's breath and see the glaze of anger in his eyes. Casinos were run by big, faceless corporations. But the guys in the trenches were a different story. They didn't like being made to look like idiots. Especially by kids from MIT.

The pit boss leaned even closer, so close Martinez could almost *taste* the whiskey. "We'll be back to make sure you're gone. If we find you in here, maybe we'll erase all the tape from our cameras. Maybe you weren't in the casino tonight, maybe you never came back to your room. Maybe you just fucking disappeared."

The man laughed, then stepped out of the bathroom.

Martinez pressed his back against the bathroom wall as the two security guards followed. The last security guard to leave patted him on his cheek with a callused hand: "Have a nice night, *Mr. Toyama.*"

When they were gone, Martinez sat down hard on the floor. It took him a full minute to catch his breath. Then he hastily began repacking the duffel, praying he could get out of there before the bastards returned to carry out their threat.

TWENTY-FIVE

The Bayou: Shreveport, LA, 1998

If Kevin had known the true story of what Martinez had gone through, he probably never would have agreed to Fisher's weekend experiment the very next Friday. As it was, Martinez had given the team a soft version of the story, keeping the details to himself. Even so, the event was disheartening. He had been barred from another casino without ever playing a hand of blackjack there.

But the rest of the weekend had gone smoothly: Martinez had composed himself and even gone to Caesars for a second shift. The team had won a remarkable two hundred thousand dollars by Sunday morning, revolving through a handful of different disguises. Martinez had gone from Japanese to Mexican to Eastern European. Kevin had traded the ponytailed acne look for "off the boat" Chinese, finally settling on a Polynesian theme that would have been a perfect fit at the Mirage. Fisher's hair had gone through three color changes and was still flecked in reddish blond, with dark black streaks at the roots.

Kevin was enjoying the subterfuge; he felt even more like James Bond, donning makeup in the bathroom at the airport, sometimes fixing himself up in the lavatory on the plane right before landing.

Martinez's barring was certainly a bad sign, but the team's overall feeling was that the costumes and makeup might keep them in action for a while longer. They just needed to avoid the more dangerous locales and open up new avenues of play.

Toward that end, Fisher's discovery seemed like a godsend.

"Shreveport, Louisiana. Paddleboats and full-service casinos just fifteen minutes from the airport. Lots of blackjack tables, high maximums, and clueless personnel. It's hicks with chips. We can't go wrong."

He had heard about the southern casinos from a friend who played on a counting team out West. The Shreveport casinos—some of them replicas of ninetenth-century paddle wheelers—were virgin territory for the MIT team, an untapped reservoir. Kevin, Fisher, Martinez, and Dylan would do a recon mission to check the place out, and if all went well, the rest of the team would fly down the following evening. It was decided that minimal camouflage would be necessary, and the four team members' disguises were limited to minor changes in hair color and skin tone.

They booked two rooms at a hotel near the Shreveport airport, then rented a four-door Toyota and made the short trip to the Red River waterfront. Their first stop was Jack Binion's Horseshoe Casino, a complex consisting of a twenty-five-floor hotel attached to a floating casino with almost thirty thousand square feet of gaming space. When they pulled up to the hotel, they were struck by its size: They had been expecting something more rustic, more representative of the ramshackle town they had driven through on the way to the waterfront. In fact, the Horseshoe was the tallest hotel structure between Dallas and Atlanta, with more than six hundred rooms.

They gave the car to a valet and stepped into the air-conditioned hotel lobby. The clientele heading into the floating casino fit more with the Deep South locale: plenty of denim shorts, overalls, baseball hats, and T-shirts. Kevin had a moment of anxiety when he realized that four part-Asian kids weren't going to blend in as easily as in Vegas; but at least their ethnicity and their attire—casual, urban, certainly Northeast—would match their big bankrolls. Nobody in a baseball hat and overalls was going to drop fifty thousand dollars at blackjack.

Once inside, they surveyed the landscape. The Horseshoe paddle-boat was three floors, with most of the blackjack tables situated on the lowest deck. They boarded the boat one at a time, at ten-minute intervals. Kevin was the last onto the boat, taking his time as he wound between the crowded tables. As Fisher had described, the table limits were five thousand dollars, and the Spotter visibility was quite good. Kevin sidled into an open seat, nodding at the other players.

He put down the minimum and began the count as low cards streamed out of the shoe. He noticed that unlike Vegas, the players were extremely friendly and talkative, often giving advice to one another and tossing comments to the dealer as he played his own hand. The southern accents made the atmosphere seem even more casual and friendly, and Kevin felt himself enjoying the camaraderie, joining in as the table helped a young woman handle a pair of nines.

By midnight he'd called Fisher in to his table twice. He didn't notice any heat coming from the smiling, cordial pit bosses who roamed the gambling area, and as far as he could tell, the team play was going completely unnoticed. When they left the boat—again staggered in ten-minute intervals—the quartet was up fifty thousand dollars. Knowing that they'd be in Shreveport all weekend, they left the money in Horseshoe chips, sealing the stash in a large plastic bag jammed into the duffel in the back of their rented Toyota.

Rather than retire to the hotel, Fisher voted to head over to another of the riverboats—a Caribbean-themed resort called the Isle of Capri. Kevin wasn't tired yet, so he acquiesced. Dylan requested a short pit stop to call Jill; then they made the quick drive.

They gave the car to the valet and entered the Capri one at a time. The Isle of Capri was smaller than the Horseshoe, and a little less well kept. Kevin dubbed it the Isle of Debris because of the lower-class element he saw strolling through the lobby. Once on the boat, he looked over the blackjack area and saw that the tables were packed a little closer together, but the maximums were still high and the visual access good. He watched Fisher, Dylan, and Martinez take positions a few tables apart, laying down minimum bets. Then he began to move in a loose circle around the gaming area.

He had made one revolution around the deck when he noticed something odd. Four pit bosses were gathered together in the center of the blackjack area, leaning over something on a small table. Usually, the pit bosses did not group together; they each had their own "turf" and conferred only at shift changes or when there was a security concern.

Kevin had a sudden, ugly feeling and moved in for a closer look. He found an angle where he could see between two of the blackjack tables, shielded behind a heavyset man in overalls who was leaning over one of the tables and trying to add up the numbers on his cards.

The pit bosses were talking to one another in low voices. All four were wearing white shirts and ties, and two had on dark jackets. Their expressions were all serious: lips turned down, brows furrowed. Something was bothering them. Kevin craned his neck, shifting his gaze to the table in front of them.

On the center of the table was a fax machine, purring as paper spewed out of its mouth. Kevin squinted, saw that the first few pages were covered in writing. Then he saw a new page come out, darker than the rest. Even from that distance, he could tell the page was split into four sections, each containing a multitoned image. One of the pit bosses tore the page from the stream of fax paper and held it up for the others to see. Kevin got a good glimpse of the four sections—and understood immediately what the images were.

Pictures. Four faces, all young males. He couldn't see many details, but two of the faces definitely looked Asian, and one of them had a crew cut.

Kevin's throat closed, and he stumbled backward. *Christ*. A fax with pictures of four young faces. A team of four counters hitting the casino for the first time. A team that had been nailed in Vegas with increasing precision over the past two weeks.

Kevin kept his eyes on the pit bosses as he moved to Fisher. Breaking rules and character, he tapped Fisher hard on the shoulder. "Get the others. We're getting out of here, now."

The back of Fisher's neck turned bright red, but he didn't turn around. Instead he nodded, almost imperceptibly.

Kevin moved quickly toward the exit. The pit bosses were still gathered around the fax machine, but one of them was dialing a cellular phone. *Calling out the reinforcements.*

Kevin reached the ramp that led to the hotel and increased his speed. A minute later, he burst out through the lobby to the valet stand. He gave the young valet a twenty-dollar bill and told him to get the car—immediately.

Martinez was the first to join him on the curb. A minute later, Fisher and Dylan raced over, both out of breath.

"What the hell is going on?" Fisher demanded.

Kevin held up a hand. They were outside, but they were still too close to the hotel for comfort. He waited until the valet skidded to a stop in front of him, and they all piled in. Kevin took the wheel, gunning the car out of the driveway. "I think they were onto us. A fax came in with four pictures on it—four young males, at least two of them Asian. One of them looked just like Fisher."

There was a moment of silence in the car. Then Fisher cleared his throat. "No way. No fucking way. We were in there ten minutes. We hadn't even made a single big bet."

"But we were at the Horseshoe all night," Kevin responded, jerking the wheel to avoid a pickup truck coming in off the interstate. "They could have nailed us, then forwarded the fax as a courtesy. The pit bosses didn't look like they'd seen any of us yet—they were probably just about to get the Eye in the Sky to scan the crowd."

Dylan leaned forward from the backseat. "If this is true—how did they get pictures of us?"

Martinez drummed his fingers against the side window. "Well, if the Grand Victoria in Chicago hired Plymouth, it's possible these riverboats are also working with the PIs. Maybe Plymouth is sending out a warning to all the casinos on its list. We get burned the minute we start to win—sometimes the minute we walk through the door."

"Then we're dinosaurs," Kevin mumbled, a heavy feeling in his chest.

"We are not fucking dinosaurs!" Fisher shouted, slamming a fist against the dash. "You don't know what was on that fax. It might have had nothing to do with us. For all we know, they might be looking for four hicks who knocked over a goddamn 7–Eleven. We didn't get barred. Hell, we took fifty thousand dollars from the Horseshoe, and they didn't even whimper."

"You think it's a coincidence?" Kevin asked.

"I think you're jumping to a conclusion," Fisher shot back. "Your head's not in the game. We should have waited until they barred us. We shouldn't have broken ranks. Now we don't know what's going on or what to do next."

Kevin shook his head, insulted by Fisher's tone. "I know exactly what we do next. We get on a plane and go back to Boston."

Fisher glared at him but didn't respond. Martinez was still tapping the side window. Kevin's mind was made up. He didn't care what Fisher thought. He wasn't going to stick around, waiting for them to get nailed. This was Louisiana, the Deep South. Kevin had no idea what sort of people ran the riverboats down here—or what they would do to a bunch of northern kids who had taken their money.

Suddenly, Dylan cursed from the backseat. "Oh, man. We've still got all those Horseshoe chips."

Kevin's fingers whitened against the wheel. He hadn't even thought of that. He looked at Fisher, then at Martinez in the mirror.

Fisher was glaring straight ahead. Martinez had his eyes closed. Kevin knew what they were thinking. Fifty thousand dollars was way too much to eat. Though he was scared, he had to agree. They had no choice but to go back to the Horseshoe.

He drove in silence, doubling back toward the giant lit-up hotel on the waterfront. When they reached the turnoff for the driveway, he turned to face Fisher.

"All right," he said quietly. "We'll park the car twenty feet from the front doors. You guys will wait while I go inside and exchange the chips."

Fisher looked like he was about to say something, then shrugged. It was Kevin's paranoia that had them on the run. If Kevin wanted to make the exchange, it was his call.

Dylan took the plastic bag full of chips out of the duffel and handed it to him. "Don't spend it all in one place."

Kevin felt like everyone was staring at him as he moved through the lobby and up the ramp that led to the riverboat. The boat seemed even more crowded than before, and he passed at least three uniformed security officers on his way to the cashier's desk. Thankfully, none of the officers gave him a second look or seemed to notice the heavy plastic bag gripped tightly in his hands.

There was a short line at the cashier's desk. It took ten minutes before the woman directly in front of him—short, with mousy brown hair teased up so high it blocked Kevin's view—reached the gated window. Kevin bit down on his lower lip as he watched her place twelve dollars in chips into the tray. With his stash, he was going to blend in like an elephant at a dog show. *An Asian elephant, at that.*

The woman got her cash—two fives and two ones—and Kevin stepped up to the window. He pushed his chips through in multiple stacks. Normally, high rollers did not cash their own chips. Someone from the casino staff took care of it, trading markers for chips or vice versa. But this was a strategic mission, a quick hit-and-run.

The cashier, a blond man with his sleeves rolled up, looked at all the purple chips, then smiled at Kevin. "One moment, sir."

He scooped the chips into a tray, then reached for a phone. Kevin's pulse quickened, even though he knew this was par for the course. Nowadays you couldn't walk out of a casino with such money without someone making a phone call. Any transaction over ten thousand dollars would be reported to the IRS. Kevin didn't like the CTR, but he wasn't overly concerned about it, since he was using a legal alias and a real Social Security number. He was more concerned about the person on the other end of the cashier's phone call.

The cashier stepped away from the window, still talking on the phone. When he came back, he still had that idiotic smile planted on his face. "This is going to take a few minutes. Kindly step to the side so I can service other customers while the boys upstairs handle your account."

Kevin nodded, his nausea building as he let the next person step up to the window. *This was taking way too long.* He considered bolting for the door—but fifty thousand dollars was too much to leave behind. He set his jaw, reminding himself that he'd done nothing wrong. He hadn't broken any laws or hurt anyone in any way. *Fuck 'em, if they didn't want his business. He'd take his money and go play somewhere else.*

Ten minutes later, two men in dark suits came from a door behind the cashier's desk. One of the men had grey hair and dark plastic-rimmed glasses. The other was younger, with a puggish nose and thin lips. The one with the glasses had a brown paper bag in his hands.

Without saying a word, he handed the bag to Kevin, then crossed his arms. Kevin glanced inside, saw the stacks of hundred dollar bills. When he looked up, the pug nose was pointing toward the exit. "You and your friends had your little fun. Now get the hell off our boat."

Kevin felt his face pale as he turned and headed toward the exit. He didn't look back. *Step by step by step.*

He passed through the exit and onto the ramp that led to the hotel. Then he was through the lobby and on the sidewalk. He passed the valet stand and started down the driveway toward the car.

He had made it five steps when a white van with darkened windows suddenly pulled up next to him, going the wrong way down the driveway. The van slowed to the same speed he was walking, staying right alongside. Kevin couldn't feel his feet anymore; he just kept moving, step by step by step. He trained his eyes straight ahead, trying not to look at the van as it moved with him. When he was ten feet from the Toyota, he broke into a sprint. The van paused, then its tires squealed as it raced past the car and out onto the interstate.

Kevin jumped inside the front passenger seat of the Toyota and threw the paper bag into the back. Fisher was in the driver's seat, craning his neck to watch the van skidding around the corner.

"Drive!" Kevin shouted. "Now!"

Fisher slammed on the gas, and the Toyota lurched forward. He had almost made it to the other end of the driveway when he was forced to hit the brake. There was a police car blocking the exit.

"Oh Jesus," Dylan said from the back. "This isn't good."

A bright spotlight stabbed at them from the front seat of the police car. Kevin had to close his eyes against the glare. He sat perfectly still, his hands visible on the dash. He hoped that Fisher and the rest knew enough to do the same. This had nothing to do with the law anymore. If four kids from Boston disappeared in Shreveport, Louisiana, it would take a long time for anyone to sort things out. *Especially four kids who play cards for a living.*

A full minute went by; then the spotlight went out. Kevin opened his eyes as the police car slowly rolled past. The cop in the passenger seat stared at him as they drove by. He had a shotgun in his lap.

Kevin blinked, hard. There was no mistaking the venom in the cop's eyes. The drive-by had been a warning. They weren't welcome in Shreveport anymore. This wasn't Boston, this wasn't even Vegas.

And this wasn't a game. This didn't have anything to do with big corporations and mathematical advantages. This was about people, and money. And what measures people would take to *protect* their money.

When the police car was gone, Kevin locked eyes with Fisher. "Don't fucking talk to me about jumping to conclusions. Those cops weren't looking for hicks. They were hunting for dinosaurs."

TWENTY-SIX

Boston, Spring 1998

Three days later, Kevin got the first letter in the mail: a sealed manila envelope with a return address in Pittsburgh, Pennsylvania.

He was sitting on the floor in his living room, eating cereal and watching *Monday Night Football* while talking on the phone with his sister in Houston. Melissa was giving him advice about the stock market when he absentmindedly picked the envelope off of a tall stack of unopened mail on the floor next to him. He tore the seal, half listening as Melissa briefed him on the future of fiber optics and the financial health of the tech industry.

Inside the envelope, he found a few pages of typed, legal-looking documents. The top page was a letter addressed to him—from the Internal Revenue Service. It was a notice of an audit. At the bottom was a phone number he was supposed to call to schedule the first meeting with an IRS investigator.

Kevin stared at the letter while Melissa droned on about Internet stocks. Then he exhaled. He started to tell Melissa about the letter, reading her the first few lines. Then he cut himself off. "Melissa, I need to call you back." He hung up the phone without waiting for her response.

He had known all along that an IRS audit was a high risk for card counters. Often the team would try to keep all of its exchanges below the ten thousand mark per twenty-four-hour period, but sometimes—such as in Louisiana—it was unavoidable. Other times the casinos filled out the forms without even informing players.

It wasn't the audit itself that was suspicious; it was the *timing* of the investigation. Coming right on the heels of the barrings in Vegas and the frightening situation down south, Kevin couldn't help but wonder if he was being targeted by someone who wanted to send him a message.

He read through the rest of the IRS papers. Then he picked up the phone and called Dylan. Dylan got Jill on the line, and the two of them talked Kevin into a state of relative calm. He hadn't done anything illegal, and he had declared all of his gambling winnings. Still, they suggested he get a lawyer. With so much money at issue, the IRS wasn't going to back off easily.

Kevin hardly slept at all that night. He felt strangely violated by the notice of audit, as if the casinos had somehow reached into his life and bared his private business. Up until then, his card-counting life had taken place outside of Boston. But this was an intrusion of one side of his double life into the other. This was an assault on his home.

When the phone rang at seven the next morning, he was almost afraid to answer it, expecting more bad news.

To his surprise, it was his father.

"Kevin, I understand you're having some trouble with the IRS. Something about an audit? What's going on?"

Kevin rubbed his eyes. Obviously, Melissa had relayed what he had told her about the letter. He could tell from his father's voice that he didn't know anything about IRS audits; he had grown up in a place where any attention from the government was a dangerous thing.

"Dad, don't worry. I'm handling it."

Jill and Dylan had given Kevin a few names of local tax-law specialists. And Martinez already had a relationship with a lawyer who was an expert on gambling law. When the team traveled through airports with large amounts of money, they frequently carried letters from the gambling lawyer to explain who they were. It wouldn't mean much to the DEA or the FBI, but it was better than nothing.

"Kevin, are you in some kind of trouble?"

Kevin closed his eyes, the phone a heavy weight against his ear. He felt emotion building up inside of him. He wanted to open up, to tell his father everything. But he couldn't. He needed his father to know that he could handle things on his own.

"It's nothing, Dad. I've made a lot of money in the stock market, a lot of capital gains. I must have set off some IRS computer. I've already got a lawyer who's going to clear everything up. There's nothing to worry about."

"Okay. You know we're here if you need us."

Kevin felt a tug of guilt as he hung up the phone. He was such a coward. He should have had the guts to tell his father the truth. He was a professional card counter. He had made almost a million dollars in the past two years. His team had made more than three million in the same time period. But something had gone wrong—and in his heart, he believed that this audit was just the beginning of his problems.

He rolled out of bed and started toward the shower. Audit or no, he had to go to work, if only to remind himself that card counting was *not* the dominant focus of his life. He had just gotten the water running when the phone rang again. This time it was Martinez. Kevin knew it had to be important if Martinez was awake before noon.

"Kevin, we think we've figured out what's going on. And it's worse than we had imagined."

Kevin looked at the letter from the IRS, tacked above his bed. "What do you mean?"

"Just meet me and Fisher at Micky Rosa's place, ten tonight. Don't tell anyone else about it. Not even Dylan or Jill."

The line went dead. Kevin sat down on the bed, listening to the dial tone above the hiss of water from the shower.

Why Micky Rosa's?

And what could be worse than what he was already imagining?

TWENTY-SEVEN

Boston, Spring 1998

Fisher and Martinez were already seated on the couch when Micky ushered Kevin out of the elevator. Kevin's hair was still wet from his shower after a swimming workout: Despite the nuisance of the audit and his long hours at work to make up for all the weekends away, he was still swimming a few times a week.

Micky seemed happy to see him, though there was obvious concern in the older man's eyes. His face was even puffier than usual, and there were dark bags visible beneath his thick glasses. He didn't look like he'd slept much in the past two days.

Fisher and Martinez didn't look much better. Martinez was wearing a hooded grey sweatshirt, and his face was so pale it almost blended into the material. Fisher looked more angry than tired; his dark pinpoint eyes smoldered with intensity. His hands were balled into fists, the muscles on his forearms tightening into ropes beneath his flesh.

"Somebody sold us out," he said as Kevin dropped onto the couch next to them. "One of our own betrayed the team."

Kevin's mouth opened. He looked at Martinez, who nodded.

Micky sat heavily on the couch across from them. "It's true. I got this directly from a source at Plymouth. Someone from MIT sold a list of both MIT teams—yours and the Amphibians—to the agency.

Names, yearbook photos, Vegas gambling schedules, estimated profits—everything."

Kevin's head swirled. "Jesus Christ."

"Twenty-five thousand dollars," Martinez said, shaking his head. "They got twenty-five grand to turn us in."

"Who—" Kevin started.

"That's the thing," Micky interrupted. "We don't know who. My source didn't have a name. Just that it was someone from MIT. It could be someone on your team or someone on mine. Or someone who just knows about us. Hell, it could be anyone."

Kevin knew now why Martinez had told him not to tell Dylan or Jill. But he was certain that they wouldn't have done this—not for twenty-five thousand dollars. They could make that much in two weekends with the team.

"Are you sure?" Kevin said. "Maybe your source got it wrong."

Micky reached toward a coffee table next to his couch and pulled out a sheaf of paper. He leaned over and tossed it into Kevin's lap.

The sheaf was twenty pages thick, stapled down one side. It was a booklet of sorts: photocopied pages split into two columns each. Running down the left side was a row of black-and-white pictures. Down the right side were stats for each picture—including real names, aliases, and other assorted pieces of information. The names did not seem to be alphabetical.

"It's arranged like a Most Wanted list. The higher the picture, the more perceived the threat."

The top photo on the first page was Micky. It was grainy, from a poor angle, most likely taken from a video still. Three photos below Micky's picture was one of Martinez. He looked years younger, his hair cropped short above his ears. He was smiling at the camera. Below him was Fisher, also much younger. His hair reached almost to his eyes.

On the top of the second page, Kevin found himself. He recognized the picture immediately. It was from his college yearbook. He was grinning in the photo, and there was a small bruise above his left eye. He had gotten that during a pickup basketball game that spring.

He shifted his gaze to the second column. He sank deeper into the couch as he read the information. Kevin Lewis. Born in Weston, MA, 1972. Graduated MIT in 1994. Next to the graduation date was his current address, followed by his work address. Then his phone number and a list of his aliases.

"They've got everything," he whispered. "They know where I live."

"They've got all of our addresses," Martinez said. "And all of our aliases. It was definitely someone who knew exactly what was going on. Someone who had access to all of the details."

Someone on our team or the Amphibians. Kevin shook his head, bewildered. He couldn't believe that any of his friends could have betrayed them. It must have been someone from the other team. Or someone who had been watching them, someone from MIT who wanted to make a quick buck at their expense. When Kevin thought about it, this explanation seemed to make the most sense. Twenty-five thousand dollars wasn't that much to a member of the MIT team.

The truth was, they might never know who had sold them out.

"So we're finished in Vegas?" Kevin asked.

Micky shook his head. "Only the casinos working with Plymouth have access to this list. In those casinos, you're marked men. Plymouth takes a very proactive stance. They've got this point guy, a tough mother named Vincent Cole. He's got a real hard-on for card counters."

Kevin pictured the gangly man with the silver hair and weathered cheeks, wondering if he was Vincent Cole.

"There's a story making the rounds about Cole," Micky continued. "I don't know if it's true or not, but it's pretty frightening. Supposedly, a year ago he back-roomed a player from an Australian team he'd been tracking for six months. First he went through the regular routine—told him to get against the wall, took a few Polaroids, made him sign a trespass act."

Kevin's eyes continued scanning the facebook while he listened. On the fourth page he found Dylan and Jill, Kianna and Tay. He imagined the man with weathered cheeks scrutinizing the same pictures, matching the faces with video stills from the casinos.

"After the guy signed the trespass act," Micky went on. "Cole told the security guards to leave and locked the door behind them. Then he pulled out a gun."

Kevin looked up from the list. Micky's face had gone dead serious.

"He asked the card counter to tell him how much he'd won over the past year. The card counter was too scared to say anything. Then Cole took a five-hundred-dollar chip out of his pocket and tossed it to the poor guy. 'You've eaten a lot of our chips over the past year,' Cole said. 'But this is the one you're going to remember.'"

Kevin tensed as he braced for the finish. Micky looked at him, then Martinez, then Fisher.

"Cole made the guy swallow it. Halfway down his throat, the thing got stuck. The guy turned as purple as the chip. He almost choked to death right there in the back room. Then, somehow, he got it down. Cole let him go, but the poor Australian never counted cards again. He learned his lesson. Probably learned it again when the chip worked its way out the other side."

Fisher shifted uncomfortably on the couch. "That's a fucking myth. That never happened."

Micky shrugged. "I don't know. Maybe it is an urban legend. But I'm telling it to you because I want you to be careful. You make mistakes, and shit happens. To all of us."

Kevin understood: Micky was making a statement, perhaps implying that if they hadn't kicked him off of their team, this might never have happened. Maybe he was right. Maybe they had been too caught up in their success. Maybe they had made mistakes.

But at least they knew now: It was never going to be the same. Kevin knew they should have been thankful; they had made a lot of money, and none of them had gotten hurt. Kevin could handle the audit. He had his job, his apartment, and his family. He didn't *need* card counting. He didn't need to go up against guys like Vincent Cole.

Then again, the thought of giving up—just like that—bit at Kevin down deep. He didn't need card counting, but he didn't want to be forced out of it by the casinos.

"So what can we do?" he asked, handing the sheaf of photos back to Micky.

Fisher looked like he was going to jump down Kevin's throat. "There are still dozens of casinos that don't work with Plymouth. We can start over."

"We get new aliases," Martinez broke in. "We tighten our security, pick our team more carefully. And we travel more. There are casinos all over the world."

Kevin touched his lips. He wished he could be as optimistic as Martinez and Fisher. But he wasn't sure the risk was worth the return. Foreign countries were guided by foreign laws. Card counting in Vegas was one thing; despite Micky's story, the practice was relatively safe. But Kevin had learned a lesson in Louisiana. And a foreign country—who knew what could happen?

"Maybe we should take some time," Kevin said, "slow down a bit."

"We get right back on the horse," Fisher said, jabbing a finger toward Kevin's face. "We find out the casinos that don't work with Plymouth, and we hit them, hard. We go to Monte Carlo, Montreal, the Bahamas—anywhere they've got blackjack. We can make just as much money as before."

Kevin rose from the couch. He didn't want a lecture from Fisher. He needed to think things through on his own. He didn't intend to give up card counting. But he felt they needed to strategize before they forged ahead. The list that had been sold to the casinos had compromised their double lives. Before they could hit Vegas as card counters and return home to their regular lives. But now at least some of the casinos knew who they were. They knew all about MIT, and the team, and the danger it posed.

"Come on, Kev," Martinez said, "you want to go to the Bahamas this weekend? Bikinis, booze, and blackjack?"

Kevin shook his head. He couldn't go to the Bahamas because he would be busy preparing for his IRS audit. Martinez sighed, and Fisher turned away in disgust. Kevin could sense the fissure that was growing between them, but at the moment he didn't see any easy solution.

He looked at Micky, who was watching the three of them, his face unreadable. An uneasy feeling came over Kevin, and he headed for the door.

"Kevin," Fisher said. "Martinez and I don't need time to think. We know what we have to do. We're card counters, like Micky. We'll always be card counters."

Kevin didn't respond. No doubt they would head to the Bahamas without him.

He prayed there wouldn't be someone waiting for them when they got there. Someone with a Polaroid camera and a twenty-five-thousand-dollar list.

TWENTY-EIGHT

Boston, Spring 1998

Kevin spent the following Saturday morning with a tax lawyer, going over all of the receipts he had gathered from the past four years as a professional card counter. Syphoning through all the trips to Vegas, all the plane tickets, restaurant receipts, and hotel reservations, Kevin found himself filled with sobering emotions. It had gone by so fast, he'd never had time to contemplate the lifestyle he'd chosen: Laid out in front of him with a tax lawyer's precision, his counting life seemed almost epic in scale.

He was brought back to a memory from New Year's Eve, just a few months earlier. He had been playing the MGM Grand with his squad, running about even with the house. Because of all the recent barrings—this was only a few months after the debacle at the Rio—he had been keeping a tight watch on the pit bosses. Although nothing had seemed out of the ordinary, as a safeguard, he had latched on to another high roller in the high-stakes pit—a man in his mid-fifties who called himself Nick, a Hispanic guy from Miami wearing a huge pinky ring and a black velvet shirt. Kevin knew from experience that a pit boss would be less likely to make a scene in front of another high roller, so he had struck up a friendship with the rich Floridian. Nick had made his millions in the import/export business and had recently retired. He now spent his life gambling in Vegas and sunning himself down in Rio. He had a wife, a mistress, and three sons, none of whom had ever worked a day in his life.

At a quarter to midnight, Nick had invited Kevin to a party in his suite to celebrate the New Year. To keep up appearances, Kevin had accepted and followed the flashy Hispanic up to his tower room.

As the clock struck midnight, Kevin shared champagne with a roomful of strangers: mostly inebriated, middle-aged men dressed in expensive clothes and surrounded by strippers in sparkling dresses and high-class escorts in Versace gowns. Enveloped by so much Vegas glitz, Kevin had experienced a sudden sense of melancholy. Was this where he belonged? Was this who he had become?

As the New Year's ball dropped, he had no one to hug or kiss or laugh with. Instead, he had teammates down in the casino who could call him in to positive shoes. He had strippers over at the Paradise who knew him by his fake names and loved to dance for his real money. He had casino hosts waiting to extend him incredible lines of credit and provide him extravagant creature comforts. He had a woman who traveled with a football team waiting for him to phone—because she knew it meant another high-profile weekend of five-star restaurants and sold-out shows. He had a family at home who didn't know him anymore, an ex-girlfriend whose heart he had broken because she didn't play blackjack.

He'd spent the last three New Year's Eves gambling in Las Vegas. He watched Nick twirl around the suite, a bottle of champagne in one hand, a tall nineteen-year-old blonde with fake breasts and a tattoo of a spider on the back of her neck in the other, and he wondered:

Is this who I've become?

"So we've got twenty trips to Vegas and fourteen to Chicago last year," the tax lawyer said, interrupting Kevin's memory. "Does that sound right?"

Kevin blinked, back in the present. Twenty trips to Vegas in a single year. Twenty weekends in casinos, consisting of close to forty hours of blackjack a weekend, with sixty hands of cards played an hour.

Altogether, that made forty-eight thousand hands of blackjack, in Vegas alone.

It was almost impossible to comprehend.

Twelve hours later and a thousand miles to the south, Martinez rubbed his sweaty palms down the sides of his untucked, bright red Hawaiian shirt. His body rocked back and forth against an intensely purple cushioned stool as his tongue clicked in tune to the soft steel tones of ubiquitous reggae music. Martinez had been glued to the stool for the better part of the evening, but he didn't feel tired at all. Rather, he was beginning to feel jumpy—perhaps the result of the three cups of coffee he had downed in his hotel room before heading up the beach to the Golden Sun Casino.

From outside, the casino was a flashback to the worst of the eighties: Festooned in bright swaths of pink and electric blue, the massive complex could have made the perfect setting for a Miami-themed disco movie. Its high point was the beachfront location—a soft white-sand stretch of coast on the eastern side of New Providence Island in the Bahamas. The casino opened up into a tropical oasis filled with palm trees, hammocks, and outdoor tiki bars, startlingly authentic to sensibilities used to the plasticine "reality" of the Vegas resorts.

But Martinez hadn't spent much time dipping his feet in the crystal-blue water or running his fingers through the alabaster sand. He and Fisher had taken a taxi straight from the airport to a dive hotel a mile down the beach from the casino, then made the trek on foot to the Golden Sun. Unlike everyone else on the island, Martinez was here to work.

He bounced his knees, keeping time with the reggae beat. He

could hear the chips shifting in his pockets, and he fought the urge to smile. He was up twelve thousand dollars already—an amazing take considering how slow the dealers in Nassau worked the cards. He wasn't sure about Fisher, but he guessed his partner was likewise up over ten grand. They had been passing tables to each other all night, taking turns minimum betting and BPing, making full use of their dual counting abilities. It wasn't anywhere near as effective as team play, but it was the best they could manage considering the situation.

Fisher had argued for bringing in the rest of the team, even without Kevin, but Martinez had wanted to keep things manageable until they had a better idea of how deep the betrayal ran. He wasn't as shell-shocked by Micky's news as Kevin, but he wasn't as fired up as Fisher, either. A small-scale assault on the Bahamas had seemed like good middle ground.

He watched as the dealer fumbled with the shoe, his chocolate fingers crawling across the cards like they were dipped in molasses. The Bahamanians moved like they spoke, lilting, unrushed, almost musically dragging out the syllables. It was beginning to drive Martinez crazy. The other players at the table didn't seem to mind: two newlywed pairs from North Carolina, much more interested in their cocktails and each other than the cards dripping out onto the table. Nassau was teeming with couples like them, so prevalent they were probably listed somewhere as a category of local fauna.

Martinez drummed his fingers as a pair of tens finally dribbled out of the shoe. He split them, just to make it interesting, and threw a glance over his shoulder. There was no sign of Fisher—strange, considering he had signaled that he was heading to the bathroom more than twenty minutes ago. Maybe the sushi from the night before had finally caught up with him. Sometimes raw fish had a habit of doing that; but like the split tens on a positive-twelve shoe, it was an acceptable level of risk.

Two sluggish hands later, Martinez started to get worried. If Fisher were ill, he would have made it out of the bathroom long enough to give Martinez a signal. One of the earliest rules Micky had taught them was that partners were supposed to look out for each other.

Despite the double-digit shoe, Martinez asked the dealer for a mark to hold his spot and got up from the table. He took his big chips with him, leaving a handful of quarters for the dealer to watch.

He crossed the casino, passing a handful of college students and cruise passengers from one of the many ships parked nearby. The casino was empty compared to the bustling Vegas resorts; the peak season wasn't for a few more months. The visitors this time of year were newly married, or eager to take advantage of the cheaper off-season deals, or a mixture of the two.

When Martinez reached the bathroom, he was surprised to see a sign hanging in the middle of the door: LAVATORY OUT OF SERVICE.

Martinez was pretty sure he had seen his partner heading in this direction. He doubted that a sign would keep Fisher from his business. He reached for the knob—and found that it was unlocked. He shrugged and pushed his way inside.

His feet echoed against the tiled floor. The main area of the bathroom looked empty, bordered on one side by a row of sinks beneath wide rectangular mirrors, on the other by chrome towel racks and funnel-shaped hot-air dryers. As he moved into the center of the room, he heard voices coming from the alley of toilet stalls that began a few feet past the last sink.

"We're gonna play a little game," he heard someone say in a brusque voice. "I'm gonna ask you some questions, and you're gonna tell me what I want to hear."

Martinez's entire body tensed up. He stepped forward, his feet light against the tiles. There was a mop with a wooden handle standing between two of the sinks, and he grabbed it with both hands. His knees were trembling as he reached the alley of stalls. Everything began to seem unreal, as if he were staring down a long tunnel.

Fisher was at the far end of the bathroom, his arms pinned behind his back by a man nearly a foot taller. Another man had him by the throat, while a third was standing off to the side, arms crossed.

Martinez's heart froze as he took in the scene. Fisher's face was a mess; there was blood streaming from his nose, and one of his eyes was starting to swell shut. He had a dark bruise on his left cheek, and his lips looked swollen. The man holding him by the throat had blood on the knuckles of both hands.

Shit. Shit. Shit.

Martinez shifted his attention from Fisher to the three attackers. Two of the men looked Bahamanian: the one holding Fisher from behind and the one gripping his throat. Both were tall and muscular, wearing khaki pants and white sleeveless T-shirts. The third man was Caucasian. Although Martinez didn't think he'd ever seen the man before, he looked somehow familiar. He was extremely tall, gangly, with silver grey hair.

"How many of your friends are here with you?" the gangly man shouted. "How much money have you won?"

Fisher struggled against the hand at his throat. The Bahamanian hauled back and hit him in the gut. Fisher grunted, his face turning bright red.

Martinez didn't think—he was beyond thought. He let instinct take over.

He gripped the mop like a baseball bat and swung it as hard as he could into one of the mirrors. There was a loud crash as the glass shattered and shards rained down to the floor. All three men spun towards him. The man with the grey hair peered at him with narrow blue eyes. Martinez stared right back at him, the mop raised high. He tried to look as big as possible. *Inside, he had turned to Jell-O.*

"I just called the police," he shouted. "And I called our lawyers. We're going to sue you and the casino for everything you've got."

There was a moment of dreadful silence. Then the man with the grey hair smiled. "Who says we work for any casino?"

He flicked his head to the side, and the two Bahamanians let go of Fisher. He crumpled to the floor, clutching his stomach.

Martinez braced himself for a fight he would surely lose. But the three men walked right past him, grinning. When they reached the bathroom door, the man with the grey hair looked back over his shoulder.

"I liked you better as a Japanese," he said.

The door swung shut behind him.

It took all of Martinez's strength to help Fisher to the sink. As he washed the blood from his friend's face, he slowly started to breathe again.

"Jesus, that was close."

Fisher looked at him with his one good eye. "Close? What the fuck do you mean close?"

"I mean it could have been a lot worse," Martinez said, putting his hands under the warm water. His palms hurt where he had gripped the mop. "You see that guy's hair? Wasn't that how Kevin described him? Do you think he's the same bastard Micky warned us about?"

Fisher spat blood. He checked one of his front teeth with two fingers, making sure it was still tightly attached to his gums. In a way, it was fortunate that Fisher had taken the beating. Fisher was a Mack truck. If it had been Martinez against the wall, he'd be in the hospital.

"Vincent Cole?" Fisher asked. "The fuck from the PI firm? No way. We're in the Bahamas."

"It's only ten hours or so by plane," Martinez said, leaning back against the wall. "We've been gambling for twelve."

"You believe that shithead?" Fisher grunted. "Right inside the casino." He turned and pointed to a corner of the ceiling. There was a video camera resting inside a black plastic bulb. "The bastards probably watched the whole thing."

"What do you bet they 'forgot' to press the record button?"

Fisher sneered. But Martinez could see he was rattled. He had been beaten up pretty good. If they had been in Vegas, Martinez would have taken him straight to the police. But they were in a foreign country with no witnesses. For all they knew, they'd get arrested for cheating. If that had been Vincent Cole, he had known exactly what he was doing. He had gotten the call from the casino—a client who had recognized them from the facebook—and had flown down to the Bahamas to teach them a lesson.

Or, Martinez thought, he had already been in the Bahamas, waiting for them to show up. *Because he knew ahead of time that we were on our way.*

Martinez shook his head, pushing the idea away. Only a few people knew about the trip: Micky, Kevin, and a few others on the team. None of them would have done this. Hell, the man probably wasn't Cole at all. There were plenty of guys with grey hair. It was crazy to assume it was Cole.

He wondered if Fisher was working through the same thought process. He watched as his friend leaned over the sink, staring at his battered face in the mirror.

"I think we need to make some changes," he said.

Martinez didn't disagree.

TWENTY-NINE

Boston, Spring 1998

Kevin barely made it into the kitchen before he lost his grip on the Tupperware. A dozen Day-Glo plastic containers of various shapes and sizes crashed to the floor, sealed tops popping off in a spray of multiethnic leftovers. It was like staring down at an edible Jackson Pollock painting, bold strokes of beef brisket punctuated by pork dumplings and candied yams, angry swaths of grilled asparagus crossing spears with conspicuously jutting teriyaki skewers. Kevin shook his head, wondering why he had let his mother load him up on his way out the door of his home in Weston. His sisters were lucky; the airlines would never let them carry on enough Tupperware to make his mother happy.

The impromptu family reunion had been just the thing to take Kevin's mind off his tax problems, Micky's revelations about the list, and the murky events Martinez had alluded to after his and Fisher's trip to the Bahamas. Rather than wallow in his apartment, trying to pry details out of Fisher about the severity of the Bahamanian barring incident, Kevin had spent the past two days competing with his sisters in a decathlon of traditional Lewis gluttony. His usual swim Monday night was going to be a real task, considering how much extra water he was going to displace from the pool.

He dropped to his knees in the kitchen and began wiping up the spilled food, using the plastic lids as makeshift trowels. He was just about to see the tiles when he realized that the phone was ringing in the living room.

He wiped his hands on his jeans and chased down the incessant sound. He found the portable jammed beneath one of the couch cushions and kicked off his shoes as he pressed the rumbling hunk of plastic against his ear. "This better be good. I'm up to my ears in brisket."

"Kevin, I just got the weirdest e-mail from Kianna."

It was Dylan, which was strange, considering the time. Dylan and Jill were both usually asleep by ten unless they were in Vegas. Kevin wondered if they were fighting again—an occurrence that had become more and more regular in the past few months.

"What sort of e-mail?" Kevin asked.

Kianna and Dylan's only common ground had to do with blackjack—and since the team hadn't met to plan any new trips since Micky's revelations, he couldn't see why Kianna would be e-mailing Dylan late on a Sunday night.

"She asked if I could send her all the playing records from the past year. When I pushed her for details, she said she needed them because she and a few of the others were heading to Vegas this coming weekend. Kevin, am I out of the loop on something?"

Kevin's eyebrows rose as he continued wiping his hands on his pants. "Not that I know of. We haven't discussed another trip since we found out about the list."

"What about Fisher and Martinez?" Dylan asked.

"They just got back from the Bahamas a week ago. And from what Martinez told me, it was a pretty bad experience. They got barred pretty hard."

"It was worse than that," Dylan broke in. "Tay saw Fisher at the gym on Friday. He had a massive black eye and a huge bruise on his cheek. He wouldn't explain what had happened, but it had something to do with the Bahamas."

Kevin was more awake now. He was concerned, but he wasn't going to jump to conclusions. Fisher had been known to get into fights. His bruises might not have happened in the Bahamas. Kianna's e-mail was more worrisome. Why would she want the playing records, unless she was planning to schedule some team play? And why hadn't Kevin heard about any trip to Vegas? He was one of the BPs. Dylan was the team's secretary. It didn't make sense.

"Let me call Fisher," Kevin said. "I'll figure this out. Stay awake for ten minutes, if you can."

He hung up the phone and dialed Fisher's number. The line clicked over to voice mail immediately, a sign that Fisher was on the phone and wasn't using his caller ID. Curiouser and curiouser. Kevin dialed Martinez—and found that his phone wasn't picking up, either.

Kevin was beginning to get concerned. There was something going on, he could feel it inside. He punched keys on his portable—a gift from the Mohegan Sun—and searched through the memory files for Kianna's number. She was the one who had sent the e-mail. And if there really was something going on, she would probably be the easiest to crack.

He found her number and activated the automatic dial. There were three rings on the other end of the line, then Kianna's voice: "Fisher? Michael's in. I haven't reached Brian yet—"

"Kianna?" Kevin broke in. His face was burning. There was *definitely* something going on. The whole fucking team was on the phone.

"Oh, Kevin. I thought you were Fisher. Listen, I'm kind of tied up right now—"

"No way," Kevin shot back. "I want to know what the hell is going on. Why did you ask Dylan for the player records? And what's this about a trip to Vegas next weekend?"

There was a long pause on the other end. Then Kianna answered quietly, "I think you better talk to Fisher."

"Fisher is a bit tied up himself. Listen, Kianna, I have a right to know what's going on. I'm part of this team, aren't I?"

His anger was rising. *Part* of the team? He was one of the Big Players. He had proved himself over years of play.

"Kevin," Kianna finally responded, "Fisher and Martinez are starting a new team. I don't think it's anything personal, they just want to make some changes—"

Kevin hung up the phone. His head was throbbing. Two weeks ago, sitting in Micky's living room, he had thought about quitting card counting. But this wasn't quitting—this was being thrown out. Of his own goddamn team.

He dialed Fisher's number and got the voice mail again. He hit the redial with his thumb and got a busy signal. Then he hit it again. And again. And again.

Fisher finally picked up on the sixth redial. His voice sounded rushed. "Kevin, I can't talk right now—"

"But you're going to, Fisher, because I deserve an answer. Are you kicking me off of the team?"

Fisher coughed. Kevin noticed that his words seemed pained—probably not because the talk was difficult emotionally, but because there was something physically wrong with his mouth.

"Not exactly. We're restructuring. You know we've been having some problems lately. Martinez and I think it's time to reposition ourselves, take things a little more seriously."

Kevin squeezed the phone. "You think I don't take things seriously?"

"Frankly, no. Come on, Kev. This is a hobby to you. This is our livelihood. You've never been willing to commit to this one hundred percent. And now we've learned that anything less is dangerous."

Kevin wondered if he understood Fisher correctly. "Are you accusing me of something?"

"Of course not. But I no longer want to play with anyone who isn't in this all the way. I've sacrificed everything for this team. I don't have anything else in my life that matters. Can you say the same?"

Kevin sat there, silent. Did Fisher have a point? Kevin did see card counting as a side passion, not as his only reason for living.

But that didn't mean he hadn't sacrificed for the game. And it sure as hell didn't mean he had done anything to endanger them. He began to wonder if there wasn't more to it. He remembered how eager Fisher was to cut Micky out of the team—because it gave him a chance to make more money.

"This isn't right, Fisher. Cutting me out behind my back."

"It's not personal . . ."

"Like hell it's not," Kevin said, growing angrier. "If you wanted a bigger share of the investment pie, you could have simply told me. If you felt I wasn't spending enough time in the planning stages, or giving enough weekends to the team, I would have made some adjustments."

"I don't want *adjustments,*" Fisher said. "I want to run the team my way. And that's exactly what I'm going to do. Kevin, you said yourself that you wanted to slow things down a bit. Take some time to think things through. Well, now you've got all the time you need."

The phone went dead. Kevin slammed it down onto the couch.

A few minutes later, he had calmed himself down to a reasonable anger level. There was some kernel of truth to what Fisher had said. But it still hurt to be kicked off the team. And the way he saw it, he had two choices. Accept Fisher's decision and give up the lifestyle altogether. Or do a little *repositioning* of his own.

The first call he made was to Dylan.

"That was more than ten minutes," Dylan said.

Kevin made his decision while he spoke "Dylan, Fisher's breaking away and taking most of the team with him. We have a choice—we can either give up blackjack, or form our own team. I know you and Jill have been going through some problems, and I know some of it is related to our lifestyle. But I'd still like to give it a shot. I guess I'm asking—are you with me?"

Dylan didn't wait to answer. "I never liked Fisher that much, anyway. He's a controlling meathead. I can't speak for Jill, but I think she'll pitch in. She likes the life too much to give it up altogether. What about the others?"

Kevin thought about it for a moment. "Obviously, Martinez and Kianna are with Fisher. Michael and Brian will go with them, too. I never had much of a relationship with any of the others—except Tay, of course. I'll call him right now."

Kevin hung up a little more confident. At least he wasn't alone. His team would be small, but it could still be effective. And with Dylan and Jill, there would be more balance. Like Fisher had said, all he and Martinez had was card counting. Kevin wanted card counting to be a choice, not a necessity.

He reached Tay on the basement line at the frat house. As usual, there was the sound of a party in the background.

"I'm a pretty popular guy tonight," Tay said, his voice slurred. It was the most inebriated Kevin had ever heard him. "First Fisher, then Kianna. Now you. I feel like a nine hundred number."

"So you've heard what's been going on?" Kevin asked.

"Civil war," Tay said over the clacking of pool balls and the shouts of drunken college kids. "Revolution, barbarians at the gate. All that crap. I feel like my parents are getting divorced."

Kevin laughed. "Listen, Tay, I'm leaving this completely up to you. You know where I stand. We're going to take things a lot slower than the old team. We're not going to push as hard, and we're not going to make as much money. But we're going to have more fun."

Tay waited so long to answer, Kevin was worried he had passed out from the alcohol.

"I love counting cards," he finally said. "But I don't want to end up turning into Fisher, or, even worse, Micky Rosa. One day I hope to get a job and an apartment and, God willing, a girlfriend. So I'm with you."

Kevin hung up the phone, relieved. His squad was still in business.

Kevin was curled up in bed, half asleep, when the phone rang again. He answered because there was only one person who it could be.

"It shouldn't have gone down like this," Martinez said by way of a greeting. "But you know it was inevitable. MIT chaos theory. Put a bunch of overly intelligent, socially inept people like us together, sooner or later you get chaos."

Kevin closed his eyes. "Maybe."

He couldn't help feeling sad about the team's breakup. It was like a good relationship ending. They had gone through some wild times together.

"I never told you why I left MIT, did I?"

Kevin opened his eyes. The dark ceiling stared back at him. He waited for Martinez to continue.

"Because I didn't belong there anyway. I had already been recruited by Micky. I knew this was the right life for me. Some people might think I'm wasting my gifts. But I believe this is what I'm supposed to do. I'm a card counter, Kevin."

After they said good-bye, Kevin sat there in the dark, thinking about what Martinez had said. It had been an apology of sorts. It had also felt like a challenge. It was the same thing Fisher had asked him, in different language.

How much was Kevin willing to sacrifice for the system? How far was *he* willing to go?

THIRTY

Las Vegas, Memorial Day 1998

Vegas had never looked better.

Kevin was spread out on a circular leather couch facing a giant picture window. Below, he could see down the entire Strip, from the radioactive green lion at the base of the MGM Grand to the glowing spire of the Stratosphere. The logjam street traffic just added to the visual effect: a thousand headlights blinking like neurons in the glowing spine that snaked down the center of the city.

"Forty-two thousand dollars," Dylan said from the recliner in the far corner of the room. His laptop was open on the ottoman in front of him. "Not a bad couple of months, all things considered."

Kevin nodded. It wasn't bad at all. There were only four of them, and they had hit Vegas just twice since the team had split up. And without Fisher driving them, they had taken time to enjoy the city between six-hour shifts. Kevin had even begun to play craps, to Dylan's dismay; he knew the odds were against him, but he enjoyed the social aspects of the game, the stimulation of the crowd. Craps was a sort of symbol of his team's new aura. He didn't mind sacrificing a little profit if it made him happy.

"How does this look?" Jill said, entering the suite from the adjoining bedroom. Her red hair was hidden under a jet-black wig. She was wearing wire-rimmed glasses and dark brown lipstick. Her skirt was leather, her stockings webbed.

"I call it my schoolteacher-goth look."

"I like it," Tay responded from the mahogany bar at the far end of the living room. "You should dress like that at work. You'd scare your clients into submission."

Kevin laughed. The atmosphere had changed dramatically since the breakup. The siege mentality was gone. With a smaller team, they felt like the chance of getting barred had gone down. And as long as Kevin continued to play craps at the level he was playing—thousands of dollars per roll—even if they got barred from blackjack, the casinos would treat them a bit better than before. A high roller who counted cards was different from a card counter who played like a high roller.

"We ready to play?" Kevin asked, rising from the couch. His reflection danced across the window, lit up by the neon from below.

"Where are we going tonight?" Dylan asked. They had chosen the MGM Grand as their home base and had agreed never to play blackjack in the casino. That left a handful of favorite places where their faces were still good. Kevin had tried to get better information on safe casinos by calling the Plymouth Associates, but he'd been unable to learn anything. He'd considered asking Micky to get his contact to help, but he'd realized that Micky would have more of an affinity to Fisher and Martinez's team. The two roommates were cut in his image.

"How about the Luxor?" Kevin asked. He had grown attached to the megaresort. He felt safe in the labyrinthine casino.

Tay downed his drink. Dylan shut the laptop. Jill straightened her skirt, trying to cover a few more inches of thigh.

"Let's hit the pyramid."

The elevator opened on the casino floor of the MGM Grand, and Kevin took two steps toward the exit—when he saw the blond wig, dark sunglasses, and denim shirt, its buttons strained by the pent-up bulk beneath the material.

Fisher was stalking the back of the MGM Grand's casino, his shades scanning back and forth as he prowled the edge of the blackjack area. Kevin had watched his act before, so he knew exactly what to expect. Fisher would get the call-in from one of his teammates, then enter the table rubbing his hands together, commenting how he had just driven in from L.A. and needed to make gas fare for the ride home. Then he'd smile and start throwing down purple chips.

"You see that?" Dylan asked, leaning over Kevin's shoulder. "I didn't know they were working the MGM. They're going to make it dangerous for us to stay here."

Jill stepped next to him. "Let's tell him to get lost. There are plenty of other casinos to play."

"This is our turf," Tay chimed in. "Let him find his own backyard."

Kevin waved them quiet. He didn't like Fisher and his team playing the MGM Grand, either. But there wasn't much they could do. He hadn't spoken to Fisher—or Martinez, for that matter—since the night the team broke up. If they had been on better terms, they could have made an agreement to work different ends of the Strip. Kevin was sure Martinez would have wanted to reach a state of harmony. But he wasn't so sure about Fisher.

He looked past Fisher to the gambling floor. He spotted Kianna and Brian at two tables near where he liked to play craps. He saw Martinez at the far end of the room, wearing jeans and a baseball cap. He shook his head. "All right, I'll talk to Fisher."

He started forward, a numb feeling growing in his throat. Over the past two months, he had tried not to think about the breakup in personal terms. But now he couldn't help it; Fisher had been his friend, a big part of his life. Then he had pushed Kevin aside without the slightest hesitation.

Kevin caught up to Fisher as he was about to slide in to Kianna's table. He put a hand on his old friend's shoulder, stopping him mid-motion. Fisher tensed, then glanced up. Kevin jerked his head toward the bathroom.

♠ ♥ ♦ ♣

As usual, they met at the last row of urinals. Fisher was the first to speak, his tone angry but subdued.

"That was stupid. You might have given us away."

"You guys need to get out of here," Kevin responded. "This is our home turf. We don't gamble here."

Fisher reached up and took off his sunglasses. Kevin could still see the fading bruises around his right eye. He had a moment of sympathy, then reminded himself that Fisher partially blamed him for what had happened in the Bahamas.

"*We* gamble wherever we want," Fisher said. "You guys are just tourists. Go stay at Circus Circus. Or Excalibur. Leave the blackjack tables to us."

Kevin realized he would have to be the bigger man. "Come on, Fisher. This is ridiculous. We don't have to be enemies. We can work together."

"You're right," Fisher said, adjusting his wig. "We don't have to be enemies. Just keep out of our way, and everything will be fine."

So that was how Fisher wanted it to be. It wasn't enough that he had kicked Kevin off of the team. He wanted to kick Kevin out of Vegas.

"There's room for both teams," Kevin countered. "Just not in the same casino."

"Then take a walk," Fisher said. "Or better yet, take Micky's advice. Know when to quit."

He put his sunglasses back on and walked out of the bathroom, leaving Kevin alone at the urinals. Kevin stared after him. *What an asshole.* He realized it was all about control. Fisher didn't like the fact that Kevin's squad was still in business—because he couldn't control them anymore. Maybe he had assumed Kevin would shrivel up and go away. If so, he had seriously misjudged him.

Fisher might have helped recruit him as a card counter, but he couldn't tell him when to quit.

Back outside at the elevators, Kevin regrouped with his squad. "He rejected my suggestion."

"The jackass," Jill hissed.

"So what do we do?" Tay asked.

"We ignore him," Kevin said, watching with the rest of them as Fisher moved through the blackjack pit. "Vegas is big enough for all of us."

But it wasn't Vegas that Kevin was worried about. It was Fisher's ego. Was it a coincidence that he was playing the MGM Grand?

Or was he trying to make a point?

THIRTY-ONE

Boston, June 1998

Kevin leaned across the table to light Dylan's cigar as the waiter opened the second bottle of wine. The marble between them was littered with empty dessert plates, ashtrays, and the skeletal remains of a vast celebratory feast. The restaurant around them had gone from bustling to deserted, and a group of busboys had gathered by the entrance to the kitchen, eyeing the two remaining diners with palpably hostile intent. It was after midnight on a sweltering Tuesday; most of the city had already gone home to their air conditioners and their beds.

But Kevin and Dylan had reason to celebrate. The new team had broken the fifty-thousand-dollar mark, proving that the more casually run foursome was viable, profitable, and effective. Apart from the run-in with Fisher at the MGM Grand, there had been no problems at all. No signs of casino heat, no potential barring situations, and most important of all, no sign of the man with the weathered cheeks and silver hair.

Kevin swirled the wine in his mouth—though he was too far gone to taste much of anything—and gave the waiter his okay. Although he had to be at work at seven the next morning, Kevin had no interest in heading home just yet. He felt reinvigorated. He believed he had finally found the balance between blackjack and the rest of his life.

"We could recruit more people," Dylan said between puffs on his cigar. "We could bring in a new crop of MIT kids."

Kevin finished his glass of wine. He noticed that the waiter had left the check on the table without being asked.

"Why bother? Let Fisher run his factory. We're sleek, streamlined, and manageable."

"Now you sound like a consultant," Dylan joked. He picked up the check and nodded toward the busboys. "We better pay this and get out of here. They look ready to mutiny."

Kevin reluctantly pulled a roll of hundred dollar bills out of his shirt pocket. He peeled three off and put them under the check. "I'm still on Vegas time. How about you—another drink at the bar?"

Dylan shook his cigar over the ashtray. "I've got a good bottle of red back at our place."

"Will Jill get mad if we keep her up late?"

"She's probably still at work. She's working on some big Internet project. And hell, she gets mad at just about everything nowadays."

They didn't wait for change. Ten minutes later, the taxi dropped them off in front of Dylan's apartment building. The doorman eyed them disapprovingly as they wobbled toward the elevator. Kevin tried to find the button but ended up hitting three wrong floors before Dylan pushed him out of the way.

Kevin's legs wobbled as the elevator rose toward the sixteenth floor. His head was spinning, but it was a nice feeling: Everything seemed soft at the edges; even his thoughts felt like they were covered in cotton. He hadn't been this drunk outside of Vegas in a while.

He followed Dylan out of the elevator and into a long hallway. He was concentrating on his feet—one step in front of the other—when he noticed that Dylan had suddenly stopped moving.

"Did you forget something at the restaurant?"

Dylan didn't answer. Instead, he pointed toward the end of the hallway.

The door to his apartment was wide open. Even from that distance, Kevin could see that the living room didn't look right.

"Oh my God," Dylan said. He rushed forward.

Kevin raced after him, still drunk but sobering fast. When they reached the entrance to the apartment, Kevin paused, taking it all in.

The place was trashed. All the shelves in the living room had been emptied onto the floor. The couch cushions were strewn everywhere, and one of them had been torn in half—white, feathery stuffing coated everything like a fine Vermont snow. The stereo had been upended, and the TV was leaning at an angle, as if someone had pushed it aside to get behind the entertainment center.

Kevin turned to face the kitchen, which was separated from the living room by a short open hallway. The kitchen was in similar shape; the cabinets were open, the pots and pans pitched all over the floor. Even the refrigerator was ajar. A carton of orange juice was lying on its side, rivulets of orange bleeding down from shelf to shelf.

"Christ," Kevin mumbled. "Looks like you've been robbed."

"But they didn't take the TV or the stereo," Dylan said. He sounded like he was in shock. "In fact, it doesn't look like they took anything. Unless— Oh, fuck."

Dylan turned and rushed toward the bedroom. Kevin followed one step behind. The bedroom was trashed, like the living room: the sheets pulled back, the mattress leaning off its bed frame, all the drawers in the dresser pulled out and dumped on the floor. But Dylan didn't seem to care about any of the mess. He headed straight for the closet by the window. The closet doors were wide, the suits pulled back to reveal a plaster wall. Halfway up, there was a hole about the size of a basketball. The plaster around the hole was cracked away, as if someone had pried something loose.

"Fuck fuck fuck!"

Kevin came up behind Dylan and put a hand on his shoulder. "What is it?"

"There used to be a safe there. It's where we kept our blackjack money."

Kevin's face hurt. He felt like he needed to sit down. "How much money?"

There was a sudden sound from the living room. Then a female shout. "Dylan! My God, what happened here?"

Dylan ran out of the bedroom, Kevin behind him. Jill was standing at the entrance to the kitchen, briefcase under one arm, holding herself up with the wall. Her face was pale.

"We were robbed," Dylan said, awkwardly standing in front of her. He looked like he didn't know what to do with his hands. "They took the safe."

Jill stared at him. Her expression suddenly went from fear to anger. "Is that all they took?"

Dylan looked around, nodding. "Looks like it."

"How much?" Kevin asked again.

"Seventy-five thousand," Jill said bitterly. Then she whirled on Dylan. "I told you we had to deposit it in the bank. I told you we shouldn't leave it lying around."

Kevin no longer felt the wine at all. Horrible thoughts were pressing down on his skull. Whoever had broken into the apartment had left the TV and the stereo. They had made off with only the safe—and seventy-five thousand dollars, probably in hundred-dollar bills. Either the thieves had been unbelievably lucky, or they had known about Dylan and Jill's blackjack career.

Jill turned toward Kevin. Her eyes were fierce. "Who knew you guys were going out to dinner?"

Kevin stared at her. "You think someone we know would have done this?"

Jill kicked a piece of the ruined couch cushion, sending a plume of feathers into the air. "Someone was looking for our stash. The only people who know we play blackjack are on the MIT team."

Kevin leaned back against the wall. He knew where she was heading. If Fisher had wanted to send them a signal, this was a hell of a way to do it. But Kevin didn't want to believe that Fisher would stoop to burglary. And though Martinez liked playing games, this wasn't his style.

Could it have been someone else on the team? Maybe the same person who'd sold Plymouth the player list?

Then Kevin had another thought.

"The list," he said. "The Plymouth facebook that Micky showed me had our pictures and home addresses. Maybe it isn't Fisher who's sending us a message. Maybe it's someone else."

"Why us?" Dylan asked. "Why our apartment?"

"Maybe because you're the easiest target. You're married, you've got a future, good jobs. You'd be the easiest to scare off."

"Or maybe we're just the beginning," Jill said.

Kevin thought about the IRS audit and the bruises on Fisher's face. If this was the beginning, he was terrified to imagine where it could end.

Twenty minutes later, Kevin arrived home to his apartment. He was relieved to find his front door still locked. He let himself in and warily moved up the steps to the main floor.

He hit the lights and stood in the entrance to his living room, making sure everything was in the right place. Unlike Dylan and Jill, he kept most of his blackjack money in the bank. *When you're under an IRS audit, you try not to keep huge sums of money lying around in your laundry basket.*

The living room looked just as he had left it. He continued through the apartment, checking every room, including the bathrooms. By the time he reached the kitchen, he had partially relaxed. Maybe he was just being paranoid. Maybe they were all being paranoid.

When the police had arrived at Dylan and Jill's, they had mentioned a number of robberies in the apartment building over the past few weeks. Although it was strange that nothing other than the safe was stolen, it was possible the robbers had been looking for cash and valuables. Maybe it had nothing to do with blackjack at all.

Still, Kevin felt shaken to the core. He crossed to the sink and ran himself a glass of cold water. His hand was trembling as he pressed the glass to his lips.

He remembered what Micky had said when they had kicked him off the team: *The most important decision a card counter ever has to make is the decision to walk away.*

This wasn't about some PI firm trying to frighten Kevin out of the business. This wasn't about an IRS audit or a twenty-five-thousand-dollar list. This wasn't about Fisher cutting him out or Micky scaring him with stories. This wasn't even about being able to look his father in the eyes without feeling like a liar.

This was about him, about his life, about his choices.

Was it time to walk away?

Was it time to end the double life?

He stepped back from the sink and turned to face the kitchen. He took one step toward the door—then stopped, his breath coming in short gasps. The glass slipped from his fingers and shattered against the floor.

There was a single purple casino chip sitting on his kitchen table.

His mind ran wild. Breathing hard, he rushed to the window. Outside, in the alley next to his apartment, he saw a lone figure standing in the shadows talking on a cellular phone.

THIRTY-TWO

Las Vegas, Hard Rock, Present Day

The casino was rock and roll.

The clientele was hip, L.A.

The music coursing from the hidden amplifiers in the ceiling throbbed loud enough to crack glass.

The air was crisp enough to burn my eyes.

I entered the circular casino like Kevin Lewis had taught me: bold, arrogant, leering at the gorgeous blonde waitresses in their tight black shorts and dark stockings, walking in long strides as if my cock ran halfway down my leg. My hair was slicked back, my silk shirt open two buttons at my neck. My jacket flowed around me like a cape, black and Armani and way too expensive to be anything but borrowed.

I paused at the head of the blackjack pit. The Hard Rock was a relatively small casino, a circle of gaming tables surrounding the trendiest bar in town. Here, it was all about the scene: gorgeous models and actresses from L.A. in for the weekend with their producer boyfriends, A-list celebrities partying with sports stars and assorted high rollers. The decor fit the scene—wood tones and plush velvet, everything loud and young and in your face, from the custom Harley-Davidson motorcycle in the lobby to the *Playboy*-style grotto pool outside. Strewn about the casino and the hotel was one of the most expansive rock memorabilia collections under one roof, but people didn't come to the Hard Rock to see what the rock stars *wore*. They came to see the rock stars themselves—or, more accurately, to try and *be* the rock stars, if only for the night.

I hadn't come to the Hard Rock to be a rock star. I was living out a different fantasy.

I started my stroll around the blackjack pit, feeling the chips bouncing in my pockets. I wasn't sure how much I had on me, just that Kevin had assured me it was enough to fit the part.

I made two sweeps of the casino before I caught sight of my partner in crime. Baseball cap pulled down tight over his forehead, thick round glasses resting on his nose, a trace of stubble on his jaw. Hunched over at the third-base position of a table at the edge of the pit, he didn't look at all like the geeky kid in the MIT sweatshirt I had met at the airport, or the polished young man who had bought me dinner at Nobu when we first arrived at the hotel. He looked like a guy who was burning his paycheck at the card table because he had nothing better to do.

Although he didn't turn his head, he seemed to know I was there. He lifted his elbows off the table, crossing his arms. I tensed up—then reminded myself who I was supposed to be. *Guys in three-thousand-dollar jackets don't get nervous.*

I slipped into the table and pulled a handful of chips out of my pocket. As I was trying to figure out what to bet, Kevin looked up at the dealer. "So I hear they got a webcam set up in the pool. Is that true?"

The dealer nodded. He had no idea Kevin had just passed me the count. *Pool,* a positive eight. I picked out a single purple chip and put it in the betting circle.

If it had been my money, I would have choked at the sight of my first card, an ugly six. But tonight I was an extension of Kevin's bankroll.

I was his Gorilla; I wasn't going to think or panic or even breathe on my own. I was just going to watch for Kevin's signals.

Over the next hour he moved my bet up and down with flicks of his hands, shifts of his arms, comments to the dealer, the passing cocktail waitresses, even the other players. He never once looked at me. And he never seemed to focus on the cards.

Pretty soon I was up five thousand dollars, and my body was so jacked up on adrenaline I could barely stay planted on my stool. I was in the groove, playing the cards like a pro. From my research, I knew enough basic strategy to take advantage of Kevin's cues. I was beginning to feel invincible—when I happened to glance past the dealer's right shoulder.

There were two men in suits standing a few feet away, watching me play. Both of the men had name tags, and one was talking into a cellular phone.

Kevin must have seen them as well, because he suddenly rose from the table.

"That's it for me," he said, coloring up his chips. As the dealer traded his blacks for purples, Kevin lifted his hat and ran his fingers through his hair. "I think I'll check out this pool everyone's talking about."

He shuffled away from the table, hands deep in his pockets. I counted sixty seconds—the longest minute of my life—and got up to follow him. The two men in suits watched me all the way across the gambling floor. I didn't start breathing again until I was outside, gasps of hot Vegas air billowing against my face.

I found Kevin in a private cabana overlooking one of the meandering lagoon's many waterfalls. He was stretched out on a lounge chair, sipping lemonade from a frosted glass. He was still wearing the baseball hat, but he had traded the round spectacles for a pair of wraparound sunglasses.

I sat down on a chair next to him and flagged down an anatomically perfect waitress wearing an aquamarine bikini and white tennis shoes. She happily added another drink to "Jamie Chin's" tab.

When she was out of earshot, I leaned toward Kevin. "Do you miss it?"

I knew it was a loaded question. It had been almost three years since the robbery, and Kevin still got uneasy when questioned about the events of his final days as a member of the MIT card-counting team. He had never conclusively figured out who had been behind the robbery or the intrusion into his own home. He had his suspicions, but he never shared them with me. I had wondered whether the betrayal circled back to the man who had started it all—Micky Rosa. Micky, after all, had been spurned by the team and was running competing squads from the same launching pad. But no one on the team—least of all Kevin—would ever voice such a thought, and there was no evidence linking Micky with the break-in.

After the robbery, Kevin had officially disbanded his squad and retired from team play. He still gambled, and sometimes he still counted cards. But the double life he had led for more than four years was over.

His shift to a more normal lifestyle hadn't been easy. Over the course of six months, he had changed jobs three times, finally joining a small start-up software firm in downtown Boston. He still spent much of his time toying with numbers—but now the numbers inhabited spreadsheets instead of blackjack shoes. As for his winnings, much of the money had gone into a downtown bar he had opened with his friends.

Even after three years, the repercussions of Kevin's double life had not entirely receded. For starters, he had recently endured a second audit by the IRS. Although he had come out clean once again, he could not shake the feeling that someone was keeping an eye on him—just in case.

As for Kevin's old teammates, he had not spoken to Fisher in three years. He still saw Martinez on occasion, but there was tension between them, and he doubted they'd ever again consider themselves friends. To his knowledge, Martinez and Fisher's team still carried on their assault on Vegas from a home base on the West Coast—though all of the original members had long ago become dinosaurs and couldn't effectively play any of the major Strip casinos anymore. Martinez and Fisher had thus recruited an entirely new crop of whiz kids; at last count, their team had as many as sixteen members and had brought in close to half a million dollars in the last year alone.

Jill and Dylan had gotten divorced six months after the robbery. Though neither of them saw blackjack as the main catalyst for their breakup, they wouldn't have discounted the effects of the Vegas lifestyle, either. Maybe the pressure had just brought them to boil a little early. Whatever the reason, they were no longer on speaking terms. Jill had moved to Hartford, Connecticut, where she was a high-priced corporate consultant. And Dylan had a burgeoning advertising career in the south of France.

Andrew Tay was still living in Boston, spending three nights a week at the frat house, fleecing unsuspecting MIT undergrads at the poker table. Sometimes, late at night on his way home to his apartment in the Back Bay, he would run into Micky Rosa in the halls of the Infinite Corridor—perhaps heading to the classroom with the drawn shades. The latest rumor was that Micky and Kianna were living together in Micky's apartment, running a handful of new teams out of MIT. A sort of poetic cycle, one that had begun before Kevin and would still be spinning long after him.

"Do you?" I repeated, feeling the spray of the faux waterfall. "Miss the thrill, the money, the game?"

Kevin looked at me through the dark lenses. "Sometimes I think about what it would be like to start again. It's different now. You saw how quickly they reacted. You have to be a lot more careful. And a hell of a lot smarter. Most important, you've got to recruit people you can trust."

"Well," I joked, smoothing out my silk shirt, "I've got the clothes, if you're asking."

Kevin smiled. "First there's this test you've got to take . . ."

HOW TO COUNT CARDS AND BEAT VEGAS

An Essay by Kevin Lewis

In the movie *Rain Man,* there's a famous scene in which Dustin Hoffman and Tom Cruise are making a killing at the blackjack tables in Caesars Palace. Dumbfounded by their success, a casino employee remarks that "no one can count into a six-deck shoe." His sentiment seems to make perfect sense: Even an autistic savant/three-time Academy Award winner can't possibly keep track of three hundred and twelve cards. Especially cards that are streaming past at casino speeds—as many as eight hands at a time!

So the question remains: How do all of the so-called professional card counters make their fortunes, and why is blackjack considered the only truly beatable game in the casino?

The answer is actually fairly simple. *Card counting* is a misnomer; the practice has nothing at all to do with the ability to *count* the cards coming out of the deck. Nor does it have anything to do with memorizing the order in which the cards are seen. Rather, professional counting is merely the practice of taking advantage of the statistical nature of blackjack.

Blackjack is the only game in the casino that is beatable over an extended period of time, because blackjack is subject to *continuous probability*. This simply means that what you see affects what you are going to see. Blackjack is a game with a memory. If an ace comes out in the first round of a blackjack shoe, that means there is one *less* ace left in the rest of the deck. The odds of drawing another ace have gone down by a calculable fraction. In other words, the past has an effect on the future.

Compare that to the games of craps and roulette. If a hot shooter rolls three elevens in a row, what are the odds of that shooter rolling another eleven on the next roll? Or if black comes up three times on the roulette wheel, how have the odds of black coming up again changed? The simple and definitive answer is that in either case, the odds haven't changed one bit. Again, blackjack is the only popular casino game where what you *see* affects what you are *going* to see.

This fact, and this fact alone, makes blackjack beatable. It's just a matter of figuring out how best to take advantage of the game's continuous probability.

To this end, in 1963, MIT professor Edward Thorp did simulations on the relative effect that each card has on the player's chances of winning. What he found was that when many low cards remained in the deck (sevens and below), the odds were in the dealer's favor. Contrarily, when there were many high cards remaining (nines, tens, face cards, and aces), the odds shifted to the player. Over the years, many different counting systems have been developed based on his work—but the simple rule of thumb preaches that low cards remaining in the deck are bad for the player, and high cards are good. All successful counting systems are based on this principle, and while there are more complicated methods that take advantage of the different relative values to the player of each individual card, the very basic hi-lo system was adopted by the MIT team.

Simply put, the hi-lo system assigns a value of plus one for all cards two through six, and a value of minus one for all tens, face cards, and aces. Sevens, eights, and nines are considered neutral and are not counted. Since this system does not take into account such important factors as a five having more negative value than a six, or an ace having more positive value than a ten, hi-lo is not the most powerful or even most advantageous counting method. However, card-counting mistakes made in the casino are infinitely more disastrous than a less-than-perfect method of counting. My teammates and I felt comfortable with our ability to execute the hi-lo system flawlessly, and did not feel that the added value of more advanced systems outweighed the potential risk of casino error.

In practice, we typically would count a six-deck shoe. We would keep a running count of the cards we saw, using the hi-lo system. A high positive count would mean that we had seen a lot of low cards and there were a lot of high cards left in the deck. A highly negative count would mean that we had seen a lot of high cards and there were a lot of low cards left in the deck. According to Thorp's work, the former situation was more advantageous and meant that we should increase our bet. The question was, how much?

We could have used the system employed by Dustin Hoffman's character in *Rain Main:* "One for bad, two for good." Instead, we decided to try something a little more advanced.

In order to figure out how much to increase our bet, we had to first find a way to understand what our count meant; we had to develop an equation that took into account how much of the deck we had seen. Clearly, a count of fourteen through the first *three* decks of a shoe is much more advantageous than a count of fifteen through just the first deck of a shoe. Therefore, we needed to adjust our count to register the number of cards left in the deck.

To do this, we divide our count by the number of decks we have *not* seen. If we had a count of fifteen with three decks remaining, our adjusted count (true count) would be five.

We then take this true count and subtract an offset from it. This offset is based on the blackjack rules at the casino and represents the disadvantage that the player is faced with when the count is neutral. In other words, as we calculate our advantage over the casino based on the count, we must take into account the *disadvantage* that is inherent in the game of blackjack. Remember, casinos wouldn't offer the game if they didn't have an advantage from the outset. In Las Vegas, however, most casinos offer the most advantageous rules for the players. These rules include Surrender, Double After Split, and Resplit Aces. Typically, our team tried to play at casinos with all of these favorable rules. At these casinos, we would subtract an offset of one from the true count.

How do we use this adjusted and offset count to make money? First we must decide on a betting unit. The size of our unit is based on many factors but, most important, on the size of our overall bankroll. Although card counting is statistically proven to work, it does not guarantee you will win every hand—let alone every trip you make to the casino. We must make sure that we have enough money to withstand any swings of bad luck.

For example, let's say that I offered you a game where I flipped a coin and paid you two dollars for every head that came up, and you paid me one dollar for every tail that came up. You would be a fool not to play this game. But if you had only three dollars, you could lose your entire bankroll on the first three flips and never have the chance to take advantage of the statistical advantage that you have over me. This same logic holds true with blackjack.

Let's assume you have roughly a 2 percent edge over the casino. That still means the casino will win 49 percent of the time. Therefore, you need to have enough money to withstand any variant swings against you. A rule of thumb is that you should have at least a hundred basic units. Assuming you start with ten thousand dollars, you could comfortably play a hundred-dollar unit.

After you've established your betting unit, you can make decisions on how much to bet given each count. Simply, you subtract your offset from your true count, then multiply that number by your basic unit. For example, with a running count of fifteen with three decks remaining, you would have a true count of five. You then subtract your offset of one, and your new offset count would be four. Multiply four by your hundred-dollar unit, and your bet would be four hundred dollars. Furthermore, as long as the count is in your favor, you should play two hands at a time, taking full advantage of the good cards. If the count is not in your favor, you play a minimum bet and a single hand.

Your minimum must be small enough to minimize your losses, while being large enough not to arouse suspicion from the casino staff. As an example, if at the end of the shoe you are betting two hands of five hundred dollars, it looks extremely strange if you drop down to one hand of ten dollars on the next round. A good rule of thumb is to bet a minimum equal to half of your betting unit. So in our case, we would never go below a minimum of fifty dollars.

Some players will initially bet a high minimum to camouflage their card counting. Normally, they will bet a large amount off the top of the shoe, knowing that at a count of zero, they are at only a small disadvantage to the casino. However, this kind of play can prove costly in the long run and greatly increases the variance of your game.

As described in *Bringing Down the House,* the MIT Blackjack Team perfected many other advanced and team strategies to maximize the return on our efforts. Rather than having one person sit a table for hours waiting on a favorable shoe, we had four to ten Spotters flitting from table to table. Big Players would be signaled in to positive counts, receiving information on the shoe through verbal and visual cues. This proved extremely profitable and prudent, as we had Spotters betting ten dollars a hand when the count was unfavorable, and Big Players betting thousands of dollars when counts were favorable.

We also developed more advanced strategies, such as tracking pockets of cards. Casinos lose money when their dealers are shuffling, so before the advent of the automatic ShuffleMaster, many casinos had very simple shuffles to minimize the time between active shoes. We were able to take advantage of these casinos, since their shuffles were not truly random. Nonrandom shuffling (or NRS) was a technique many of us mastered, whereby we would track packets of cards from a half deck to a full deck. We would monitor these packets of cards as they moved through the shuffle, calculating the exact number of *other*-card infiltration. This technique was quite lucrative.

Other advanced games we played probably seemed like magic tricks to the uninitiated. Many of us could cut exactly fifty-two cards of a deck every time. If we caught a glimpse of the back card on the deck during the shuffle rollover, we could cut the deck so that the known card would be dealt at a predesignated time. If the card turned out to be an ace, we would time it so that it landed on our hand. If it turned out to be a ten, we'd use it to make the dealer bust. Other times we would track the exact location of aces within the shoe and memorize sequences of cards surrounding those aces. Then we could predict when whole sequences would come out of the deck.

The golden age of card counting came to a close when the casinos began to crack down on us—and, eventually, installed continuous shuffling machines. Although it is much more difficult to make money on a large scale playing blackjack nowadays, it is still possible. It's just a matter of picking and choosing your target casinos.

Keep in mind, card counting isn't gambling. We spent hours refining our art and left as little as possible to chance. In my five years of blackjack, our team never had a losing year. In fact, we never had a year where we returned less than 30 percent for our investors.

You find a stockbroker or trader who can claim that!

About the Author

BEN MEZRICH graduated magna cum laude from Harvard in 1991. Since then, he has published six novels with a combined printing of more than a million copies in nine languages (*Threshold, Reaper, Fertile Ground, Skin,* and, under the name Holden Scott, *Skeptic* and *The Carrier*). His second novel, *Reaper,* was turned into TBS's premiere movie, *Fatal Error,* starring Antonio Sabato, Jr., and Robert Wagner. *Bringing Down the House* is his seventh book and his first foray into nonfiction.